the

Unfolding

of

Romans

OBSERVATIONS IN FORM

WAYNE OLSON

A Division of WINEPRESS PUBLISHING

Printed in the United States of America

Packaged by Pleasant Word, a division of WinePress Publishing, PO Box 428, Enumclaw, WA 98022. The views expressed or implied in this work do not necessarily reflect those of Pleasant Word, a division of WinePress Publishing. Ultimate design, content, and editorial accuracy of this work are the responsibilities of the author.

All boldface type is author's emphasis.

Unless otherwise noted, all Scriptures are taken from the King James Version of the Bible.

Verses marked NIV are taken from the Holy Bible, New International Version, Copyright © 1973, 1978, 1984 by the International Bible Society. Used by permission of Zondervan Publishing House. The "NIV" and "New International Version" trademarks are registered in the United States Patent and Trademark Office by International Bible Society.

ISBN 1-4141-0159-7
Library of Congress Catalog Card Number: 2004103451

Dedication

I dedicate this book to Pat my faithful wife for twenty-four years and mother of my four children. Her theme song was "Living for Jesus." In life she showed us how to live for him and in death she showed us how to die a Christian. She was faithful to the end.

Table of Contents

Acknowledgments

This study has been in progress for eleven years. From the very beginning others have encouraged and contributed. Without their help it is doubtful that I could have completed this monumental task.

In the very beginning it was Pastor Lawrence Manzer and Pastor Stephen Wilson, who not only encouraged me to write this book but also were the ones that counseled me to write it as a thesis.

My brothers and sisters in Christ at Bethany Baptist Church have been an encouragement. Many of them have read portions of the manuscript and given me much needed feedback. I would especially like to thank the church staff for helping me get through the publication process, and Maria Bergstrom who helped with editing, especially with the introduction.

Some of my coworkers, at Houghton County Medical Care, have also helped by reading portions of the manuscript and giving feedback.

To all of these people I give a hardy thank you.

How This Paper Came to Be

After high school I joined the U.S. Navy. In the winter of 1964–65, a shipmate and I got together for Bible study. That winter, on patrol off northern Russia, we studied Romans together. Ever since then, Romans has been a treasured book for me. When teaching various biblical topics, I have often gone there for information. In spite of this, Romans remained somewhat of a mystery. I could not follow Paul's argument from beginning to end. Besides that, there were those nagging questions that could not be answered with certainty: is Romans one continuous document, or are there parenthetical sections? Is the good of Romans 8:28 one specific good, or is it a general good? In chapter seven Paul describes his earlier struggle with sin; did he struggle as a believer or as an unbeliever? As a result of these things I did not teach Romans, but used it as a resource. In 1991–1992 I was working with a new believer and decided that a study of Romans would be helpful for him. It was while we were studying Romans together that I observed the two ends of a macro inverted system. I set out to find the rest and complete that system. In the process I found pieces of other systems that needed completing also.

There were many obstacles to overcome as I began this work, the first being my ignorance of the topic. Upon discharge from the U.S. Navy, I attended Grand Rapids School of the Bible and Music. In spite of this training I had never heard of inverted parallelism or of chiasmus. I bought a plain Bible (no notes or references) and with that Bible, my original observation and a prayer, I began what would be over a decade of study.

The second obstacle to overcome was personal hardship. About the time that I started this study my wife took sick. Two years later, on my fifty-third birthday, she went home to be with the Lord. When she passed away, two of our four children were in college and two were still at home. Shortly after this, the place where I worked closed, and I was unemployed for a period. In time my children have grown up and are on their own. The Lord heals the brokenhearted, and a new job meets my financial needs. In spite of these hardships, this study remained active. I was not always able to spend lots of time, but I always managed to devote some to it.

My wife's home-going brought into focus a third obstacle. She requested that some of her life insurance money be used to buy a computer. She wanted us to have it to help the children with their schoolwork and me with my project. With these tools in hand, however, I still faced a seemingly insurmountable challenge. I could not write. I am a deep dyslectic-dysgraphic, and if there are any other words in the English language that start with "dys", I am probably all of the above. I finished high school functionally illiterate, but with a determination that I would learn. By the time I was twenty-eight I was a good reader, but unable to write. When my wife passed away I wanted to write a letter to our family doctor but was unable, so a Christian friend wrote it for me. Even though my study of Romans continued, the documentation of my observations did not. Everything was kept in my mind. When my youngest daughter went to college in 1996, I let her take the computer with her. I was depressed, because in the two years that we had the computer, I had not managed to write anything. I continued my study, learning much but writing nothing.

One night in the fall of 1997, Pastor Steve Wilson stopped by unexpectedly. He gave me a copy of *Chiasmus in the New Testament* by Nills Lund. For the first time I had a name, some definitions and some examples. The first obstacle, my ignorance of the whole field of chiasmus, soon vanished before my eyes. What a gift!

With the gift came a challenge, however. According to Lund, chiastic systems had to be balanced, with the same amount of text on each side. My systems were terribly unbalanced. The system that I first observed and that started me on this study had three chapters on one side and thirteen on the other. The systems that Lund described were very balanced but very short. I had not observed such small inverted systems, but once I was introduced to them I began finding them myself.

The final obstacle came when I read other authors. Lund's book helped me become aware of these authors. Over time I have obtained some of their works. I did not have the benefit of them while researching and writing most of this paper, because I obtained them after the fact. Before reading them, I did not know that these systems were divided into micro and macro-chiasmus, and that the existence of macro-chiasmus in the New Testament was debated. I had observed two complete systems and parts of others. One of these systems encompassed the whole book of Romans and the other about eighty percent of Romans. I could not understand how anyone could question the existence of such systems. As I read these authors, I realized they were not referring to systems the size of mine. To them, macro meant anything greater than fifteen verses. To me greater than fifteen wasn't macro, but a system that encompassed the whole book of Romans was normal. In time, I have come to agree in principle with Lund and those authors, that chiasma are balanced and very small. At the same time I have been able to reconcile this with my larger unbalanced systems, because my large systems are fundamentally different from chiasmus. They are similar in that they have a clear pattern of inversion, but differ in other ways. They form different categories of inverted systems.

In 1998 I bought a new computer, and at age fifty-seven, I sat down once again before my personal mountain. As I did, I asked God to give me that mountain. Progress was disappointing. What I authored was poor at best; but I was writing. In time my writing improved and now I can say that God is gracious. He has given me most of that mountain.

When I am aware that another author has previously demonstrated a chiasmus in a passage that I am using, I footnote, giving credit. I do this even when my arrangement differs from his. I do not have extensive resources and I am therefore not always aware of everything that has been done. When I fail to give credit it is not intentional. Without the contributions of those who have labored before, it is doubtful that I could have completed my research.

This paper is not the consolidation of what others have set forth. I am thankful for them and have benefited from them, but this paper is primarily my observations from the Word of God. I try to dress these observations in the terms of the profession, but when I made such observations I did not know these terms. I propose some systems that are outside of the box and set forth new paradigms for Romans and for chiastic literature. I do this in a spirit of respect and humility. I am convinced that my God has given me an assignment. The desire of my heart is to finish that assignment. The task that he gave me to do was beyond my personal capacity. Therefore the credit must be his.

I tell you all this so that you will know that this paper is not the product of a great academic. It is the product of God's grace. This north-woods preacher, who supports himself with a day job and conducts his ministry after hours, is not capable of writing such a thesis. One of my friends says, "It is the book that should never have been." I testify unto you that, "There is nothing too hard for the LORD" (Genesis 18:14).

Not by might, nor by power,
but by my spirit, saith the LORD of hosts.

(Zechariah 4:6b)

A Historical and Spiritual Sketch

Paul's letters are both reflections of who he is, and his intended audience. Paul was a Jew, trained at the feet of Gamaliel in Jerusalem and at the feet of Jesus in the desert. When he wrote to the Corinthians he wrote as unto babes and gave them milk. When he wrote unto the Ephesians, he wrote as to mature believers and fed them the strong meat of the Word. Before presenting this thesis regarding the structure of Romans, I would like to look at what we know concerning the people to whom it was written. Knowing something about the believers at Rome will help us understand why Paul would write this very meaty letter to them.

The early church consisted of Jews, proselytes, and Gentiles. While these people loved the Lord, they struggled to understand the relationship between *law* and *grace*. In due time God chose Saul of Tarsus, not only to be his instrument for taking the gospel to the Gentiles, but also to clarify the relationship between these two important concepts in the Word of God.

God chose Saul of Tarsus to reveal to the church the grace of God in salvation. The early church was very much a sect within Judaism. As salvation by faith without the works of the law was proclaimed, those Jews who trusted in the Law reacted. They reasoned that this amounted to teaching that people should *"do evil that good may come."*[1] A very heated debate followed.

---

[1] Romans 3:8

As Jews came to Jerusalem to worship they got introduced to this controversy, took sides and carried it back home, where such debates flourished. Once such intellectual and spiritual fires are started they tend to consume more and more. As the controversy continued, those who claimed to be believers became divided as well. The Jerusalem council [2] was called to settle the issue for believers. At about the same time Claudius, the Roman Caesar, was called upon to deal with this controversy. The situation had become so heated within the city of Rome, that the Roman peace was threatened. Incensed that this should happen in the capital city of Rome, he ordered all Jews to leave and the synagogues within the city closed. Approximately two years later, Paul arrived at Corinth. Some of the Jews expelled from Rome had made their new home at Corinth; Paul stayed with one of these exiled families, Priscilla and Aquila. [3] The controversy concerning salvation by faith without works was a matter of ongoing debate. The arrival of the Jews from Rome added fuel to this debate at Corinth. Then Paul and his party came to Corinth and for a year and a half he reasoned in the synagogue every Sabbath. It is important to remember that there were many Jews from Rome in the audience, some receiving instruction from Paul and others opposing him. Next, Paul went to Ephesus for three years and taught in the school of Tyrannus for two of those years. In the year fifty-four, which was about halfway through Paul's ministry at Ephesus, Claudius was assassinated and Nero became Caesar. One of Nero's first official acts was to issue a decree allowing the Jews to return to the city of Rome and allowing worship in the synagogues to resume. The returning Jewish believers had benefited from three or four years of Paul's teaching ministry. Paul says "I have written you quite boldly on some points, *as if to remind you of them again*, because of the grace God gave me" (emphasis added). [4]

It is a reminder because many of them heard these truths directly from Paul during their exile. It is very possible that Romans contains, at least in part, the curriculum Paul taught in the school of Tyrannus. These people would have been familiar with both the message and Paul's presentation of it. Paul left Ephesus about one year after Nero's decree was given, but while still at Ephesus he expressed his desire to go to Rome. [5] Priscilla and Aquila, with whom he stayed at Corinth, had returned to Rome, as had Epaenetus.

---

[2] Acts 15
[3] Acts 18:2–4
[4] Romans 15:15 NIV
[5] Acts 19:21

In chapter sixteen Paul names many other people that he knew at Rome.[6] All of them were probably with him at Corinth or at Ephesus. Paul wrote this letter from Corinth around the year A.D. 60.

While there is much that we do not know about the church at Rome, there are some things that we do know.

1. The church at Rome consisted of both Jews and Gentiles.

    > Know ye not, brethren, (for I speak to them that know the law) [7]
    > For I speak to you Gentiles . . . [8]

2. This church had mature leadership. When listing those present at Pentecost we read:

    > . . . Rome, Jews and proselytes,[9]

While we don't know if these people were still at Rome, we do know that there were some believers in Rome who dated back close to that time.

> Salute Andronicus and Junia, my kinsmen, and my fellowprisoners, who are of note among the apostles, who also were in Christ before me. [10]

Since Paul's conversion was about three years after Acts 2, these people came to Christ sometime in those first three years. When Paul wrote this letter, about twenty-seven years had elapsed since Acts chapter two.

The very first New Testament book written was the gospel of Mark. This gospel was written before Paul went on his first missionary journey, and was sent to the church at Rome. The gospel of Mark makes an interesting comment in 15:21: "And they compel one Simon a Cyrenian, who passed by, coming out of the country, the father of Alexander and Rufus, to bear his cross."

We then read in Romans 16:13, "Salute Rufus chosen in the Lord . . ."

---

[6] Romans 16:6–15
[7] Romans 7:1
[8] Romans 11:13
[9] Acts 2:10
[10] Romans 16:7

Historians have agreed that this is the same Rufus mentioned in Mark. This man was obviously a believer and well known to believers in Jerusalem and Rome at the time this gospel was written. We can not tell from the information we have just when Rufus became a Christian, but with certainty it was in the early days of the church. Like Andronicus and Junia, he may have been in Christ before the conversion of Paul. We must therefore regard him as a mature believer.

3. They were obedient.

> But God be thanked, that ye were the servants of sin, but ye have obeyed from the heart that form of doctrine which was delivered you. Being then made free from sin, ye became the servants of righteousness [11] and for your obedience is come abroad unto all men.[12]

4. They had a good testimony.

> First, I thank my God through Jesus Christ for you all, that your faith is spoken of throughout the whole world.[13]

5. They were both experienced and capable laborers for Christ. In Romans 16 they are referred to as servants, helpers, and laborers in the Lord. We also read:

> and I myself also am persuaded of you, my brethren, that ye also are full of goodness, filled with all knowledge, able also to admonish one another. [14]

Considering the internal evidence, Paul and many of the believers at Rome had a well-established relationship. In the past they had prayed together, ministered together, and faced the enemy of their faith together. Many in this church had sat at the feet of the apostle Paul and learned from him. Paul had lived with one of these families for a year and a half. It is therefore reasonable to assume that the leadership of this church was mature enough to receive this letter and familiar enough with Paul's literary style to make use of it. The thesis of this paper has to do with Paul's literary style, which is his mechanism for conveying his message. I trust that as you, the reader of this paper, get a fresh view of Romans, it will do for you what Paul wanted his letter to do for the believers at Rome.

---

[11] Romans 6:17–18
[12] Romans 16:19
[13] Romans 1:8
[14] Romans 15:14

Introduction

THE THESIS STATEMENT

The prevailing literary form of Romans is inverted parallelism, sometimes called chiasmus, and its many inverted systems are placed together so as to form multiple inverted parallelisms, two of which encompass the whole of Romans. Therefore, every part is part of the whole, and the whole is not complete without every part.

In the following paper I will support the above thesis with evidence from within the text of Romans. All quotations are from the KJV unless otherwise noted.

The thesis of this paper asserts that Romans was written in inverted parallelism. In this paper, "inverted parallelism" is used as the broad term, and "chiasmus" as one of four sub-categories within inverted parallelism.

Chiasmus is a relatively short and highly balanced inverted parallelism in which the ideas proceed to a point of inversion, after which the same ideas are presented in reverse order. Usually the same word is used on both sides of inversion and most often there are identical or nearly identical phrases and the same literary style. Sometimes this literary style is unique to the corresponding parts and does not occur in the rest of the chiasmus. There are however, cases of the same ideas being expressed with different words. These examples are extremely rare, concise, and detailed enough to be very clear. Sometimes two corresponding elements in a chiasmus are expressed in different words, but because the remainder of the inverted system is detailed and very clear, we can still identify these elements. Without the rest of the system there would not be enough evidence to say that they correlate. If a chiasmus of these types is not obvious, it probably does not exist. The reader should not view the second half of a chiasmus as a repeat of the first. There is a shift in thought at the middle, and the author then develops that new thought. As the author does this, he brings ideas from the first half forward and weaves them into the fabric of the second half. He starts with the most recent idea and works back from the center, producing the inversion. Each idea that is brought forward is carefully worked into the development of the new idea.

As far back as 400 B.C. the Greeks used the term chiasmus to describe this form of writing. They named this literary style after the Greek letter *chi*, which looks much like an X. They had noticed that in the one-sentence examples, lines could be drawn between parallel parts creating a *chi*. For example:

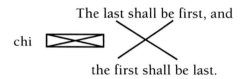

The Greeks used this term for larger inverted systems as well, but for them chiasmus was a seldom-used style of speaking and writing. Long before this term came to be, the Jews had developed this literary style far beyond that of the Greeks. The Greek definition does not adequately define its Jewish predecessor and counterpart, which is much broader in scope. Bible scholars have never come to a consensus concerning this term, resulting in much disagreement and confusion. It would be a huge step forward if scholars were to come to a consensus concerning the term *chiasmus*.

From the early church to the Reformation, chiasmus was used for poetry, hymns, and church liturgy in both the Western and Eastern Church. The Reformation Bible scholars were therefore familiar with chiasmus, but did not realize the extent to which it was used in Scripture. In time, they began to see it in the Psalms and thought that it was unique to the Psalms, but as time went on they began to observe it elsewhere in the Old Testament. It was then thought to be something that was exclusively Old Testament. In 1742, Bengal published his commentary on the New Testament. In it he suggested that Romans was written in this format. No one took him seriously but his students began looking at other New Testament books and found examples. Bible scholars have been slow to acknowledge that major portions of the New Testament are written in chiasmus, but the evidence is mounting. I am hopeful that the publication of this book will be the turning point.

People sometimes ask, "Is chiasmus peculiar to a particular translation?" No, it can be observed in any translation and in the Greek and Hebrew texts. In some instances, the translation loses some of the detail, making it harder to detect and identify chiasmus, but enough of the form is retained that the determined student can still identify these systems. My work has been done using the King James Version and readily available study helps. In the majority of instances the detail is retained so that the translation presented no problem. This would be true for other translations as well. The one exception to this would be a paraphrase. In a paraphrase, the translator asks *what does this mean* and then states this perceived thought in his own words. In this case, form is not necessarily preserved.

One of the ways a chiasmus is detected is by a word being used repeatedly in a passage, but not in the surrounding text.

My first example of this rises from the fact that there is not always equivalent vocabulary in both languages. In Greek, the word translated *righteous* has the full range of forms, but our English word *righteous* does not have a verb form. We would not say that a person is *righteousfied*. When the verb form appears in the Greek, it is translated *justified*. Therefore, when reading in the English, the reader may not detect the repetitive use of the Greek word that would cause him to look for a chiastic structure.

The translators of the King James Version were educated and knew what was considered good literature in the Western world. In the Western world it was not acceptable to use the same word too often in the same passage. Sometimes the translators tried to fix what they saw as a problem, by translating a word that was used repeatedly in more than one way. In chapter four of Romans, the Greek word translated *impute* is also translated *reckoned* and *counted*. The only reason for this was to avoid using the same word too frequently. This obscures the real fact that in the Greek the same word is used repetitively, which would help the student identify the literary form. In spite of these obstacles the form can be identified with a little work.

There is a standard system of notation used by scholars to present their findings. Parallel passages are labeled with the same letter; for example, (A). If the person labeling these passages sees them as comparative in nature, a single prime (') is placed after the second. For example A, A'. If they are seen as being in contrast to one another a double prime (") is placed after the second. For example, A, A".

The Greek term *chiasmus* is singular. The plural form is *chiasma*. The Greek word *colon* is also singular and its plural form is *cola*. These terms will occur often in this paper.

In addition to chiasmus there are large inverted systems that encompass many smaller systems. While they display a clear pattern of inversion, they are usually not balanced and are sometimes asymmetrical. Because this paper will be concerned with inverted parallelisms in the broad sense, these systems will be included. In addition to chiasmus there are three types of inverted systems presented in this paper: extended chiasma, transitional inverted parallelisms and extended transitional inverted parallelisms. These three depend on chiasma for their existence, but lack sufficient balance to qualify as chiasmus. The following is a brief description of each type of the macro-systems proposed in this paper.

Extended Chiasma

Often, the central chiasmus in a series of chiasma has an influence through the whole series. This happens when the pattern of inversion connected with that central chiasmus extends in both directions to include the whole series. These extensions are not always balanced, but the pattern of inversion is clear. I call these systems *extended chiasma*.

Transitional Inverted Parallelisms: TIP

When placing a number of chiasma in series, it could be very choppy, with abrupt change between chiasma. In music and literature, that which makes a smooth transition between parts without pause is called a *segue*. Paul makes this segue by introducing an idea at the end of one system, and then repeating it in the beginning of the following system. Paul sometimes uses a segue as the center of another inverted parallelism. The systems of this type are fundamentally different from chiasmus and form a separate category of inverted parallelism. In these systems the secondary side is an amplification of the primary side and is very unbalanced. Several of these systems will be presented as we go through Romans. Because they have a segue for a center, I call them *transitional inverted parallelisms* or TIP. The last element of a chiasmus often introduces the next chiasmus but with TIP, the last element introduces multiple chiasma or groups of chiasma, providing an outline for the coming section.

Extended Transitional Inverted Parallelisms: E-TIP

With E-TIP, the primary side of a transitional inverted parallelism is not restricted to the end of the previous extended chiasmus, or to the whole system, but extends back towards the beginning of the document, as far as the author wishes. Because they exist simultaneously with each other and with chiasmus, there can be multiple statements indicating what a coming chiasmus is about. These E-TIP systems are viewed as intentional and serve a different purpose. It is doubtful that Paul intended the casual reader to be aware of them, but I am convinced that he expected the serious student to find at least some of them, and to share what he found with others. In time, believers would learn chiasmus in the same way Paul learned it in the school of Gamaliel.

This paper is presented with the conviction that the awareness of form enhances our understanding of the text. Awareness of form in Romans will do several things for us: It will answer some long-standing questions. Does Romans have a parenthetical section? In chapter seven, did Paul struggle with sin as a believer or as an unbeliever? Is the good of 8:28 a general good, or is it one specific good? It helps us follow Paul's logic and clarify some otherwise confusing passages. Our understanding of some doctrinal areas is improved, especially our understanding of salvation in the Old Testament. New doors are opened for study and understanding. It also demonstrates God's preservation of his Word.

To the best of my ability, I have sought to make this paper readable to the serious lay student. Not everybody is for the Word of God, but the Word of God is for everybody. The obvious can be learned and verified through observation. The experienced eye always sees things that the inexperienced eye does not, but when the obscure is pointed out, it becomes obvious even to the inexperienced. Much of what is in this paper will be obvious, and can be verified through observation.

The Jews, starting with Abraham, used chiasmus extensively. It was not called chiasmus then, but it was the way they thought, talked, and wrote. Different scholars have used various terms to describe their basic thought unit. In this paper I use the term *bicolon*. A bicolon consists of two nearly identical clauses, called a *colon* (part). These mental building blocks are placed in comparison or in contrast with each other. As an introduction to my study of Romans, I will first discuss the basic nature of Jewish parallelism, with examples from the Scriptures, in and out of Romans. I will discuss chiasmus, with examples from the Old and New Testaments, including Romans, and macro-inverted parallelisms, with two examples from outside of Romans and four from within.

A. The Nature of Jewish Parallelism

Jewish parallelism is a system of thought that is based on comparison and contrast. Truth is compared to unleavened bread and falsehood to leavened bread. Israel is compared to the grapevine and unfaithfulness to the Lord is compared to adultery. This comparison and contrast extends all the way from the most basic thoughts to the most complex thoughts.

Psalms 24:1   The earth is the LORD'S, and the fulness thereof;
           The world, and they that dwell therein.

The second statement strengthens, intensifies or completes the first. "The earth" becomes "the world" and, "the fulness thereof" becomes "they that dwell therein." The second clarifies what was meant by the first.

Psalms 24:2   For he hath founded it upon the seas,
           and established it upon the floods.

"Founded" becomes "established" and "seas" becomes "floods," giving a more complete picture of what is meant.

Psalms 34:1   I will bless the LORD at all times:
           His praise shall continually be in my mouth.

It takes both cola to have a complete thought.

Sometimes the cola come in threes. This is called a *tricolon*. The tricolon forms two complete thoughts because the middle colon is shared with the other two.

Psalms 29:3 The voice of the LORD is upon the waters:
The God of glory thundereth:
the LORD is upon many waters.

Proverbs 3:3 Let not mercy and truth forsake thee:
Bind them about thy neck;
Write them upon the table of thine heart:

Two bicola or two tricola are often placed in comparison or contrast to each other, building a larger thought.

Proverbs 3:5–6 Trust in the LORD with all thine heart;
And lean not unto thine own understanding.
In all thy ways acknowledge him,
And he shall direct thy paths.

Psalms 24:7–10

A.[7] Lift up your heads, O ye gates;
And be ye lift up, ye everlasting doors;
And the King of glory shall come in.

B.[8] Who is this King of glory?
The LORD strong and mighty,
The LORD mighty in battle.

A'.[9] Lift up your heads, O ye gates;
Even lift them up, ye everlasting doors;
and the King of glory shall come in.

B'.[10] Who is this King of glory?
The LORD of hosts,
He is the King of glory. Selah.

In this case the matched pairs are displaced from each other, but they still form a new complete thought. The second element strengthens, intensifies, or completes the first.

Chiasmus is the natural outgrowth of this basic thought process. In chiasmus the second half is given in the reverse order. For example:

Isaiah 22:22   And the key of the house of David will I lay upon his shoulder;

> So he **shall open**,
>> and none **shall shut**;
>> and he **shall shut**,
> and none **shall open**.

Verse twenty-two is inverted but these next four are not. I am not convinced that the writers of Scripture saw these as two separate forms of writing, but as two variations of the same form.

Isaiah 22:23–25

A. [23] And I will fasten him as a nail in a sure place; and he shall be for a glorious throne to his father's house.

B. [24] And they shall hang upon him all the glory of his father's house, the offspring and the issue, all vessels of small quantity, from the vessels of cups, even to all the vessels of flagons.

A'. [25] In that day, saith the LORD of hosts, shall the nail that is fastened in the sure place be removed, and be cut down, and fall;

B'. and the burden that was upon it shall be cut off: for the LORD hath spoken it.

This pattern of inversion that we saw in verse twenty-two can be extended over larger passages.

Zechariah 1:13–17

A. [13] And the LORD answered the angel that **talked with me with good words and comfortable words.**

B. [14] So the angel that communed with me said unto me, **Cry thou, saying, Thus saith the LORD of hosts;**

C. I am jealous for Jerusalem and for Zion with a great jealousy.

D. [15] And **I am very sore displeased with the heathen that are at ease:**
E. for **I was but a little displeased,**

D'. and **they helped forward the affliction.**

C'. [16] Therefore thus saith the LORD; **I am returned to Jerusalem with mercies:**my house shall be built in it, saith the LORD of hosts, and a line shall be stretched forth upon Jerusalem.
B'. [17] **Cry yet, saying Thus saith the LORD of hosts;**

A'. My cities through prosperity shall yet be spread abroad; and **the LORD shall yet comfort Zion,** and shall yet chose Jerusalem.

B. Basic Jewish Parallelism in Romans

a. Did Paul write in the sentence format of Greek, or did he use the colon-bicolon approach? It would take an extensive review of Romans and Paul's other writings to answer this definitively, but here are some examples from Romans.

[11:6] And if **by grace,** then *is it* no more **of works:**
otherwise **grace** is no more **grace.** But
if *it be* of **works,** then is it no more **grace:**
otherwise **work** is no more **work.**

This is two bicolons with the second completing the first. The form of the above passage is unique to it, and is not found anywhere else in Romans.

[11:16] For if the firstfruit *be* **holy,** the lump *is* also **holy:**
and if the root *be* **holy,** so *are* the branches.

[8:15] For ye have **not received the spirit of bondage** again to fear;
but **ye have received the Spirit of adoption,** whereby we cry, Abba, Father.

Fear is in contrast to Abba, Father. The above passages are bicolons, and the following is two bicola placed together to make a larger thought unit.

> 7:3 So then if, while *her* **husband liveth,**
> **she be married to another man,** she shall be **called an adulteress:**
> but if **her husband be dead,** she is free from that law;
> so that **she is no adulteress,** though **she be married to another man.**

One of the things that stands out with Hebrew thought and with chiasmus in particular, is its repetitive nature. Notice the repetition in the following:

> 14:6 He that regardeth the day, regardeth *it* unto the Lord;
> and he that regardeth not the day, to the Lord he doth not regard *it.*
> He that eateth, eateth to the Lord, for he giveth God thanks; and
> he that eateth not, to the Lord he eateth not, and giveth God thanks
> 7 For none of us liveth to himself, and no man dieth to himself.
> 8 For whether we live, we live unto the Lord;
> and whether we die, we die unto the Lord
> whether we live therefore, or die, we are the Lord's.

b. These cola are sometimes arranged as direct comparisons or contrasts.

> A.28 **For he is not a Jew,**
> which is one **outwardly;**
>
> > B. neither *is that* **circumcision,**
> > which is **outward** in the flesh:
>
> A".29 But **he** *is* **a Jew,**
> which is one **inwardly;**
>
> > B". and **circumcision** *is that* **of the heart,**
> > in the spirit, *and* not in the letter
> > whose praise *is* not of men, but of God.

I often hear people say that they find the Bible hard to read. Could it be that the problem is not with the text, but with the way we read the text. For best results the Bible should be read as it was written. These examples clearly indicate that

Paul was using the colon-bicolon Hebrew approach. As we observe many chiasma in Romans, we will have opportunity to note many more examples.

In the coming section I will demonstrate chiasmus throughout the Word of God with special attention to the writings of Paul, including Romans. I want you, the reader of this paper, to get a good feel for chiasma and to establish the extensive use of this literary form in Scripture. I have chosen familiar passages and in some cases these are extended. The extended portions demonstrate that chiasmus is the primary form and not something that was used sparingly. Chiasma are rarely used in modern times and when they are, they are very short. Some modern examples of chiasma are as follows.

c. Chiasmus

1. **Modern Examples**

When the *going* gets **tough**,
the **tough** get **going**.

Some people **work** to **live**,
others **live** to **work**.

Everything in its **place** and
A **place** for **everything**.

Are you **working hard** or
hardly working?

Figures don't **lie** but
liars do **figure**.

The **ideal** is not **real**
And the **real** is not **ideal**.

These chiastic statements are short and to the point. They are easy to remember and hard to forget. We use them sparingly in a thought process that starts at the beginning and continues in a straight line until finished. In chiastic literature, inversion is the norm, with the thought patterns folding back and forth. In systems of four or more elements, there is a definite conclusion. The conclusion is in the center.

2. **Chiasmus in the Old Testament**

The following systems are from my own study unless otherwise noted. Scholars are not always in agreement as to what constitutes a chiasmus. I doubt therefore that every system will meet with everybody's approval. For the most part I have chosen passages that I do not find in the literature that I have in my possession.

Chiasmus is very common in the Old Testament and may well be its prevailing literary form. First, we will look at some very simple examples of chiasmus.

Exodus 33:20–23

A. And he said, **Thou canst not see my face:** for there shall no man see me and live.

B. [20] And the LORD said,
[21] Behold, there is a place by me,
and **thou shalt stand upon a rock:**
[22] And it shall come to pass, while my glory passeth by,

A.	Thou canst not see my face
B.	Thou shalt stand upon a rock
B'.	I will put thee in a cleft of the rock
A'.	My face shall not be seen

B'. that **I will put thee in a cleft of the rock,** and will cover thee with my hand while I pass by: [23] And I will take away mine hand,

A'. and thou shalt see my back parts: but **my face shall not be seen.**

Note that "Thou canst not see my face" and "my face shall not be seen" are nearly identical statements. Again "Thou shalt stand upon a rock" and "I will put thee in a cleft of the rock" are very close. Most chiasma will have some correlating elements that are nearly identical statements. This is not to say that there cannot be chiasma without nearly identical statements, but the examples where nearly identical statements are not present are very limited. These nearly identical statements have helped me identify many chiasma.

Exodus 34:1–5

A. 1 And **the LORD said unto Moses,**

B. a. **Hew thee two tables of stone like unto the first**: and I will write upon these tables

> A. The LORD said
> B.   Hew two tables of stone
> C.   Neither let any man
> C'. Neither let the flocks
> B'. He hewed two tables of stone
> A'. Proclaimed the name of the LORD

the words that were in the first tables, which thou brakest.

  b. [2] And be ready in the morning, and **come up in the morning unto mount Sinai**, and present thyself there to me in the top of the mount.

C. [3] And no man shall come up with thee,
   neither let any man be seen throughout all the mount;

C'. neither let the flocks nor herds feed before that mount.

B'. a'. [4] And **he hewed two tables of stone like unto the first**;
    b'. and **Moses rose up early in the morning, and went up unto mount Sinai**, as the LORD had commanded him, and took in his hand the two tables of stone.

A'. [5] And the LORD descended in the cloud, and stood with him there, and **proclaimed the name of the LORD.**

Next compare correlating parts, this is called the chiastic reading.

A. And the LORD said unto Moses,

A'. proclaimed the name of the LORD.

B. a. Hew thee two tables of stone like unto the first:
   b. come up in the morning unto mount Sinai

B'. a'. And he hewed two tables of stone like unto the first;
    b'. and Moses rose up early in the morning, and went up unto mount Sinai

C . neither let any man be seen throughout all the mount;

C'. neither let the flocks nor herds feed before that mount.

In addition to nearly identical statements, the correlation most often includes the same literary form. By this I mean that if an element has a certain number of cola, bicola, etc., then the correlating element will have the same. If one is arranged as a chiasmus or in some unique way, its correlating element will be arranged in the same way. Not every set of correlating elements will be this way, but most chiasmus will have some that are. This will become clearer as we look at increasingly complex systems.

Exodus 3:13–15

A. a. [13] And **Moses said unto God**,

b. Behold, when I come unto **the children of Israel**, and shall **say unto them**,

c. **The God of your fathers hath sent me unto you;**

> A. Moses said unto God . . .
> The God of your fathers hath sent me unto you
> B. What is his name?
> B'. I AM THAT I AM
> A'. God said unto Moses . . .
> The LORD God of your fathers . . . hath sent me unto you

B. and they shall say to me, **What is his name?** What shall I say unto them?

B'. [14] And God said unto Moses, **I AM THAT I AM**: and he said, Thus shalt thou say unto the children of Israel, **I AM hath sent me unto you.**

A'. a'. [15] And **God said moreover unto Moses,**

b'. Thus shalt thou **say unto the children of Israel**,

c'. **The LORD God of your fathers**, the God of Abraham, the God of Isaac, and **the God of Jacob, hath sent me unto you**: this is my name for ever, and this is my memorial unto all generations

The Chiastic reading:

A. a. [13] And Moses said unto God,

   b. Behold, when I come unto the children of Israel, and shall say unto them,

   c. The God of your fathers hath sent me unto you

A'. a'. [15] And God said moreover unto Moses,

   b'. Thus shalt thou say unto the children of Israel,

   c'. The LORD God of your fathers, the God of Abraham, the God of Isaac, and the God of Jacob, hath sent me unto you: this is my name for ever, and this is my memorial unto all generations,

B. and they shall say to me, What is his name? What shall I say unto them?

B'. [14] And God said unto Moses, I AM THAT I AM: and he said, Thus shalt thou say unto the children of Israel, I AM hath sent me unto you.

Genesis 12:1–5

Now the LORD had said unto Abram,

A. a. [1] **Get thee out of thy country,**

   b. and **from thy kindred,**

   b'. and **from thy father's house,**

> A. Get thee out of thy country
>   B. a. I will bless thee
>   b. Thou shalt be a blessing
>   B.' a'. I will bless them that bless thee
>   b'. In thee shall all families
>   of the earth be blessed
> A'. Abram departed, as the LORD had spoken
>   unto him

   a'. **unto a land** that I will shew thee:

B. a. [2] And I will make of thee a great nation, and I will **bless thee,**

   b. and make thy name great; and **thou shalt be a blessing:**

B'. a'. [3] And **I will bless them** that **bless thee,** and curse him that curseth thee:

   b'. **and in thee shall all families of the earth be blessed.**

A'. a. [4] So **Abram departed**, as the LORD had spoken unto him;

> b. and **Lot went with him** and Abram was seventy and five years old when he departed out of Haran.
>
> b'. [5] And Abram took Sarai his wife, **and Lot his brother's son**, and all their substance that they had gotten in Haran;

> a'. and **they went forth** to go into the land of Canaan; and into the land of Canaan they came.

A and A' are small chiastic systems that are elements of a larger system. I call this em*bedded chiasmus.* Notice how these elements are both arranged with their own inverted system. This is not required, but occurs often.

The chiastic reading:

A. a. [1] Get thee out of thy country,

> b. and **from** thy kindred,
>
> b'. and **from** thy father's house,

> a'. unto a land that I will shew thee:

A'. a. [4] So Abram departed, as the LORD had spoken unto him;

> b. and Lot went with him: and Abram was seventy and five years old when he departed out of Haran.
>
> b'. [5] And Abram took Sarai his wife, and Lot his brother's son, and all their substance that they had gotten in Haran;

> a'. and they went forth to go into the land of Canaan; and into the land of Canaan they came.

B. a. [2] And I will make of thee a great nation, and I will bless thee,

> b. and make thy name great; and thou shalt be a blessing:

B'. a'. [3] And I will bless them that bless thee, and curse him that curseth thee:

> b'. and in thee shall all families of the earth be blessed.

In the following chiasmus, each set of correlating elements has multiple identical or nearly identical statements and the same literary form.

Exodus 33:12–17

A. [12] And **Moses said unto the LORD**, See, thou sayest unto me, Bring up this people:

    a. and **thou hast not let me know whom thou wilt send with me. Yet thou hast said,**

A.	I know thee by name
	B. I have found grace in thy sight
	C. My presence shall go with thee
	C'. If thy presence go not with me
	B'. That I and thy people have found grace in thy sight?
A'.	I know thee by name

    b. **I know thee by name, and thou hast also found grace in my sight.**

B. [13] Now therefore, I pray thee,

    a. if I have found **grace in thy sight,**

      b. shew me now **thy way,**

      b'. that I may **know thee,**

    a'. that I may **find grace in thy sight:**
and **consider that this nation is thy people.**

C. [14] And he said,

    a. **My presence shall go with thee,** and

    b. **I will give thee rest.**

C'. [15] And he said unto him,

    a'. **If thy presence go not with me,**

    b'. **carry us not up hence.**

B'. [16] For wherein shall it be known here

    a. that **I and thy people** have found **grace in thy sight?**

   b. Is it not in that **thou goest with us?**
   b'. So shall we be **separated,**

   a'. **I and thy people,** from all the people that are upon the face of the earth.

A'. [17] And **the LORD said unto Moses,**

   a'. **I will do this thing also that thou hast spoken:**
   b'. for thou hast **found grace in my sight,** and **I know thee by name.**

In verse seventeen the LORD says, "I will do this thing also that thou hast spoken." What did Moses say that God is going to do? The answer is in the correlating element, "thou hast not let me know whom thou wilt send with me." We therefore know that God is going let Moses know who is going with him.

The chiastic reading:

A. [12] And **Moses said unto the LORD,** See, thou sayest unto me, Bring up this people:

   a. and **thou hast not let me know whom thou wilt send with me.** Yet thou hast said,
   b. **I know thee by name,** and **thou hast also found grace in my sight.**

A'. [17] And **the LORD said unto Moses,**

   a'. **I will do this thing also that thou hast spoken:**
   b'. for thou hast **found grace in my sight,** and **I know thee by name.**

B. [13] Now therefore, I pray thee,

   a. if I have found **grace in thy sight,**

      b. shew me now **thy way,**
      b'. that I may **know thee,**

   a'. that I may **find grace in thy sight:**

and **consider that this nation is thy people.**

B'. [16] For wherein shall it be known here

    a. that **I and thy people** have found **grace in thy sight?**

        b. Is it not in that **thou goest with us?**
        b'. So shall we be **separated,**

    a'. **I and thy people,** from all the people that are upon the face of the earth.

C. [14] And he said,

    a. **My presence shall go with thee,** and
    b. **I will give thee rest.**

C'. [15] And he said unto him,

    a'. **If thy presence go not with me,**
    b'. **carry us not up hence.**

When content and form correlate, it is much easier for the one being addressed to detect and make use of the chiastic structure. If the same general truth is present but not expressed in these specific correlations, it is doubtful that the listener or reader would be able to detect and benefit from the correlation.

The writings of Moses set the standard for the rest of the Old Testament. Chiasmus is not found just in the writings of Moses, but throughout the Old Testament. Examples from Ezekiel and 1 Samuel are given later in the complete presentation of Romans. Consider now another Old Testament passage. Again, I have chosen a very familiar passage.

Isaiah 6:9–11

A. [9] **And he said, Go, and tell** this people,

    B. [10] Make the **heart** of this people fat, Hear ye indeed, but understand not; and see ye indeed, but perceive not.

C. and make their **ears** heavy,

D. and shut their **eyes**;

D'. lest they see with their **eyes**,

A.   Go, and tell this people
   B.   Make the **heart** of this people fat
     C.   Make their **ears** heavy
        D.   Shut their **eyes**; lest they
        D'. see with their **eyes**
     C'. Hear with their **ears**
   B'. Understand with their **heart**
A'. How long?

C'. and hear with their **ears**,

B'. and understand with their **heart**, and convert, and be healed.

A'. [11] **Then said I, Lord, how long?** [15] And he answered, Until the cities be wasted without inhabitant, and the houses without man, and the land be utterly desolate.[16]

This is an example of one-word correlation. Because they are packed into one verse, one word is sufficient for the reader to recognize the pattern.

When chiasma are based on one-word correlations, they are very short systems. They are effective because they are so short.

3. Chiasmus in the New Testament

Matthew 19:30

> But many that are *first* shall be *last*;
> and the *last* shall be *first*.

Parallelisms were the primary thought pattern in Jewish culture. In Jewish literature the inverted parallel system is used more than the direct parallelism. In the inverted order, there is a rhyme of thought, but not of the sounds that express the thought. Alan Culpepper has provided us with an excellent example of chiasmus in the gospel of John.[17]

[15-16] Isaiah 6:10 is presented as chiasmus in *The Shape of Biblical Language,* pg 31, John Breck, St. Vladimir's Seminary Press, Crestwood, New York. 1994
[17] Pg. xv, preface to *Chiasmus in the New Testament,* Nils W. Lund, Hendrickson, Peabody, Mass. Reprint 1992

A. 1:1–2 The Word as theos with God

   B. 1:3 Creation came through the Word

      C. 1:4–5 We have received life from the Word

         D. 1:6–8 John was sent to testify

            E. 1:9–10 Incarnation and the response of the world

               F. 1:11 The Word and his own (Israel)

                  G. 1:12a Those who accepted the Word

                     H. 1:12b He gave authority to become the children of God

                  G'. 1:12c Those who believed the Word

               F'. 1:13 The Word and his own (believers)

            E'. 1:14 Incarnation and the response of the community

         D'. 1:15 John's testimony

      C'. 1:16 We have received grace from the Word

   B'. 1:16 Grace and truth came though the Word

A'. 1:18 The Word as theos with God

To get a good feel for the symmetry, compare each matched pair.

A. The Word as theos with God

A'. The Word as theos with God

B. Creation came through the Word

B'. Grace and truth came through the Word

C. We have received life from the Word

C'. We have received grace from the Word

D. John was sent to testify

D'. John's testimony, etc.

In this example of chiasmus, the two halves of the matched pair A, A' are just as closely related in thought as G, G' even though G, G' are in the same verse and A, A' are eighteen verses apart. These paired units of thought serve to bring past ideas to the forefront and apply them to the related material. They also give commentary on each other. In extended chiasmus (more than six elements), the *conclusion is in the middle*, and there is often a *shift in thought* at that juncture.

A second area of emphasis is found at the extremes. In the prologue to the gospel of John, the conclusion is "He gave authority to become the children of God." The first half presents "the Word." The thought then shifts to "those who believe." An additional emphasis of "The Word was with God," is in the two extremes. In spite of the shift in thought, balance is maintained.

To support my assertion that parallelism is the primary form in Paul's letters, I would like to consider some examples from the third chapter of each of 1 and 2 Corinthians and Galatians. In restricting our study to the third chapter of each of these epistles, I cannot pick those passages that best support my position and skip those that do not. This should help you know that I am representing the situation accurately.

1 Corinthians 3:1–4

A. [1] And I brethren, could not speak unto you as unto spiritual, but as unto carnal,

> A. Speak unto you . . . as unto carnal
> B. as unto babes in Christ
> B'. I have fed you with milk
> A'. Ye are yet carnal

B. even as unt **babes in Christ.**

B'. [2] **I have fed you with milk,** and not with meat: for hitherto ye were not able to bear it, neither yet now are ye able.

A'. [3] **for ye are yet carnal:**

    a. for whereas there is among you **envying, and strife, and divisions,**

    b. **are ye not carnal**, and walk as men?

  a'. [4] For while **one saith**, I am of Paul; and another, I am of Apollos

    b'. **are ye not carnal?**

Paul has been talking about babes in Christ and will segue to planting and watering. He makes this segue by introducing the names, Paul and Apollos, in **A'** and restates them in **A** of the following chiasmus. For example:

A'. [4] For while one saith, I am of **Paul**; and another, I am of **Apollos**;
A. [5] Who then is **Paul**, and who is **Apollos**,

1 Corinthians 3:5–10a

A. a. [5] **Who then is Paul, and who is Apollos,**

    b. but **minis-**
    ters by
    whom ye
    believed,

A.	Who then is Paul, and who is Apollos
B.	God gave the increase
B'.	God gave the increase
A'.	We are labours together with God

    b'. even as **the**
    Lord gave
    to every man?

  a'. [6] I have planted, Apollos watered;

B. but **God gave the increase.** [7] So then neither is he that **planteth** any thing, neither he that **watereth**;

B'. but **God gave the increase.** [8] Now he that **planteth** and he that **watereth** are one: and **every man shall receive his own reward** according to his own labour.

A'. a. [9] For **we are labourers together with God:**

    b. ye are God's husbandry, ye are **God's building.**
    b'. [10] according to the grace of God which is given unto me, as a **masterbuilder,**

  a'. I have laid the foundation, and **another buildeth** thereon.

Segue: **A'.** [10b] I have laid the **foundation**, and another **buildeth** thereon.

    A. But let every man take heed how he **buildeth** thereupon.

    [11] For other **foundation** can no man lay than that is laid, which is Jesus Christ.

A. a. But **let every man take heed how he buildeth thereupon**.

> **A.** Let every man take heed how he buildeth thereupon
> **B.** Every man's work shall be made manifest
> **B'.** If any man's work abide
>   If any man's work shall be burned
> **A'.** If any man defile the temple of God, him shall God destroy

    b. [11] For other **foundation** can no man lay than that is laid,

    b'. which is Jesus Christ

  a'. [12] Now **if any man build** upon this foundation

      1. **gold, silver, precious stones,**
      2. **wood, hay, stubble;**

B. a. [13] **Every man's work** shall be made manifest: for the day shall declare it,

    b. because **it shall be revealed by fire**; and the fire shall try every man's work of what sort it is.

B'. a'. [14] **If any man's work abide** which he hath built thereupon, he shall receive a reward.

    b'. [15] **If any man's work shall be burned**, he shall suffer loss: but he himself shall be saved; yet so as by fire.

A'. a. [16] Know ye not that **ye are the temple of God,**

    b. and that the **Spirit of God dwelleth in you?**

    b'. [17] **If any man defile the temple of God, him shall God destroy;**

  a'. for the **temple of God is holy**, which temple ye are. [18]

Segues are constructed in a similar fashion as the center of a system. They have the same repetitive nature. Notice that the above segue has a pattern of inversion built in. This pattern of inversion appears to continue. Consider the following.

3:6–15

God gave the increase
   [7c] every man shall receive his own reward
      foundation
         buildeth
         buildeth
      foundation
   [14] he shall receive a reward
 [15] he himself shall be saved . . .

This example is not as detailed as some that will come later, but should demonstrate that a segue between two systems can double as the center for a third system which is fundamentally different in nature. For those who doubt this there will be better examples coming.

2 Corinthians 3:1–5

A. [1] **Do we begin to commend ourselves?** Or need we, as some others, epistles of commendation to you?

B. [2] **Ye are our epistle written in our hearts**, known and read of all men:

C. [3] For as much as ye are manifestly **declared to be the epistle of Christ** ministered by us,

A.	Do we begin to commend ourselves
B.	Ye are our epistle
	C. The epistle of Christ
B'.	Written with the spirit . . .
A'.	Not that we are sufficient of ourselves

---

[18] 3:16–17 is presented as chiasmus in, *The Shape of Biblical Language*, pg. 245, by John Breck, St. Vladimir's Seminary Press, Crestwood, New York. 1994

B'. **Written** not with ink, but with the Spirit of the living God;
Not in tables of stone, but **in fleshly tables of the heart.**

A'. [4] And **such trust have we through Christ to Godward:** [5] Not that we are **sufficient** of **ourselves** to think any thing as of **ourselves;** but our **sufficiency is of God;**

2 Corinthians 3:6–15

A. [6] Who also hath made us able ministers of the **New Testament;** not of the letter, but of the spirit: for the letter killeth, but **the spirit giveth life.**

B. [7] **But if the ministration of death,** written an engraven in stones, was glorious, **so that the children** of Israel could not stedfastly **behold the** face of **Moses** for the glory of his countenance; which glory was to be done away:

A.	New Testament
B.	so that the children of Israel could not stedfastly behold the face of Moses
C.	For if the ministration of condemnation be of glory, much more doth the ministration of righteousness exceed in glory
D.	had no glory in this respect
D'.	by reason of the glory that excelleth
C'.	For if that which is done away was glorious, much more that which remaineth is glorious
B'.	Moses, which put a veil over his face, that the children of Israel could not stedfastly look
A'.	Old Testament

C. [8] How shall not **the ministration of the spirit be rather glorious?**
[9] **For if the ministration of condemnation be of glory,** much more doth **the ministration of righteousness exceed in glory.**

D. [10] For even that which was made glorious **had no glory** in this respect,

D'. by reason of the **glory that excelleth.**

C'. [11] **For if that which is done away was glorious,** much more **that which remaineth is glorious,**

B'. [12] **Seeing then that we have such hope,** we use great plainness of speech: [13] And not as **Moses,** which put a veil over his face, **that the children of Israel could not stedfastly look to the end of that which is abolished:**

A'. [14] But their minds were blinded: for until this day remaineth the same veil untaken away in the reading of the **Old Testament**; which **veil is done away in Christ.**

[15] But even unto this day, when Moses is read, **the veil is upon their heart.**

Galatians 3:1–7

A. [1] O foolish Galatians, who hath bewitched you, that ye should not obey the truth, before whose eyes Jesus Christ hath been evidently set forth, crucified among you?

A.   Not obey the truth
B.   a. Received ye the Spirit
b. By the works of the law
c. or by the hearing of faith?
C.   Are ye so foolish?
C'. If it be yet in vain
B'. a'. Ministereth to ye the Spirit
b'. . . . doeth he it by the works of the law
c'. or by the hearing of faith?
A'. Abraham believed God

B. [2] This only would I learn of you,

   a. **Received ye the Spirit**

   b. **by the works of the law**

   c. **or by the hearing of faith?**

C. [3] Are ye so **foolish?** Having begun in the Spirit, are ye now made perfect by the flesh?

C'. [4] Have ye suffered so many things in **vain?** If it be yet in **vain.**

B'. [5] He therefore that

    a'. **ministereth to ye the Spirit, and worketh miracles among you,** doeth he it

    b'. **by the works of the law,**

    c'. **or by the hearing of faith?**

A'. [6] Even as **Abraham believed God, and it was accounted to him for righteousness.**

    [7] **Know ye therefore that they which are of faith, the same are the children of Abraham.**

        Segue: the same are **the children of Abraham.**
        They which be of **faith** are **blessed with Abraham.**

In the following system, faith is the main theme. It is found at both ends and in the middle. There is an additional emphasis of "the blessing of Abraham" which is in the first and last panel. The conclusion is, "the Just shall live by faith, and the law is not of faith."

Galatians 3:8–14

A. [8] And the scripture, forseeing that God would **justify the heathen through faith,** preached before the **gospel** unto Abraham, saying, In thee shall all **nations** be **blessed.** [9] So then they which be of **faith** are **blessed with Abraham.**

A.	Blessing	
	B.	Curse
		C. Live by faith
		C'. Law not of faith
	B'.	Curse
A'.	Blessing	

B. [10] For as many as are of the works of the law are under the **curse:** For it is written, **Cursed is every one that continueth not in all things** which are written in the book of the law to do them.

C. [11] But that no man is justified by the **law** in the sight of God, it is evident: for, **The just shall live by faith.**

C'. [12] **And the law is not of faith:** but The man that doeth them shall live in them.

B'. [13] Christ hath redeemed us from the **curse of the law**, being made a **curse** for us: for it is written, **Cursed is every one that hangeth on a tree:**

A'. [14] That the **blessing of Abraham** might come on the **Gentiles** through Jesus Christ; that we might receive the promise of the Spirit through **faith**.

Nations, verse eight and *Gentiles* in verse fourteen, are the same in the Greek.

Segue: Promise

Covenant

Galatians 3:15–17

A. [15] Brethren, I speak after the manner of men;

  a. Though it be but a man's **covenant**, yet if it be confirmed,
  b. no man **disannulleth**, or addeth thereto.

B. [16] Now to Abraham and his **seed** werethe **promises** made. He saith not, And to seeds, as of many, but as of **one**,

B'. And to **thy seed, which is Christ.**

A'. a. [17] And this I say, that the **covenant**, that was **confirmed** before of God in Christ,

  b. the law, which was four hundred and thirty years after, **cannot disannul**, that it should make the **promise** of none effect.

Segue: **Promise** of none effect
God gave it to Abraham by **promise**

Galatians 3:18–29

A. ¹⁸ For if the inheritance be of the law, it is no more of promise: but **God gave it to Abraham by promise.**

> | A. | a. Covenant |
> |----|----|
> | | b. No man disannulleth |
> | B. | seed as of one |
> | B'. | That seed was Christ |
> | A'. | a'. covenant |
> | | b'. cannot disannul |

B. ¹⁹ **Wherefore then serveth the law?**

  a. It was added because of transgressions, till the seed should come to whom the promise was made;
  b. and it was ordained by angels in the hand of a mediator. ²⁰ Now a mediator is not a mediator of one, but **God is one.**

C. ²¹ **Is the law then against the promises of God?** God forbid:
  a. for if there had been a law given which could have given life,

  b. verily righteousness should have been by the law.
  b'. ²² But the scripture hath concluded all under sin, that the promise by faith of Jesus Christ might be given to them that believe.

  a'. ²³ But before faith came, **we were kept under the law,** shut up unto the faith which should afterwards be revealed.

B'. a'. ²⁴ 1. wherefore **the law was our schoolmaster** to bring us unto Christ,

> | A. | . . . God gave it to Abraham by promise |
> |----|----|
> | B. | Wherefore then serveth the law? |
> | C. | Is the law then against the promises of God? |
> | B'. | The law was our schoolmaster |
> | A'. | are ye Abraham's seed and heirs according to the promise. |

  2. that we might be justified by faith.
  2'. ²⁵ But after that faith is come,

      1'. we are no longer under a schoolmaster.

    b'. 1. [26] For ye are all the **children of God by faith** in Christ Jesus. [27] For as many of you as have been baptized into Christ have put on Christ.

        2. [28] There is neither Jew nor Greek, there is neither bond nor free, there is neither male nor female: for **ye are all one in Christ Jesus.**

  A'. [29] And if ye be Christ's, then are ye **Abraham's seed** and heirs according to the **promise.**

This has been a long series of examples. Other authors have demonstrated chiasmus in the New Testament including examples from the pastoral epistles. The above examples demonstrate that chiasmus was Paul's normal way of writing. If Paul wrote the third chapter of all of these epistles in chiasmus, then it is reasonable to assume that he wrote the epistles, including Romans, in this form.

Paul is not the only New Testament writer to use chiasmus extensively.

Matthew 6:24

  A. "No man can **serve two masters:**

    B. For either he will **hate** one,

      C. and **love** the other;

      C'. Or else he will **hold** to the one,

    B'. and **despise** the other.

  A'. Ye cannot **serve God and mammon.**"

Usually the same word is used on both sides of inversion. In this example different words are used to express similar ideas.

> Two masters: God and mammon
> Hate: despise
> Love: hold

The above system can be viewed in light of other words within the chiasmus.

Matthew 6:24

A. "No man can **serve** two masters:

B. For either he will hate **one**,
and love the **other**;

B'. Or else he will hold to the **one**,
and despise the **other**.

A'. Ye cannot **serve** God and mammon."

The words *one* and *other* refer to the two masters the believer must choose between.

3 John 1–14

A. The elder **unto the wellbeloved Gaius**, whom I love in the truth.

B. [2] Beloved, I wish above all things that thou **mayest prosper** and be in health, **even as thy soul prospereth.**

A. Greeting
  B. I desire your good
    C. Your good testimony
      D. Your faithful service to the brethren
        E. Receive the brethren
          F. Diotrophies does not receive us
        E'. Diotrephes does not receive the brethren
      D'. Follow good not evil
    C'. Demetrius's good testimony
  B'. I desire your good
A'. Greeting

C. [3] For I rejoiced greatly, when the **brethren came and testified of the truth that is in thee**, even as thou walkest in the truth. [4]I have no greater joy than to hear that **my children walk in truth.**

D. [5] **Beloved, thou doest faithfully** whatsoever thou doest to the **brethren, and to strangers;** [6]Which have borne witness of thy charity before the church: whom if thou bring forward on their journey after a godly sort, thou shalt do well:

E. [7] Because that for his name's sake they went forth, taking nothing of the Gentiles. [8] **We therefore ought to receive such,** that we might be Fellow helpers to the truth.

F. [9] I wrote unto the church: but **Diotrephes,** who loveth to have the preeminence among them, **receiveth us not.**

E'. [10] Wherefore, if I come, I will remember his deeds which he doeth, prating against us with malicious words: and not content therewith, **neither doth he himself receive the brethren,** and forbiddeth them that would, and casteth *them* out of the church.

D'. [11] **Beloved, follow not that which is evil, but that which is good.** He that doeth good is of God: but he that doeth evil hath not seen God.

C'. [12] **Demetrius hath good report of all** *men,* and of the truth itself: yea, and we *also* bear record; and ye know that our record is true.

B'. [13] I had many things to write, but I will not with ink and pen write unto thee:[14] But I trust I shall shortly see thee, and we shall speak face to face.

Peace *be* **to thee.**

A'. *Our* **friends salute thee. Greet the friends** by name.

In the following example each point has three phrases, but there is still inversion and balance.

John 1:8–10

    A. If we say that we have no sin,
       we deceive ourselves,
       and the truth is not in us.

        B. [9] If we confess our sins,
           he is faithful and just to forgive us *our* sins,
           and to cleanse us from all unrighteousness.

   A'. [10]If we say that we have not sinned,
       we make him a liar,
       and his word is not in us.

4. Chiasmus in Romans

In the complete presentation of Romans it will be shown that the whole of Romans is written in Jewish parallelism, primarily in chiasmus. I will give a few examples here of chiasmus, starting with small, simple systems and working up to the larger and more complex.

10:5–13 [19]

    A. [5] For Moses **describeth the righteousness of the law,** [6] **But the righteousness which is of faith speaketh** on this wise

        B. [9] if thou shalt **confess with thy mouth** the Lord Jesus

           C. [10] and shalt **believe in thine heart** that God hath raised him from the dead, thou shalt be saved.

A.	Moses describeth the righteousness of the law, The righteousness which is of faith speaketh
B.	Confess with thy mouth
C.	Believe in thine heart
C'.	with the heart man believeth
B'.	With the mouth confession is made
A'.	Call upon the name

C'. For **with the heart man believeth** unto righteousness,

B'. and **with the mouth confession** is made unto salvation.

A'. [13] For whosoever shall **call upon the name of the Lord** shall be saved.

These verses are the center of three macro-systems. Since the center of a system is the conclusion and main emphasis, there is a lot of emphasis put on these verses.

The chiastic reading:

A. [5] For Moses **describeth the righteousness of the law**, [6] **But the righteousness which is of faith speaketh** on this wise

A'. [13] For whosoever shall **call upon the name of the Lord** shall be saved

B. if thou shalt **confess** with thy mouth the Lord Jesus

B'. and with the mouth **confession** is made unto salvation

C. and shalt believe in thine **heart** that God hath raised him from the dead, thou shalt be saved.

C'. For with the **heart** man believeth unto righteousness,

15:22–29

A. [22] For which cause also I have been much hindered from **coming** to you. [23] But now having no more place in these parts, and having a great desire these many years to **come unto you**;

B. [24] Whensoever **I take my journey into Spain,**
I will come to you: for I trust to see you in my journey, and to be brought on my way thitherward by you, if first I be somewhat filled with your *company*.

---

[19] Romans 10:6–12 is listed as chiasmus in, *The Shape of Biblical Language* pg. 54., by John Breck, St. Vladimir's Seminary Press, Crestwood, New York. 1994

C. ²⁵ But now I go unto Jerusalem to minister unto the saints.
²⁶ For **it hath pleased** them of Macedonia and

> A.   Having a great desire . . . to come unto you
>   B.   Whensoever I take my journey into Spain, I will come to you
>   C.   It hath pleased them of Macedonia
>   C'.   It hath pleased them
>   B'.   I will come by you into Spain
> A'.   When I come unto you

Achaia to make a certain contribution for the poor saints which are at Jerusalem.

C'. ²⁷ **It hath pleased** them verily; and their debtors they are. For if the Gentiles have been made partakers of their spiritual things, their duty is also to minister unto them in carnal things.

B'. ²⁸ When therefore I have performed this, and have sealed to them this fruit, **I will come by you into Spain.**

A'. ²⁹ And I am sure that, when I **come unto you**, I shall **come** in the fulness of the blessing of the gospel of Christ.

The correlation in this chiasmus is not highly detailed but very clear just the same. Partly, the clarity comes from the use of words and phrases that are not used through the body of the letter. This passage will also correlate to chapter one where Paul says that he desires to come and visit them.

The chiastic reading:

A. ²² For which cause also I have been much hindered from coming to you. ²³But now having no more place in these parts, and having a great desire these many years to come unto you;

A'. ²⁹ And I am sure that, when I come unto you, I shall come in the fulness of the blessing of the gospel of Christ.

B. ²⁴ Whensoever I take my journey into Spain, I will come to you: for I trust to see you in my journey, and to be brought on my way thitherward by you, if first I be somewhat filled with your *company*.

B'. [28] When therefore I have performed this, and have sealed to them this fruit, I will come by you into Spain.

C. [25] But now I go unto Jerusalem to minister unto the saints. [26]For it hath pleased them of Macedonia and Achaia to make a certain contribution for the poor saints which are at Jerusalem.

C'. [27] It hath pleased them verily; and their debtors they are. For if the Gentiles have been made partakers of their spiritual things, their duty is also to minister unto them in carnal things.

13:8–10

A. [8] Owe no man any thing, but to **love one another**: for he that **loveth another hath fulfilled the law**.

    B. [9] For this,
    Thou shalt not commit adultery,
    Thou shalt not kill,
    Thou shalt not steal,
    Thou shalt not bear false witness,
    Thou shalt not covet; and

    B'. if *there be* any other commandment, it is briefly comprehended in this saying, namely, **Thou shalt love thy neighbour as thyself.**

> A. He that loveth another hath fulfilled the law
> B. Thou shalt not
> B'. Thou shalt love thy neighbour as thyself
> A'. Love is the fulfilling of the law

A'. [10] **Love** worketh no ill to his neighbour: therefore **love** *is* **the fulfilling of the law**.

This system has a list in B. When a list appears in an element, there is often an imbalance.

The chiastic reading:

A. [8]Owe no man any thing, but to **love one another**: for he that **loveth another hath fulfilled the law**.

A'. [10] **Love** worketh no ill to his neighbour: therefore **love** *is* **the fulfilling of the law.**

B. [9] For this, **Thou shalt not** commit adultery, **Thou shalt not** kill, **Thou shalt not** steal, **Thou shalt not** bear false witness, **Thou shalt not** covet; and

B'. if *there be* any other commandment, it is briefly comprehended in this saying, namely, **Thou shalt love thy neighbour as thyself.**

8:35–39

A. [35] Who shall **separate us from the love of Christ?**

B. *shall* tribulation, or distress, or persecution, or famine, or nakedness, or

A.	Who shall separate us from the love of Christ?
B.	Shall tribulation, or distress
	C. We are more than conquerors
B'.	For I am persuaded, that neither death, nor life . . . Shall be able to
A'.	Separate us from the love of God

peril, or sword? [36] As it is written, For thy sake we are killed all the day long; we are accounted as sheep for the slaughter.

C. [37] Nay, in all these things **we are more than conquerors** through him that **loved** us.

B'. [38] For I am persuaded, that neither death, nor life, nor angels, nor principalities, nor powers, nor things present, nor things to come, [39] Nor height, nor depth, nor any other creature,

A'. shall be able to **separate us from the love of God,** which is in Christ Jesus our Lord.

This system has a list in both **B** and **B'** resulting in a balanced system. Different words are used in these lists but there should be no doubt that they correlate. The love of Christ and the love of God correlate demonstrating that Christ's love is God's love. God's love for Israel will be expressed through Paul in chapter nine. The main theme is in verse thirt-seven.

The chiastic reading:

A. [35]Who shall separate us from the love of Christ?

A'. shall be able to separate us from the love of God, which is in Christ Jesus our Lord.

B. *shall* tribulation, or distress, or persecution, or famine, or nakedness, or peril, or sword? [36]As it is written, For thy sake we are killed all the day long; we are accounted as sheep for the slaughter.

B'. [38]For I am persuaded, that neither death, nor life, nor angels, nor principalities, nor powers, nor things present, nor things to come,[39]Nor height, nor depth, nor any other creature,

C. [37]Nay, in all these things we are more than conquerors through him that loved us.

I will now present a series of chiasma from the midsection of Romans, so that we can see Paul's segue as well as illustrate some very detailed chiasma.

6:15–23

[15]What then? **Shall we sin**, because we **are not under the law, but under grace**? God forbid.

A. [16]Know ye not,
that to whom ye yield
yourselves servants
to obey, his servants ye
are to whom ye obey;
whether of **sin unto
death**, or of **obedience
unto righteousness**?

    B. [17]But God be thank-
ed, that **ye were the
servants of sin**, but
ye have **obeyed**

> A. his servants ye are to whom ye obey; whether of sin unto death, or of obedience unto righteousness
>   B. Ye were servants of sin; Ye became the servants of righteousness.
>   C. ye have yielded your members servants to uncleanness and to iniquity unto iniquity;
>   C'. even so now yield your members servants to righteousness unto holiness
>   B'. Ye were servants of sin . . . And become servants of God
> A'. The wages of sin is death . . . The gift of God is eternal life

from the heart that form of doctrine which was delivered you. [18] **Being then made free from sin, ye became the servants of righteousness.**

C. [19] I speak after the manner of men because of the infirmity of your flesh: for as ye have **yielded your members servants to** uncleanness and to **iniquity unto iniquity**;

C'. even so now **yield your members servants to righteousness unto holiness.**

B'. [20] **For when ye were the servants of sin, ye were free from righteousness.** [21] What fruit had ye then in those things whereof ye are now ashamed? For the end of those things *is* death. [22] But **now being made free from sin, and become servants to God,** ye have your fruit unto holiness, and the end everlasting life.

A'. [23] For the **wages of sin** *is* **death**; but **the gift of God** *is* eternal life through Jesus Christ our Lord.

Notice how detailed the correlation between parts is, and that the basic construction is that of the colon-bicolon used in Hebrew.

B. [17] But God be thanked, that ye were the servants of sin, but ye have obeyed from the heart that form of doctrine which was delivered you. [18] Being then made free from sin, ye became the servants of righteousness.

B'. [20] For when ye were the servants of sin, ye were free from righteousness [22] But now being made free from sin, and become servants to God . . .

C. . . . yielded your members servants to uncleanness and to iniquity unto iniquity;

C'. even so now yield your members servants to righteousness unto holiness.

Segue:

a. wages of sin is death
b. the gift of God is eternal life through Jesus Christ our Lord

a'. The first husband (Law)

b'. The second husband (Christ)

7:1–6

A. ¹Know ye not, brethren, (for I speak to them that know the law,) how that the **law hath dominion** over a man as long as he liveth?

B. ² For the woman which hath an husband is bound by the law to *her* husband so long as he liveth; but **if the husband be dead, she is loosed from the law of** *her* **husband**.

> A. How that the law hath dominion over a man as long as he liveth?
> B. if the husband be dead, she is loosed from the law of *her* husband
>> C. She be married to another man, she shall be called an adulteress
>> C'. So that she is no adulteress, though she be married to another man
> B'. Ye also are become dead to the law by the body of Christ
> A'. But now we are delivered from the law

C. ³ So then if, while *her* husband liveth, **she be married to another man,** she shall be called an adulteress:

C'. but if her husband be dead, she is free from that law; so that she is no adulteress, though **she be married to another man**.

B'. ⁴Wherefore, my brethren, **ye also are become dead to the law by the body of Christ**; that ye should be married to another, *even to* him who is raised from the dead, that we should bring forth fruit unto God.

A'. ⁵ For when we were in the flesh, **the motions of sins, which were by the law**, did work in our members to bring forth fruit unto death. ⁶**But now we are delivered from the law, that being dead wherein we were held**; that we should serve in newness of spirit, and not *in* the oldness of the letter.

The chiastic reading:

A. ¹Know ye not, brethren, (for I speak to them that know the law,) how that the law hath dominion over a man as long as he liveth?

A'. ⁵For when we were in the flesh, the motions of sins, which were by the law, did work in our members to bring forth fruit unto death. ⁶But now we are delivered from the law, that being dead wherein we were held; that we should serve in newness of spirit, and not *in* the oldness of the letter.

B. ²For the woman which hath an husband is bound by the law to *her* husband so long as he liveth; but if the husband be dead, she is loosed from the law of *her* husband.

B'. ⁴Wherefore, my brethren, ye also are become dead to the law by the body of Christ; that ye should be married to another, *even* to him who is raised from the dead, that we should bring forth fruit unto God.

C. ³So then if, while *her* husband liveth, she be married to another man, she shall be called an adulteress:

C'. but if her husband be dead, she is free from that law; so that she is no adulteress, though she be married to another man.

The segue from 7:6 to 7:7 will be presented later.

7:7–12

A. ⁷What shall we say then? *Is the law sin?* God forbid. Nay, I had not known sin, but by the law: for I had not known lust, except the law had said, Thou shalt not covet.

A. Is the law sin
  B. Sin, taking occasion by the commandment
    C. Sin was dead
      D. I was alive
      D'. I died
    C'. The commandment . . . I found to be unto death
  B'. Sin taking occasion by the commandment
A'. The law is holy . . . just and good

B. [8]But **sin, taking occasion by the commandment**, wrought in me all manner of concupiscence.

    C. For without **the law sin *was* dead.**

        D. [9]For **I was alive** without the law once:

        D'. but when the commandment came, sin revived, and **I died.**

    C'. [10]And **the commandment**, which *was ordained* to life, **I found** *to be* **unto death.**

B'. [11]For **sin, taking occasion by the commandment**, deceived me, and by it slew *me.*

A'. [12]Wherefore the **law *is* holy**, and the commandment holy, and **just**, and **good.**

The chiastic reading:

A. [7] Nay, I had not known sin, but by the law: for I had not known lust, except the law had said, Thou shalt not covet.

A'. [12]Wherefore the law *is* holy, and the commandment holy, and just, and good.

B. [8]But sin, taking occasion by the commandment, wrought in me all manner of concupiscence.

B'. [11]For sin, taking occasion by the commandment, deceived me, and by it slew *me.*

C. For without the law sin *was* dead.

C'. [10]And the commandment, which *was ordained* to life, I found *to be* unto death.

D. [9]For I was alive without the law once:

D'. but when the commandment came, sin revived, and I died.

Segue:

[12] Wherefore the **law** *is* holy, and the commandment holy, and just, and **good**. Was then that which is **good** the law made death unto me? God forbid.

7:13–23

[13] Was then that which is good the law made death unto me? God forbid.

A. But sin, that it might appear sin, **working death in me** by that which is good; that **sin by the commandment might become exceeding sinful.**

> A.   That sin by the commandment might become exceeding sinful
> B.   I am carnal, sold under sin
> > C.   For that which I do I allow not: it is no more I that do it, but sin that dwelleth in me
> > > D.   I know that in me . . . dwelleth no good thing
> > C'. For the good that I would I do not Now if I do that I would not, it is no more I that do it, but sin that dwelleth in me
> B'. When I would do good, evil is present with me
> A'. I delight in the law of God after the inward man

B. [14] For we know that the law is spiritual: but **I am carnal**, sold under sin.

C. [15] For that which I do I allow not: for what I would, that do I not; but what I hate, that do I. [16] If then I do that which I would not, I consent unto the law that *it is* good. [17] Now then **it is no more I that do it, but sin that dwelleth in me.**

D. [18] For **I know that in me** (that is, in my flesh,) **dwelleth no good thing**: for to will is present with me; but *how* to perform that which is **good** I find not

C'. [19] For the **good** that I would I do not: but the **evil** which I would not, that I do. [20] Now if I do that I would not, **it is no more I that do it, but sin that dwelleth in me**

B'. [21] I find then a law, that, when I would do **good, evil is present with me.**

A'. [22] For **I delight in the law of God** after the inward man: [23] But I see another law in my members, warring against the law of my mind, and bringing me into captivity the law of sin which is in my members.

These sets of elements vary in the degree of correlating detail, but those elements that have detailed correlation help us identify the system and the less-detailed elements. In the above chiasmus, B and B' are not highly correlated, but C and C' are.

C. [15] For that which I do I allow not: for what I would, that do I not; but what I hate, that do I.

C'. [19] For the good that I would I do not: but the evil which I would not, that I do.

And

C. [17] Now then it is no more I that do it, but sin that dwelleth in me.

C'. [20] Now if I do that I would not, it is no more I that do it, but sin that dwelleth in me.

The format of verses fifteen and nineteen is unique to this passage and does not appear anywhere else in Romans. This highly detailed correlation serves as a marker. Once these elements are identified, the center of the chiasmus is halfway between them.

The following chiasmus is an alternating one, alternating between the old Adam and the new Adam. It also has the main theme in both extremes and in the center.

a. Death reigned
b. Him that was to come

    a. Death reigned by one
    b. Righteousness shall reign in life by one

a. Sin hath reigned unto death

b. even so might grace reign

5:14–21

A. a. [14] Nevertheless **death reigned** from Adam to Moses, even over them that had not sinned after the similitude of Adam's transgression,

b. **who is the figure of him that was to come.**

```
A.   Death reigned
     . . . him that was to come
  B.   Through the offence of one
       Much more the grace
    C.  by one to condemnation
        Many offences unto justification
      D.  Death reigned by one
          Righteousness shall reign in life
          by one
    C'.  Judgment came upon all men to
         condemnation
         The free gift came upon all men unto
         justification of life
  B'.  By one man's disobedience
       Grace did much more abound
A'.  Sin hath reigned unto death
     Grace rein . . . unto eternal life by Jesus Christ
```

B. a. [15] But not as the offence, so also *is the free gift.* For if through the **offence of one many** be dead,

b. **much more the grace** of God, and **the gift by grace,** *which is* **by one man,** Jesus Christ, hath abounded unto many.

C. a. [16] And not as *it was* by one that sinned, *so is* the gift: for the judgment *was* by one to **condemnation,**

b. but the *free gift is* of many offences unto **justification.**

D. a. [17] For if by one man's offence **death reigned by one;**

b. much more they which receive abundance of grace and of the gift of **righteousness shall reign** in life **by one** Jesus Christ.

C'. a'. [18] Therefore as by the offence of one *judgment came* upon all men to **condemnation;**

b'. even so by the righteousness of one *the free gift came* upon all men unto **justification** of life.

B'. a'. [19] For as by **one man's disobedience** many were **made sinners,** so **by the obedience of one** shall many be **made righteous.**

  b'. [20] Moreover the law entered, that the offence might abound. But where sin abounded, **grace did much more abound:**

A'. a'. [21] That as sin hath **reigned unto death,**

  b'. even so might **grace reign** through righteousness unto eternal life by **Jesus Christ our Lord**

The chiastic reading:

A. a. [14] Nevertheless death reigned from Adam to Moses, even over them that had not sinned after the similitude of Adam's transgression,

  b. who is the figure of him that was to come.

A'. a'. [21] That as sin hath reigned unto death,

  b'. even so might grace reign through righteousness unto eternal life by Jesus Christ our Lord.

B. a. [15] But not as the offence, so also *is* the *free gift.* For if through the offence of one many be dead,

  b. much more the grace of God, and the gift by grace, *which is* by one man, Jesus Christ, hath abounded unto many.

B'. a'. [19] For as by one man's disobedience many were made sinners, so by the obedience of one shall many be made righteous.

  b'. [20] Moreover the law entered, that the offence might abound. But where sin abounded, grace did much more abound:

C. a. [16] And not as *it was* by one that sinned, *so is* the gift: for the judgment *was* by one to condemnation,

  b. but the *free gift is* of many offences unto justification.

C'. a'. [18] Therefore as by the offence of one *judgment came* upon all men to condemnation;

  b'. even so by the righteousness of one *the free gift came* upon all men unto justification of life.

D. a. [17] For if by one man's offence death reigned by one;

   b. much more they which receive abundance of grace and of the gift of righteousness shall reign in life by one Jesus Christ.

C. Paul's Thought Process

A question often asked is, did the authors of scripture think in chiasmus and other aspects of parallelism as their first thought process? In this paper I am especially concerned with Paul. To answer this as it applies to Paul, I will look at two passages of Scripture where Paul speaks extemporaneously. When we speak extemporaneously we do not have time to plan our presentation, and cannot revise or edit what we say. We must rely on the thought processes that come naturally to us. Much of the way we organize our extemporaneous thoughts happens in the subconscious.

In this first passage, Paul is on Mars Hill in Athens, Greece. His Gentile audience is not familiar with the extensive use of chiasmus. If ever Paul was going to choose to use the thought process of the Greek culture, it seems that this would be it. Paul speaks here in Greek, but he does not use the form that his audience is most familiar with but the form with which he personally is most comfortable. Regardless of what language he was using, he thought in chiasmus, which is then expressed in both his written and spoken communication. He does not have time to contemplate or to plan out a presentation. He is asked to speak and this is what he said:

Acts 17:23–31

For as I passed by, and beheld your devotions, I found an altar with this inscription, TO THE UNKNOWN GOD. Whom therefore ye ignorantly worship, him declare I unto you.

A. [24] **God that made the world and all things therein,**

B. seeing that he is Lord of heaven and earth, **dwelleth not in temples made with hands;**

A. God that made the world
   B. Dwelleth not in temples made with hands
   B'. Neither is worshipped with men's hands
A'. Hath made of one blood all nations of men

B'. [25] **Neither is worshipped with men's hands**, as though he needed any thing, seeing he giveth to all life, and breath, and all things;

A'. [26] And **hath made of one blood all nations of men** for to dwell on all the face of the earth,

A. and **hath determined the times before appointed and the bounds of their habitation;**

B. [27] **That they should seek the Lord,** if haply they might feel after him, and find him, though he be not far from every one of us:

A.	The times before appointed	
B.	They should seek the Lord	
	C.	For we are also his offspring
	C'.	. . . we are the offspring of God
B'.	Commandeth all men every where to repent	
A'.	He hath appointed a day	

C. [28] For in him we live, and move, and have our being; as certain also of your own poets have said, **For we are also his offspring.**

C'. [29] **Forasmuch then as we are the offspring of God,** we ought not to think that the Godhead is like unto gold, or silver, or stone, graven by art and man's device.

B'. [30] And the times of this ignorance God winked at, but **now commandeth all men every where to repent:**

A'. [31] **Because he hath appointed a day, in the which he will judge the world in righteousness by that man whom he hath ordained;** whereof he hath given assurance unto all men, in that he hath raised him from the dead.

In the second passage, Paul has just been beaten and arrested. He asks the soldiers for permission to speak to his accusers. This is an extremely emotional setting.

Acts 22:3–21

A. ³ I am verily a man *which am* a Jew, **born in Tarsus, a city in Cilicia,** yet brought up in this city at the feet of Gamaliel, and taught according to the perfect manner of the law of the fathers, and was zealous toward God, as ye all are this day.

> A.   A Jew, born in Tarsus in Cilicia
> B.   I persecuted this way unto the death
> C.   Suddenly there shone from heaven a great light round about me
> D.   What shall I do Lord?
> E.   I could not see
> F.   Ananias
> E'. Receive thy sight
> D'. Thou shalt be his witness unto all men
> C'. I was in a trance
> B'. Stephen
> A'. I will send thee far hence unto the Gentiles

B. a. ⁴ And **I persecuted this way unto the death, binding and delivering into prisons both men and women.**

   b.   ⁵ As also the **high priest doth bear me witness.**

   b'. And **all the estate of the elders: from whom also I received letters** unto the brethren,

 a'. and went to Damascus, to **bring them which were there bound unto Jerusalem, for to be punished.**

C. ⁶ And it came to pass, that, as I made my journey, and was come nigh unto Damascus about noon,

   a.   **suddenly there shone from heaven a great light round about me.**

   b.   ⁷ **And I fell unto the ground, and heard a voice saying unto me, Saul, Saul, why persecutest thou me?**

   b'. ⁸ And I answered, Who art thou, Lord? And he said unto me, I am Jesus of Nazareth, whom thou persecutest.

a'. ⁹ And they that were with me **saw** indeed the light, and were afraid; but they **heard not** the voice of him that spake to me.

D. ¹⁰ And I said, **What shall I do Lord?** And the Lord said unto me, Arise, and go into Damascus: and there **it shall be told thee of all things which are appointed for thee to do.**

E. ¹¹ and **when I could not see for the glory of that light**, being led by the hand of them that were with me, I came into Damascus.

F. ¹² And one Ananias, a devout man according to the law, having a good report of all the Jews which dwelt there, ¹³ Came unto me, and stood, and said unto me,

E'. **Brother Saul, receive thy sight.** And the same hour I looked up upon him. ¹⁴ And he said, the God of our fathers hath chosen thee, that thou shouldest know his will, and see that Just One, and shouldest hear the voice of his mouth.

D'. ¹⁵ For **thou shalt be his witness unto all men of what thou hast seen and heard.** ¹⁶ And now why tarriest thou? Arise, and be baptized, and wash away thy sins, calling on the name of the Lord.

C'. a. ¹⁷ And it came to pass that, when **I was come again to Jerusalem**,

b. even while I prayed in the temple, **I was in a trance;**

b'. ¹⁸ And **saw him saying unto me,**

a'. **Make haste, and get thee quickly out of Jerusalem:** for they will not receive thy testimony concerning me.

B'. [19] And I said, Lord, they know that

>> a. **I imprisoned and beat in every synagogue them that believed on thee:**
>>
>>> b. [20] And when the blood of thy **martyr Stephen** was shed,
>>>
>>> b'. I also was standing by, and **consenting unto his death,**
>>
>> a'. and **kept the raiment** of them that slew him.

A'. [21] And he said unto me, Depart: **for I will send thee far hence unto the Gentilles.**

Verses four and twenty correlate. We therefore know that when he said, "And I persecuted this way unto the death," he was referring to the death of Steven. C and C' correlate because the Lord appears to Saul in both.

I conclude that Jewish parallelisms, especially chiasma, were Paul's natural and preferred thought patterns. To think in any other form would require a conscious decision or a very definite stimulus. He would otherwise think in Jewish parallelisms. Of the various forms of Jewish parallelism, Paul definitely prefers chiasmus.

The position of this paper is that, in inverted parallelism, chiasma are the primary literary units and are short enough to allow a complete system to be held in the working memory of most people. Seldom will they exceed fourteen elements, seven on a side. A maximum length of fifteen verses has been suggested for chiasmus. The fifteen-verse limit is debatable, but fifteen is a good approximate number. Of the many chiasma proposed in this paper, one is sixteen verses long, and another fifteen. The remaining chiasma are thirteen verses or less and average between seven and eight verses. In the introduction of this paper, Paul's defense in Acts 22 is nineteen verses, the prologue to the gospel of John is eighteen verses, and 3 John is fourteen verses. The remaining chiasma are thirteen verses, or less.

D. Macro-systems

Since the writing of the New Testament, scholars have believed that there are large inverted systems; but, as they have sought to find them, their efforts have been to little or no avail. This lack of evidence has resulted in a controversy concerning macro-chiasma. This controversy has been fueled by the lack of convincing evidence and by abuse. By abuse I mean that macro-chiasma have been proposed where there is no evidence to support the claim. There is a rising swell of objection to such claims, even questioning the legitimacy of large systems. Some question whether the authors of Scripture actually intended to create large systems, or are they the product of the reader's mind?

Much of the abuse has taken advantage of the fact that chiasmus is a rhyme of thought, and need not be expressed in the same words. The norm is to express correlating parts in the same words, phrases, or the same unique literary construction. It seems that the questionable claims of macro-chiasma usually have none of the above, but rely on wording provided by the finder. Not that it is wrong to summarize, but there are inherent dangers, and care must be taken to accurately represent both the message and the form.

To avoid the problems that come with summarizing a text, I will quote the whole text as much as possible. When presenting systems that are much too large for that, select portions will be quoted so as to use the wording to the text. Occasionally, I will summarize, stating the text in my own words, but this will be the exception not the rule.

Generally, scholars have believed that macro-systems are identical to micro-chiasma but larger. The position of this paper is that most macro-systems are fundamentally different from chiasma. They share some of the same characteristics, but have their own unique differences as well.

Examples of Macro-systems

Examples of chiasma are increasingly being documented in scripture. A small but dedicated group of scholars have worked hard to document macro-systems. In the Old Testament there has been moderate success, but in the New Testament, success has been minimal. This effort has increased in the past few decades, but macro-systems have been elusive; therefore, good New Testament examples are difficult to find. In the last decade

John Breck has shown that the book of Ruth is chiastic; Wayne Brower has done the same with John 13–17.

a. Macro-systems in the Old Testament

The following example is from my own study and covers Jeremiah 23–33.

A.   I will raise unto David a righteous Branch . . .
this is his name whereby he shall be called, THE LORD OUR RIGHTEOUSNESS
    B.   For the land is full of adulterers . . . For both prophet and priest are profane
        C.   I will build them, and not pull them down, and
           I will plant them, and not pluck them up
           D.   they shall be my people, and I will be their God
               E.   these nations shall serve the king of Babylon seventy years
                  F.   they fetched forth Urijah out of Egypt, and . . . Jehoiakim . . . slew him
                     G.   cast his dead body into the graves of the common people
                        H.   Make thee bonds and yokes, and put them upon thy neck
                           I.   Bring your necks under the yoke of the king of Babylon
                         I'.   I have broken the yoke of the king of Babylon
                      H'.   Then Hananiah the prophet took the yoke from off the prophet Jeremiah's neck, and brake it
                  G'.   I cast thee from off the face of the earth
                F'.   this year thou shalt die
             E'.   after seventy years be accomplished at Babylon I will visit you
          D'.   ye shall be my people, and I will be your God
      C'.   so will I watch over them, to build, and to plant, saith the LORD
    B'.   which my covenant they brake, although I was an husband unto them
A'.   I cause the Branch of righteousness to grow up unto David . . .
this is the name wherewith she shall be called, The LORD our righteousness

Jeremiah 23–33

A.   ^{23:5} Behold, the days come, saith the LORD, that **I will raise unto David a righteous Branch**, and a King shall reign and prosper, **and shall execute judgement and justice in the earth.** ⁶ **In his days Judah shall be saved, and Israel shall dwell safely:** and this is his name whereby he shall be called, **THE LORD OUR RIGHTEOUSNESS.**

B.   ¹⁰ For the land is full of **adulterers** . . . ¹¹ For both prophet and priest are **profane** . . . ¹³ And I have seen **folly** in the prophets of Samaria . . . ¹⁴ I have seen also in the prophets of Jerusalem **an horrible thing** . . .

C. ^{24:6} For **I will set mine eyes upon them for good**, and I will bring them again to this land: and **I will build them**, and not pull them down, and **I will plant them**, and not pluck them up.

D. ⁷ And I will give them an heart to know me, that I am the LORD: **and they shall be my people, and I will be their God**: for they shall return unto me with their whole heart.

E. ^{25:11} And this whole land shall be a desolation, and an astonishment; and these nations shall serve the king of Babylon **seventy years**. ¹² And it shall come to pass, when **seventy years** are accomplished, that I will punish the king of Babylon, and that nation, saith the LORD, for their iniquity, and the land of the Chaldeans, and will make it perpetual desolations.

F. ^{26:23} And they **fetched forth Urijah** out of Egypt, and brought him unto Jehoiakim the king; who **slew him** with the sword,

G. and **cast his dead body into the graves of the common people**.

H. ^{27:2} Thus saith the LORD to me; **Make thee bonds and yokes, and put them upon thy neck** . . .

I. ¹² I spake also to Zedekiah king of Judah according to all these words, saying, **Bring your necks under the yoke of the king of Babylon**, and serve him and his people, and live.

I'. Hananiah spake unto Jeremiah in the house of the LORD. ^{28:2} Thus speaketh the LORD of hosts, the God of Israel, saying, **I have broken the yoke of the king of Babylon:** 3 Within two full years will I bring again into this place all the vessels of the LORD'S house, that Nebuchadnezzar took away from this place, and carried them to Babylon . . .

H'. [10] Then **Hananiah the prophet took the yoke from off the prophet Jeremiah's neck, and brake it** . . . [13] Go and tell Hananiah, saying, thus saith the LORD; Thou hast broken the yokes of wood; but thou shalt make for them yokes of iron . . .

G'. [16] Therefore thus saith the LORD; Behold, I **cast thee from off the face of the earth:**

F'. **this year thou shalt die,** because thou hast taught rebellion against the LORD. [17] So **Hananiah the prophet died** the same year in the seventh month.

E'. [29:10] For thus saith the LORD, That after **seventy years** be accomplished at Babylon I will visit you, and perform my good word toward you, in causing you to return to this place.

D'. [30:22] And ye **shall be my people, and I will be your God.**

C'. [31:28] And it shall come to pass, that like I have watched over them, to pluck up, and to break down, and to throw down, and to destroy, and to afflict; **so will I watch over them, to build,** and **to plant,** saith the LORD.

B'. [31] Behold, the days come, saith the LORD, that I will make a new covenant with the house of Israel, and with the house of

Judah: [32] Not according to the covenant that I made with their fathers in the day that I took them by the hand to bring them out of the land of Egypt; **which my covenant they brake, although I was an husband unto them**, saith the LORD . . .

A'. [33:14] Behold, the days come, saith the LORD, that I will perform good that thing which I have promised unto the house of Israel and to the house of Judah. [15] In those days, and at that time, will **I cause the Branch of righteousness to grow up unto David; and he shall execute judgment and righteousness in the land.** [16] **In those days shall Judah be saved, and Jerusalem shall dwell safely**: and this is the name wherewith she shall be called, **The LORD our righteousness.**

This system is very balanced with a great amount of detail between parallel parts. In most of these sets of information the subject matter does not occur anywhere else in Jeremiah. The one exception is **D.** and **D'.** This statement appears five times in Jeremiah and four of these are in this system. (See 7:23, 31:33, and 32:38.) This system does not need these two elements to be a valid system, but I included them because they fit well in the already-established system. Undoubtedly, some will prefer not to include them.

It is thought that some chiasma were subconscious. Chiasmus was so much a part of the culture that it just happened.[20] This is probably true of many of the smaller systems, but the large chiastic systems presented in this paper could only be the product of conscious planning and effort. Paul would have had to plan the presentation of his early verses so as to reflect what he intended to do in the rest of the system. The Holy Spirit was moving Paul, but he was still aware of the form.

b. **Macro-systems in the New Testament**

I have recently begun a chiastic study of the book of Revelation. The following system is from that study. It is not balanced, because there are two

---

[20] *Chiasmus in the New Testament,* 1992 Preface xxv Nils W. Lund, Hendrickson, Peabody, Mass. Reprint 1992

chapters on one side and one on the other, but there is a pattern of inversion and symmetry. This system focuses on Christ as he is revealed in chapter one, and how he presents himself to the angels of the seven churches in chapters two and three.

Revelation 1–3

[1:4] . . . Grace be unto you, and peace, from him which is, and which was, and which is to come; [the Father]

   A. and from the seven Spirits which are before his throne; [the Spirit]

      B. [5] and from Jesus Christ, [the Son]

         C. who is the faithful witness, and the first begotten of the dead, and the prince of the kings of the earth.

            D. [14] . . . his eyes were as a flame of fire: [15] and his feet like unto fine brass, as if they burned in a furnace . . .

               E. [16] . . . out of his mouth went a sharp twoedged sword . . .

                  F. [17] . . . Fear not; I am the first and the last:[18] I am he that liveth, and was dead; and, behold, I am alive for evermore,

                     G. [20] . . . The seven stars which thou sawest in my right hand, and the seven golden candlesticks.

                       H. The seven stars are the angels of the seven churches: and the seven candlesticks which thou sawest are the seven churches.

                     G'. [2:1] . . . he that holdeth the seven stars in his right hand, who walketh in the midst of the seven golden candlesticks: [Ephesus]

                  F'. [8] . . . the first and the last which was dead and is alive; [Smyrna]

E'. [12] . . . he which hath the sharp sword with two edges; *[Pergamos]*

D'. [18] . . . the Son of God, who hath his eyes like unto a flame of fire, and his feet are like fine brass; *[Thyatira]*

A'. [3:1] . . . he that hath the seven Spirits of God, and the seven stars . . . *[Sardis]*

B'. [7] . . . he that is holy he that is true, he that hath the key of David . . . *[Philadelphia]*

C'. [14] . . . the amen, the faithful and true witness, the beginning of the creation of God[21] *[Laodicea]*

I am in the early stages of this study and there is much to be done, but for groups of seven, the division of the first four and the last three is common in Revelation. For example, the first four seal judgements are announced by the four beasts of 4:6–9, but the last three are not. The last three trumpet judgments; are woe judgments, the first four are not.

In the temple menorah, the last three lamps are a mirror image of lamps two through four. When the presentation shifts to the last three lamps, it also shifts from inversion to a direct comparison.

---

[21] In chiastic literature an author will sometimes make a comparison to something that the reader is expected to know. The author or speaker does not restate this material, which constitutes the primary side, but presents the secondary side only. The vision of chapter one is an example of this. Consider the following:

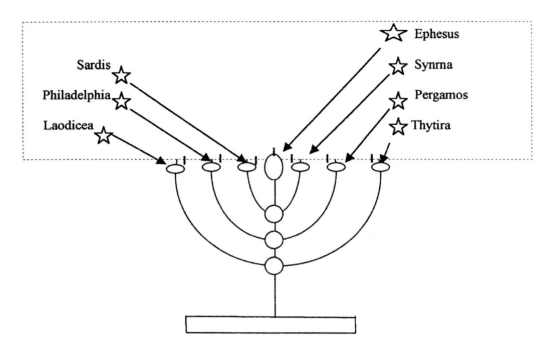

The first eleven chapters of Revelation follow the imagery of the daily sacrifice. In the Jewish temple, the day began with the slaying of the sacrificial lamb. This took place as the first rays of sunlight came over the horizon. The cleansing of the golden altar was timed to take place at the same time. It was at this time that the doors to the court of Israel were also opened, allowing the worshipers to

---

Daniel

A. ^{10:5} Then I lifted up mine eyes, and looked,

  B. and behold a certain man clothed in linen, whose loins were girded with fine gold of Uphaz:

    C. ⁶ His body also was like the beryl, and his face as the appearance of lightning,

      D. and his arms and his feet like in colour to polished brass,

        E. and the voice of his words like the voice of a multitude.

          F. ⁷ and I Daniel alone saw the vision . . . ⁹ Yet heard I the voice of his words: and when I heard the voice of his words, then was I in a deep sleep on my face, and my face toward the ground.

            G. ¹⁰ And, behold, an hand touched me, which set me upon my knees and upon the palms of my hands.¹¹ And he said unto me, O Daniel, a man greatly beloved, understand the words that I speak unto thee, and stand upright: for unto thee am I now sent. And when he had spoken this word unto me, I stood trembling.

              H. ¹² Then said he unto me, Fear not, Daniel: for from the first day that thou didst set thine heart to understand, and to chasten thyself before thy God, thy words were heard, and I am come for thy words. (continued on page 81)

come in. The next event was the lighting of the menorah. This was timed to take place when the blood of the daily sacrifice was being applied to the altar of sacrifice. The center lamp was always trimmed, oiled, and lit first. After this the priest trimmed and oiled the other six lamps, but lit only four of them, leaving two to be lit later in the service. He did the three on the right first starting with the one next to the center lamp and moving outward. After this the priest returned to the center lamp, and starting with the one next to it on the left, again moving outward. The risen Christ introduced himself to Ephesus as, "he that holdeth the seven stars in his right hand, who walketh in the midst of the seven golden candlesticks."

After lamp four, which is Laodicea, he returns to center lamp. He then introduces himself to Sardis as, "he that hath the seven Spirits of God, and the seven stars . . ."

We are told in 4:5, ". . . And there were seven lamps of fire burning before the throne, which are the seven Spirits of God."

The seven lamps of fire are the heavenly menorah, while the seven churches are the earthly representation of the same. This being true, Christ introduces

---

Revelation

A'. [1:12] And I turned to see the voice that spake with me. And being turned, I saw seven golden candlesticks;

  B'. [13] And in the midst of the seven candlesticks one like unto the Son of man, clothed with a garment down to the foot, and girt about the paps with a golden girdle.

    C'. [14] His head and his hairs were white like wool, as white as snow; and his eyes were as a flame of fire;

      D'. [15] And his feet like unto fine brass, as if they burned in a furnace;

        E'. and his voice as the sound of many waters. [16] And he had in his right hand seven stars: and out of his mouth went a sharp twoedged sword: and his countenance was as the sun shineth in this strength.

          F'. [17] And when I saw him, I fell at his feet as dead.

            G'. And he laid his right hand upon me

              H'. saying unto me, Fear not; I am the first and the last: [18] I am he that liveth, and was dead; and, behold, I am alive for evermore, Amen; and have the keys of hell and of death.

There are other aspects to this comparison, but the above is enough to illustrate that the author used an expected knowledge base as one side of this comparison.

himself to Sardis as he did to Ephesus. This helps the reader know that the presentation has returned to the center and is starting out again.

c. **Macro–systems in Romans**

1. Extended Chiasmus

There are several extended chiasma in Romans. Some of them are much too large to include here. I will give two examples that take about one page each to present. The rest can be found in the main paper.

Starting in Romans 4:1 there is a reoccurring phrase, "What shall we say then?" I remember my teacher in Bible school commenting on this, saying that Paul does this only in Romans and that there is no known reason for him doing this.

There is another reoccurring phrase later in Romans: "I say." This system centers in 10:5–13, which focuses on the speech of the repentant sinner. The primary side tells us what the speech of the believer should be, and the secondary side tells us what Paul's speech was. All this is in contrast to the speech of unbelievers in 3:8–20, who hold the truth in unrighteousness.

An Atypical Extended Chiasmus 4:1–12:8

(A.) [4:1] **What shall we say then** that Abraham our father, as pertaining to the flesh, hath found? [2] **He hath** *whereof* **to glory**; but not before God.

> (B.) **a.** [6:1] **What shall we say then?** Shall we continue in sin, that grace may abound? [2] **God forbid** [Death, burial and resurrection]
>
> > **b.** [15] What then? Shall we sin, because we are not under the law, but under grace? **God forbid** . . . even so now **yield** your members servants to **righteousness unto holiness**.
>
> > (C.) [7:7] **What shall we say then?** *Is* the law sin? **God forbid.** Paul covets, but God does not reject him

(D.) [8:31] **What shall we then say** to these things? If God *be* for us, who *can be* against us? . . . What can separate us from the love of God?

(E.) [9:14] **What shall we say then?** *Is there* unrighteousness with God? God forbid.

(F.) [30] **What shall we say then?** That the Gentiles, which followed not after righteousness, have attained to righteousness, even the righteousness which is of faith. [10:1]Brethren, my heart's desire and prayer to God for Israel is, that they might be saved.

Chiasmus 10:5–13[22]

(G.) A. [5] For Moses **describeth** the righteousness of the law, [6]But the righteousness which is of faith **speaketh** on this wise

(H.) B. [9] if thou shalt **confess** with thy mouth the Lord Jesus

(I.) C. and shalt believe in thine **heart** that God hath raised him from the dead, thou shalt be saved.

(I'.) C'. [10] For with the **heart** man believeth unto righteousness,

(H'.) B'. and with the mouth **confession** is made unto salvation]

---

[22] Romans 10:6–12 is listed as chiasmus in, *The Shape of Biblical Language,* pg. 54, by John Breck, St. Vladimir's Seminary Press, Crestwood, New York. 1994

(*G'.*) A'. [13]For whosoever shall **call** upon the name of the Lord shall be saved

(*F'.*) [9:1] **I say** the truth in Christ, I lie not, [3] For I could wish that myself were accursed from Christ for my brethren, my kinsmen according to the flesh

(*E'.*) [10:18] **But I say**, have they not heard?

(*D'.*) [19] **But I say**, did not Israel know?

(*C'.*) [11:11] **I say then**, hath God cast away his people? **God forbid**

(*B'.*) [11] **I say then**, have they stumbled that they should fall? **God forbid:**

(*A'.*) [12:3] **For I say**, through the grace given unto me, to every man that is among you, **not to think** *of himself* **more highly than he ought to think**; but to think soberly, according as God hath dealt to every man the measure of faith.

The above system is atypical for two reasons. The first "I say" comes before the last "What shall we say then," and it is hard to see how (*E*) and (*D*) correlate with (*E'*) and (*D'*). It is not hard to see the correlation between the other sets such as "glory" in 4:1 and "not to think of himself more highly than he ought to think" in 12:3, but no such relationship is apparent with these other two sets of correlation.

Extended Chiasmus (2)
Our Sinful Speech and God's Wrath

Romans 2:17–3:31 consists of five literary units. Four of these units are chiasma and the last is three rhetorical questions with short answers. The center chiasmus dominates this series, by extending its pattern of inversion through the whole series.

(A.) a. 2:17 Makest thy **boast** in God [23] **boast** in the law

   b. [17]Thou art called a **Jew**

   c. [23] and [27] Through breaking the **law**

  (B.) a. 3:1 Given the **oracles of God**

    b. 1. [3] Will their lack of faith nullify **God's faithfulness?** (NIV)

      2. [5] **Is God unrighteous** who taketh vengeance?

      3. [6 & 7] **Why yet am I also judged as a sinner?**

Chiasmus 3:8–20

(C.) A. And not rather, (as we be slanderously reported, and as some affirm that we say,) Let us do evil, that good may come? Whose damnation is just.

  (D.) B. [9]What then? are we better *than they?* No, in no wise: for we have before proved both **Jews and Gentiles,** that they are **all under sin;**

    (E.) C. [10]As it is written, There is **none righteous,** no, not one:

      (F.) D.[11]There is none that **understandeth,** there is none that **seeketh after God.**

        (G.) E. [12]They are all **gone out of the way,** they are together become unprofitable;

          (H.) F. there is **none that doeth good,** no, not one.

            (I.) G.[13]Their **throat** *is* an open sepulchre; with their **tongues** they have used deceit;

(*I'.*) **G'.** The poison of asps *is* under their lips: [14] Whose **mouth** *is* full of cursing and bitterness:

(*H'.*) **F'.** [15]Their feet *are* **swift to shed blood:**

(*G'.*) **E'.** [16]Destruction and misery *are* in their **ways:**

(*F'.*) **D'.** [17]And the way of peace have **they not known:**

(*E'.*) **C'.** [18]There is **no fear of God** before their eyes.

(*D'.*) **B'.** [19]Now we know that what things soever the law saith, it saith to them who are **under the law:**

(*C'.*) **A'.** [20]**That every mouth may be stopped,** and **all the world may become guilty before God.**

(*B'.*)   **a'.** [21] Righteousness . . . of God witnessed by **the law and the prophets**

     b'. [25] **Whom God hath set forth** to be a propitiation through faith in his blood

       1. **To declare his righteousness** for the remission of **sins that are past**, through the forbearance of God;

       2. [26] **To declare, I say, at this time his righteousness that he might be** just, and **the justifier of him which believeth in Jesus.**

(*A'.*)   **a'.** [27] Where is **boasting** then?

     b'. [29] Is he the God of the **Jews** only?

     c'. [31] Do we make void **the law** through faith?

2. Transitional Inverted Parallelism (TIP)

As previously stated, the last element often contains a statement that is in some way repeated in the beginning of the next system. These two statements segue, that is, make a transition between systems. These two statements can also be used as a center to a new system. In this paper such a system is called a transitional inverted system.

For example:

> A'. 6:14 . . . for ye are **not under the law, but under grace.**
>
> A. 6:15 . . . **shall we sin because we are not under the law, but under grace?**
>
> A'. 7:12 Wherefore **the law is** holy, and the commandment holy, just, and **good.**
>
> A. 7:13 Was then that which is **good** made death unto me?

[7:5]For when we were in the flesh, the motions of sins, which were by the law, did work in our members to bring forth fruit unto death. [6]But now we are delivered from the law, that being dead wherein we were held; **that we should serve in newness of spirit, and not *in* the oldness of the letter.**

> A. [6] That we should serve in newness of spirit,
>
> > B. That we should serve . . . not *in* the oldness of the letter.
> >
> > B'. [7–23] Paul's attempt to serve Christ by the oldness of the letter.
>
> A'. [7:24–8:30] Serving Christ in newness of spirit.

In this case, Paul makes two statements and presents these topics in the inverse order. Most often there is only one of these at a time, but there are times when there are multiple systems operating simultaneously.

The three rhetorical questions of 3:27–31 (Where is **boasting** then? Is he the God of the **Jews** only? And do we make void **the law** through faith?) segue into the next two chiasma.

The Righteousness of God Was Imputed to Past Believers 4:1–5:21

A comparison between 3:27–31 and chapter four

A. [3:27]Where *is* **boasting** then? It is excluded. By what law? Of works? Nay: but by the law of faith. [28]Therefore we conclude that a man is **justified** (declared righteous) **by faith** without the deeds of the law.

    B. [29]*Is he* **the God of the Jews only?** *Is he* not also of the Gentiles? Yes, of the Gentiles also: [30]Seeing *it is* one God, which shall justify (declare righteous) **the circumcision** by faith, and **uncircumcision** through faith.

        C. [31] **Do we then make void** the law through faith?God forbid: yea, **we establish the law.**

A'. [4:1]What shall we say then that Abraham our father, as pertaining to the flesh, hath found? [2]For if Abraham were justified (declared righteous) by works, **he hath *whereof* to glory**; but not before God. [3]For what saith the scripture? **Abraham believed God,** and it was **counted unto him for righteousness.**

    B'. [9]*Cometh* **this blessedness** then upon the circumcision *only*, or upon the uncircumcision also? For we say that faith was reckoned to Abraham for righteousness.

        C'. [13] For the promise, that he should be the heir of the world, *was* not to Abraham, or to his seed, through the law, but through the righteousness of faith. [14]For if they which are of the law *be* heirs, **faith is made void, and the promise made of none effect:** [20] He staggered not at the promise of God through unbelief; but was strong in faith, **giving glory to God;**

3. **Extended Inverted Parallelism (E-TIP)**

The three questions with their corresponding parts are the center for the extended transitional system presented on the following page. This system was my original observation. To see what I observed in the beginning, first compare Romans 1:1–2:3 with Romans 14:1–16:27.

A. 1:1 Paul, a **servant** . . .

  B. [9] . . . That without ceasing I make mention of you always **in my prayers** . . .

    C. [10–11] Making request, if by any means now at length I might have a prosperous journey by the will of God to **come unto you**. For I long to see you . . .

      D. [8] I thank my God . . . [9] I serve . . . I make mention [10] I might have a prosperous journey [11] I long to see you . . . I may impart [12] I may be comforted [13] I would not have you ignorant . . . I purposed . . . I might have [14] I am debtor [15] I am ready [16] I am not ashamed

        E. [21] They (Gentiles) **glorified him not** neither were **thankful**

          F. [2:1] Therefore thou art **inexcusable, O man, whosoever thou art that judgest:**

            G. [2] But we are sure that **the judgment of God is according to truth**
            [3] And thinkest thou this, O man, . . . that thou shalt **escape the judgment of God?**

            G'. [14:10] . . . we shall all **stand before the judgment seat of Christ** [11] For it is written, *As I live, saith the Lord, every knee shall bow to me, and every tongue shall confess to God.* [12] So then every one of us shall give account of himself to God.

          F'. [14:4] **Who art thou that judgest another man's servant?**

        E'. [15:1] in him shall the **Gentiles trust** [9] that the Gentiles might **glorify God** [10] **Rejoice, ye Gentiles** [11] **Praise the Lord, all ye Gentiles**

> **D'.** [14] I myself also am persuaded [15] I have written [16] That I should be [17] I have therefore . . . I may glory [18] I will not dare [19-33] ["I" appears in this section fifteen more times.]

> **C'.** [24] Whensoever I take my *journey* into Spain, **I will come to you** . . . [28] . . . **I will come** by you into Spain.

> **B'.** [30] now I beseech you . . . that ye strive together with me in **your prayers** . . .

> **A'.** [16:1-3] . . . Phebe . . . which is a **servant** . . . Greet Priscilla and Aquila **my helpers** . . . [6] Greet Mary, who bestowed **much labor** . . . [9] Greet Urbane, **our helper** . . . [12] Salute Tryphena and Tryphosa, **who labor** . . . Salute the beloved Persis, which **labored much** . . . [18] . . . **serve not** our Lord Jesus Christ . . . [21] Timotheus

The first half focuses on man's unrighteousness and the second half on God's righteousness that can be ours through faith.

Generally, large systems like this have the greatest comparative detail at the extremes and center of the system. Now, consider the two extremes of this system.

Compare Romans 1:1–6 with Romans 16:25–27.

A. [1:1] . . . separated unto the gospel of God,

A'. [16:25] . . . to stablish you according to my **gospel,**

B. [3] . . . concerning **his son** . . .

B'. and the preaching of **Jesus Christ, to be the son of God** with power, . . . by the resurrection from the dead:

C. [3-4] . . . which was made of the **seed of David** according to the flesh; **declared**

C'. [25] . . . according to the **revelation of the mystery,** which was kept secret since the world began,

D. [2] Which he had **promised afore by his prophets in the holy scriptures,**

D'. [26] But now **is made manifest, and by the scriptures of the prophets,**

E. **for obedience to the faith among all nations**

E'. [26] . . . made known **to all nations for the obedience of faith:**

F. [5] . . . **for his name**

F'. [27] **To God only wise, be glory** through Jesus Christ for ever. Amen.

It is fairly common for a system to be asymmetrical in a limited way. The above comparison is asymmetrical because either verses two or twenty-six are out of order. There is enough correlation to establish the proposed relationship without these two points. The proposed system should not be dependent on the rearrangement of its parts.

Those familiar with literary style will recognize that the above two passages are an example of inclusion. Inclusion is when a document begins and ends in the same way.

The center of this system is between Romans 3 and 4.

E-TIP (2) 1:1–16:27

A. $^{1:1-7}$ Paul's gospel

   B. Called to be an apostle

      C. $^{8-10}$ Paul's prayer ministry

         D. $^{11-15}$ Paul's planned visit

           E. $^{16-20}$ Paul's confidence

              F. $^{21-32}$ Gentiles fail to give glory or to be thankful

                 G. $^{2:1-3}$ Judging others

                    H. $^{1-3}$ The judgement of God is according to truth

                       I. $^{7-10}$ Principles of judgement and blessing; good and evil . . .

                          J. ^{16} God shall judge the secrets of men by Jesus Christ . . .

                             K. $^{13-15}$ Law written in the heart

                               L. ^{11} For there is no respect of persons with God $^{9-10}$ . . . to the Jew first, and also to the Gentile

M. [17] Call thyself a Jew [28] He is not a Jew, which is one outwardly He is a Jew, which is one inwardly

N. [27] . . . if it fulfil the law

O. [16-24] Jews breaking the law causes the name of God to be blasphemed

P. [24-29] Circumcision of the heart (a love relationship Deut. 30:6) [29] . . . in the spirit, and not in the letter;

Q. [3:8] Doing evil that good may come

R. [8-20] Sinful behavior

S. [21-26] Righteousness of God declared

a. [25] For past sins

b. [26] At this present time [27-31] Three questions

S'. [4:1-25] God's righteousness imputed

a'. [for past sin] [organized around the three questions]

b'. [5:1-11] [for present sin]

R'. [12-21] [Sin nature]

Q'. $^{6:1-12}$ Shall we continue in sin … [gospel] $^{13-23}$ Shall we sin [personal experience]

P'. $^{7:1-6}$ Marriage [Christ is the new husband, righteousness shall reign] ^{6} That we should serve in newness of spirit, and not *in* the oldness of the letter.

O'. $^{7-24}$ Saul tries to serve *in* the oldness of the letter; Saul breaks the law

N'. $^{8:4}$ Righteousness of the law fulfilled in us [by the Spirit]

M'. $^{9:3}$ My kinsmen according to the flesh ^{6} They are not all Israel, which are of Israel ^{8} The children of promise are counted for the seed

L'. $^{10:12}$ For there is no difference between the Jew and the Greek: for the same Lord over all is rich unto all that call upon him. $^{9:1-10:18}$ To the Jew first $^{10:19-11:32}$ To the Gentile

K'. $^{11:27}$ This is my covenant

J'. $^{12:19-13:5}$ God-ordained powers

I'. $^{12:1-13:14}$ Good and evil

H'. $^{14:9-12}$ Christ shall judge

G'. $^{14:1-13}$ Judging your brother

F'. $^{15:1-13}$ Gentiles give glory and are thankful

E'. $^{15:14}$ Paul's confidence

D'. [15:22–29] Paul's visit

C'. [30–33] Paul's prayer request

B'. [16:7] Andronicus and Junia . . . who are of note among the apostles

A'. [25–27] Paul's gospel

Extended Transitional Inverted Parallelism

This system, extending from Romans 3:25–15:14, is the most extended inverted parallelism that I am aware of. There are seventy-four correlating elements. The following is a one-page representation of it.

A. 3:25–4:25

B. 3:1–25

C. 5:1–13

D. a. [18] Therefore as by the offence of one *judgment came* upon all men to **condemnation**;

b. even so by the righteousness of one *the free gift* [*dorea*] *came* upon all men unto **justification** of life.

E. [17] For if by one man's offence **death reigned by one**; much more they which receive abundance of grace [*charis*] and of the gift of **righteousness shall reign in life by one** Jesus Christ.

F. [20] Moreover the **law entered, that the offence might abound.**

G. **But where sin abounded, grace** [*charis*] **did much more abound:**

G'. Shall we continue in sin, **that grace may abound?** [14] For sin shall not have dominion over you: for ye are not under the law, but under grace.

F'. [6:1–14] **Shall we sin, because we are not under the law, but under grace? 6:15–23** [23] For the **wages**

of sin *is* **death**; but **the gift** [*charis*] **of God** *is* **eternal life** through Jesus Christ our Lord.

 E'. ^{7:1–6} Marriage

  1. First husband [Law and Death]
  2. Second husband [Christ]

D'. ^{7:7} **What shall we say then?** *Is the law sin?* ⁹ but when the commandment came, sin revived, and **I died.** ¹² Wherefore the **law** *is* **holy,** and the commandment holy, and **just,** and **good.**

 C'. 7:24–8:39

B'. 9:1–11:36

A'. 12:1–15:14

With seventy-four correlating elements, this system is much too large to present the whole system here, but we will compare **B** and **B'** as an example of this E-TIP.

A comparison between
(B) 3:1–4:25 and (B') 9:1–11:36
For a more complete presentation, see pg. 150.

B.

a. [3:1-2] unto them were committed the **oracles of God.**

b. [3-4] shall their unbelief make the **faith of God without effect?**

c. [5] *Is God* **unrighteous** who taketh vengeance?

d. [7-8] as we be **slanderously reported,** [20] that every mouth may be stopped

e. [22] the righteousness of God *which is* by **faith**

f. for **there is no difference:** [23] For all have sinned, and come short of the glory of God;

g. [23] Being justified freely by his **grace:**

h. [27-28] Where is **boasting?**

i. [29-30] God of Jews only?

B'.

a'. [9:3-5] Who are Israelites; to whom *pertaineth* the adoption, and the glory, and the covenants, and the giving of the law, and the service *of God*, and the promises; Whose *are* the fathers, and of whom as concerning the flesh Christ *came,*

b'. [6] Not as though the word of God hath taken none effect.

c'. [14] *Is there* **unrighteousness** with God? God forbid

d'. [20] who art thou that **repliest against God?**

e'. [32] Because *they sought it* not by **faith,** [10:6] But the righteousness which is of faith . . .

f'. [12-13] For **there is no difference** between the Jew and the Greek:

g'. [11:5-6] the **election of grace.**

h'. [18] **Boast** not against the branches

i'. [17-24] Natural and unnatural branches

In the above system there is a series of contrasts starting with the two Adams in chapter five. Students of Romans often find these difficult. In our Western way of thinking, we take our thoughts and express them logically. Then, if we think that the reader may have trouble understanding our presentation, we illustrate it. In Romans, these contrasts are not illustrations of a thought process, they are the thought processes.

The complete presentation of Romans that follows can be used as a study guide or as a reference work. When using it as a study guide it is recommended that the student not get bogged down with each inverted order. Note the inversion and symmetry, identify the points of emphasis, and move on. If the reader is studying some portion of Romans in depth, he or she may wish to pay more attention to the detail. For the most part commentary is kept to a minimum so that the focus can be on form and Paul's argument. A short section at the end of this document entitled *The Value of Inverted Parallelism*, looks at how these systems affect our understanding of the text. When there is background information that would help the reader to follow Paul's presentation, that background information is presented in the appendix.

E. A Challenge

The first psalm tells us of a man who is blessed, a man who meditates in God's law day and night. The following analysis of Romans has taken literally thousands of hours to produce. My burden to share what I found had its difficulties. Chiastic systems each develop a theme. In the case of macro-systems there can be many at the same time, each developing their own theme. At the peak of Paul's presentation, which is in chapters nine through eleven, there are eight macro-systems simultaneously developing their own line of thought. This is in addition to the micro-systems. To help the reader keep all of this straight, I am providing a feature that I call, "correlations." This feature will remind you of the input from such systems and tell you where it is coming from. It has been a real challenge for me to present this aspect in an acceptable fashion and it will be a challenge for you to keep this all straight. Even with this help, it will take time and effort. May God bless you as he has blessed me.

THE UNFOLDING OF ROMANS

Observations in Form

I

Paul's Introduction 1:1–20

THE GOSPEL OF JESUS CHRIST 1:1–7

A. ¹Paul, a **servant** of **Jesus Christ**,

   B. **called** *to be* **an apostle**, separated unto the gospel of God,

      C. ²Which he had **promised** afore by his **prophets** in the holy scriptures,

A.	A servant of Jesus Christ	
	B.	Called to be an Apostle
		C. Promised afore by his prophets
		D. His son . . . according to the flesh
		D' Son of God . . . according to the spirit of holiness
		C'. Grace and apostleship
	B'. Called to be saints	
A'.	. . . the Lord Jesus Christ	

         D. ³Concerning **his Son** Jesus Christ our Lord, which was made of the **seed of David according to the flesh**;

         D'. ⁴And declared *to be* the **Son of God** with power, **according to the spirit of holiness**, by the resurrection from the dead:

      C'. ⁵By whom we have received **grace and apostleship**, for obedience to the faith among all nations, for his name:

B'. [6] Among whom are ye **also the called** of Jesus Christ: [7] To all that be in Rome, beloved of God, **called** *to be* **saints:**

A'. Grace to you and peace from God our Father, and the **Lord Jesus Christ.**

The chiastic reading:

A. [1:1]Paul, a servant of Jesus Christ,

A'. Grace to you and peace from God our Father, and the Lord Jesus Christ.

B. called *to be* an apostle, separated unto the gospel of God,

B'. [6]Among whom are ye also the called of Jesus Christ: [7]To all that be in Rome, beloved of God, called *to be* saints:

C. [2] Which he had promised afore by his prophets in the holy scriptures,

C'. [5]By whom we have received grace and apostleship, for obedience to the faith among all nations, for his name:

D. [3]Concerning his Son Jesus Christ our Lord, which was made of the seed of David according to the flesh;

D'. [4]And declared *to be* the Son of God with power, according to the spirit of holiness, by the resurrection from the dead:

Correlations: Servant

1:1 Paul a servant of Jesus Christ
1:7 The Lord Jesus Christ
16:1 Phebe our sister, which is a servant of the church at Cenchrea

Called

1:1 Called to be an apostle
1:6 Among whom are ye called of Jesus Christ
1:7 Called to be saints
16:7 Salute Andronicus and Junia . . . who are of note among the apostles

The second parallel element strengthens, intensifies, or completes the first. Paul is a servant, but so is Phebe. Paul is called to be an apostle, but the believers at Rome are called to be saints; two of their number are called to be apostles.

Gospel

> 1:3 The gospel concerning his Son is
> 1:5 For obedience to the faith among all nations
> 16:26 Made known to all nations for the obedience of the faith

The central idea in Paul's thesis is the gospel of Jesus Christ leads to obedience. This truth is challenged in 3:8. The gospel resulted in the believers at Rome being obedient to the faith (6:16–23). Paul restates this purpose in 15:18 and 16:26.

PAUL'S PRAYER 1:8–13

¹:⁸ First, I thank my God through Jesus Christ for you all, that your faith is spoken of throughout the whole world.

A. ⁹ For God is my witness, whom **I serve** with my spirit in the gospel of his Son, that without ceasing I make mention of you always in my prayers;

> A.   God . . . whom I serve
> B.   Come unto you
> C.   Ye may be established
> C'. Comforted together with you
> B'. Come unto you
> A'. Have some fruit among you

B. ¹⁰ Making request, if by any means nowat length I might have a prosperous journey by the will of God to **come unto you.**

C. ¹¹ For I long to see you, that I may impart unto you some spiritual gift, to the end **ye may be established**;

C'. ¹² That is, that **I may be comforted together with you** by the mutual faith both of you and me.

B'. ¹³ Now I would not have you ignorant, brethren, that oftentimes I purposed to **come unto you**, (but was let hitherto,)

A'. that I might **have some fruit** among you also, even as among other Gentiles.

The chiastic reading:

A. [1:9] For God is my witness, whom I serve with my spirit in the gospel of his Son, that without ceasing I make mention of you always in my prayers;

A'. that I might have some fruit among you also, even as among other Gentiles.

B. [10] Making request, if by any means now at length I might have a prosperous journey by the will of God to come unto you.

B'. [13] Now I would not have you ignorant, brethren, that oftentimes I purposed to come unto you, (but was let hitherto,)

C. [11] For I long to see you, that I may impart unto you some spiritual gift, to the end ye may be established;

C'. [12] That is, that I may be comforted together with you by the mutual faith both of you and me.

Correlations:

Prayer

> 1:9 without ceasing I make mention of you always in my prayers
> 15:30 that ye strive together with me in *your* prayers to God for me

Prayer is mutual. Paul prays for the church and the church prays for Paul.

Come unto you

> 1:10 I might have a prosperous journey by the will of God to **come unto you.**
> 1:13 Now I would not have you ignorant, brethren, that oftentimes I purposed to **come unto you,** (but was let hitherto,)
> 15:24 Whensoever I take my journey into Spain, **I will come to you**
> 15:28 **I will come** by you into Spain.

Paul's desire in chapter one to visit the believers at Rome becomes his plan in chapter fifteen. Chapter fifteen completes his thought.

Established

> 1:11 To the end ye may be established
> 16:25 Now to him that is of power to stablish you

The gospel is shared in chapter one because God's power works through it to save the lost and to establish the believer. Chapter sixteen strengthens chapter one.

A. ^{1:14} I am debtor both to the
Greeks, and to the Barbarians;
both to the wise, and to the
unwise. ¹⁵ So, as much as
in me is, I am ready to preach
the **gospel** to you that are at
Rome also. ¹⁶ For I am not
ashamed of the **gospel** of

> A. The gospel of Christ . . . the power of God unto salvation
> B. The righteousness of God revealed
> B'. The wrath of God is revealed
> A'. The invisible things of him . . . are clearly seen . . . even his eternal power and Godhead

Christ: for it is the **power of God unto salvation** to every one that believeth; to the Jew first, and also to the Greek.

B. ¹⁷ For therein is **the righteousness of God revealed from faith to faith**: as it is written, the just shall live by faith.

B'. ¹⁸ For **the wrath of God is revealed from heaven against all ungodliness and unrighteousness of men**, who hold the truth in unrighteousness;

A'. ¹⁹ Because **that which may be known of God** is manifest in them; for God hath shewed *it* unto them. ²⁰ For the **invisible things of him** from the creation of the world **are clearly seen**, being understood by the things that are made, *even* his **eternal power and Godhead**; so that they are without excuse:

The chiastic reading:

A. ^{1:14} I am debtor both to the Greeks, and to the Barbarians; both to the wise, and to the unwise. ¹⁵ So, as much as in me is, I am ready to preach the gospel to you that are at Rome also.¹⁶ For I am not ashamed of the gospel of Christ: for it is the power of God unto salvation to every one that believeth; to the Jew first, and also to the Greek.

A'. ¹⁹ Because that which may be known of God is manifest in them; for God hath shewed *it* unto them. ²⁰ For the invisible things of him from the creation of the world are clearly seen, being understood by the things that are made, *even* his eternal power and Godhead; so that they are without excuse:

B. [17] For therein is the righteousness of God revealed from faith to faith: as it is written, The just shall live by faith.

B'. [18] For the wrath of God is revealed from heaven against all ungodliness and unrighteousness of men, who hold the truth in unrighteousness;

Greeks

[1:14] I am debtor both to the Greeks, and to the Barbarians; both to the wise, and to the unwise. [15] So, as much as in me is, I am ready to preach the gospel to you that are at Rome also

[16] That I should be the minister of Jesus Christ to the Gentiles, ministering the gospel of God, that the offering up of the Gentiles might be acceptable, being sanctified by the Holy Ghost.

The first twenty verses are Paul's thesis statement, and are the seedbed from which the whole book of Romans will spring forth.

The following system encompasses the whole in outline form. E-TIP (2) encompasses the whole of Romans in more detail, but E-TIP (3) presents most of Romans in great detail.

E-TIP (1) Paul's Outline

A. Paul a Servant 1:1

B. [1:1–15] Calling

   a. [7–12] Believers at Rome called to be saints
   b. [13–15] Paul called to be an apostle

C. [16] I am not ashamed of the gospel of Christ

   a. Power of God unto salvation to every one that believeth;
   b. To the Jew first,
   c. and also to the Greek.

D. [17] **The righteousness of God is revealed**

   a. From faith to faith:

   b. As it is written, The just shall live by faith.

E. [18] **The wrath of God is revealed from heaven**

   a. Against all ungodliness

   b. And unrighteousness of men,

   c. Who hold the truth in unrighteousness;

E'. [1:21–3:31] **The wrath of God is revealed from heaven**

   a'. [1:21–32] Against all ungodliness

      1. [21–23] When they knew God, they glorified him not as God

      2. [24–27] God gave them up to uncleanness and vile affections

      3. [28–32] They did not like to retain God in their knowledge

   b'. [2:1–29] And unrighteousness of men,

      1. [1–16] Knowing the judgment of God they become judge

      2. [17–29] The truth of the gospel held in unrighteousness

   c'. [3:1–31] Who hold the truth in unrighteousness

      1. [1–8] Is God unrighteous?

      2. [21–31] The wrath of God on his son declared his righteousness

D'. [4:1–8:30] **The righteousness of God is revealed**

   a'. [1–25] From faith to faith. The righteousness of God imputed

      1. [1–25] To past believers [Abram and David]

      2. [5:1–7:23] To present-day believers

   b'. [6:1–8:30] As it is written, The just shall live by faith. [6:1–7:23] The righteousness of God demonstrated. [7:24–8:30] By the Holy Spirit and the Father.

C'. [8:31–11:36] **Whosoever believeth in him shall not be ashamed; The power of God unto salvation**

   a'. [9:6–29] To the Jew first

   b'. [10:1–18] Whosoever shall call . . .

   c'. [10:19–11:32] To the Gentile

B'. [12:1–16:27] **Called to be saints**

   a'. [12:1–2] Living sacrifices

   b'. [15:14–33] Paul an apostle

A'. [16:1–27] Believers at Rome servants

II

The Wrath of God Is Revealed 1:21–3:31

THE KNOWLEDGE OF GOD
EXTENDED CHIASMUS (1)

(A.) [1:14–16] The gospel

    (B.) [17–18] A two-fold revelation of God's righteousness

        (C.) [19–20] Without excuse

Correlations

1:18 Against all ungodliness.

Chiasmus 1:21–32

(D.) A. [21]Because that, **when they knew God,**

    a. they **glorified him not as God,** neither were thankful;

A.	When they knew God, they glorified him not as God
	B. God also gave them up to uncleanness
	B'. God gave them up unto vile affections
A'.	They did not like to retain God in their knowledge

      b. but became **vain** in their imaginations, and their **foolish** heart was darkened.

      b'. [22] **Professing themselves to be wise,** they became **fools,**

   a'. [23] And **changed the glory of the uncorruptible God** into an image made like to corruptible man, and to birds, and fourfooted beasts, and creeping things.

(E.) **B.** [24] Wherefore **God also gave them up** to uncleanness through the lusts of their own hearts, to dishonour their own bodies between themselves: [25] Who changed the truth of God into a lie, and worshipped and served the creature more than the Creator, **who is blessed for ever.** Amen.

(E'.) **B'.** [26] For this cause **God gave them up** unto vile affections: for even their women did change the natural use into that which is against nature: [27] And likewise also the men, leaving the natural use of the woman, burned in their lust one toward another; men with men working that which is unseemly and receiving in themcich was meet.

(D'.) **A'.**   a. [28] And even as they **did not like to retain God in** *their* **knowledge, God gave them over to a reprobate mind,** to do those things which are not convenient;

         b. [29] Being **filled** with all unrighteousness, fornication, wickedness, covetousness, maliciousness;**full** of envy, murder, debate, deceit, malignity; whisperers, [30] Backbiters, haters of God, despiteful, proud, boasters, inventors of evil things, disobedient to parents,

         b'. [31] **Without** understanding, covenantbreakers, **without** natural affection, implacable, unmerciful:

        a'. [32] **Who knowing the judgment of God,** that they which commit such things are worthy of death, not only do the same, but have pleasure in them that do them.

(C'.) [2:1–4] Inexcusable

(B'.) [5–12] A two-fold revelation of God's righteous judgement

(A'.) [16] According to my gospel

The chiastic reading for 1:21–32

A. [1:21] Because that, when they knew God,

> a. they glorified *him* not as God, neither were thankful;

>> b. but became **vain** in their imaginations, and their foolish heart was darkened.
>> b'. [22] Professing themselves to be wise, they became fools,

> a'. [23] And changed the glory of the uncorruptible God into an image made like to corruptible man, and to birds, and fourfooted beasts, and creeping things.

A'. a. [28] And even as they did not like to retain God in *their* knowledge, God gave them over to a reprobate mind, to do those things which are not convenient;

>> b. [29] Being filled with all unrighteousness, fornication, wickedness, covetousness, maliciousness; full of envy, murder, debate, deceit, malignity; whisperers, [30]Backbiters, haters of God, despiteful, proud, boasters, inventors of evil things, disobedient to parents,

>> b'. [31] Without understanding, covenantbreakers, without natural affection, implacable, unmerciful:

> a'. [32] Who knowing the judgment of God, that they which commit such things are worthy of death, not only do the same, but have pleasure in them that do them.

B. [24] Wherefore God also gave them up to uncleanness through the lusts of their own hearts, to dishonour their own bodies between themselves: [25] Who changed the truth of God into a lie, and worshipped and served the creature more than the Creator, who is blessed for ever. Amen.

B'. [26]For this cause God gave them up unto vile affections: for even their women did change the natural use into that which is against nature: [27]And likewise also the men, leaving the natural use of the woman, burned in their lust one toward another; men with men working that which is unseemly and receiving in themselves that recompence of their error which was meet.

Correlations

No hope

1:24 God also gave them up to uncleanness
1:26 God gave them over to vile affections
1:28 God gave them over to a reprobate mind

[15:4] For whatsoever things were written aforetime were written for our learning, that we through patience and comfort of the scriptures might have hope.

Gentiles glorify God

[1:21] Because that, when they knew God, they glorified *him* not as God, neither were thankful;

[15:6] That ye may with one **mind** *and* one **mouth glorify God**, even the Father of our Lord Jesus Christ

[15:9] And that the Gentiles **might glorify God** for *his* mercy; as it is written, For this cause I will confess to thee among the Gentiles, and sing unto thy name.

[15:10] And again he saith, **Rejoice**, ye Gentiles, with his people.

[15:11] And again, **Praise** the Lord, all ye Gentiles; and **laud him**, all ye people.

[15:12] And again, Esaias saith, There shall be a root of Jesse, and he that shall rise to reign over the Gentiles; in him shall the Gentiles **trust**.

Correlations
Knowing the judgment of God . . . do the same. 1:32

A. a. ²·¹ Therefore thou art **inexcusable, O man, whosoever thou art that** judgest: for wherein thou judgest another, thou condemnest thyself; for thou that judgest doest the same things.

   b. ² But we are sure that **the judgment of God is according to truth** against them which commit such things.

a'. ³ And thinkest thou this, O man, **that judgest them which do such things, and doest the same, that thou shalt** escape the judgment of God?

B. ⁴ Or despisest thou the riches of his goodness and

> A. The judgment of God is according to truth
>   B. The goodness of God leadeth thee to repentance?
>   C. Treasurest up unto thyself wrath against the day of wrath
>   D. Render to every man according to his deeds
>   E. In well doing seek for glory and honour and immortality
>   F. But unto them that are contentious
>   F'. Tribulation and anguish, upon every soul of man that doeth evil
>   E'. But glory, honour, and peace, to every man that worketh good
>   D'. For there is no respect of persons with God
>   C'. For as many as have sinned . . . shall perish
>   B'. The doers of the law shall be justified
> A'. And thinkest thou this, O man . . . that thou shalt escape the judgment of God?

forbearance and longsuffering; not knowing that the goodness of God **leadeth thee to repentance?**

C. ⁵ But after thy hardness and impenitent heart treasurest up unto thyself wrath against the **day of wrath** and **revelation of the righteous judgment of God;**

D. ⁶ Who will render to **every man** according to his deeds:

E. [7] To them who by **patient continuance in well doing** seek for glory and honour and immortality, eternal life:

F. [8] But unto **them that are contentious, and do not obey the truth**, but obey unrighteousness, indignation and wrath,

F'. [9] Tribulation and anguish, upon every soul of **man that doeth evil**, of the Jew first, and also of the Gentile;

E'. [10] But glory, honour, and peace, to every man that **worketh good**, to the Jew first, and also to the Gentile: [23]

D'. [11] For there is **no respect of persons** with God.

C'. [12] For as many as have sinned without law shall also **perish without law**: and as many as have sinned in the law shall be **judged by the law**;

B'. [13] For not the hearers of the law *are* just before God, but **the doers of the law shall be justified**.

A'. a'. [14] For when the Gentiles, which have not the law, do by nature the things contained in the law, these, having not the law, are a law unto themselves:

b'. [15] Which shew the work of the law written in their hearts, their conscience also bearing witness, and *their* thoughts the mean while **accusing** or else **excusing** one another;

c'. [16] In the day when **God shall judge** the secrets of men by Jesus Christ according to my gospel.

The chiastic reading:

A. a. [2:1] Therefore thou art inexcusable, O man, whosoever thou art that judgest: for wherein thou judgest another, thou condemnest thyself; for thou that judgest doest the same things.

b. [2] But we are sure that the judgment of God is according to truth against them which commit such things.

---

[23] Romans 2:7–10 is presented as chiasmus on pg. XV in the 1992 preface to *Chiasmus in the New Testament,* by Nils W, Hendrickson, Peabody, Mass. Reprint 1992

a'. [3] And thinkest thou this, O man, that judgest them which do such things, and doest the same, that thou shalt escape the judgment of God?

A'. a'. [14] For when the Gentiles, which have not the law, do by nature the things contained in the law, these, having not the law, are a law unto themselves:

b'. [15] Which shew the work of the law written in their hearts, their conscience also bearing witness, and *their* thoughts the mean while accusing or else excusing one another;

c'. [16] In the day when God shall judge the secrets of men by Jesus Christ according to my gospel.

B. [4] Or despisest thou the riches of his goodness and forbearance and longsuffering; not knowing that the goodness of God leadeth thee to repentance?

B'. [13] For not the hearers of the law *are* just before God, but the doers of the law shall be justified.

C. [5] But after thy hardness and impenitent heart treasurest up unto thyself wrath against the day of wrath and revelation of the righteous judgment of God;

C'. [12] For as many as have sinned without law shall also perish without law: and as many as have sinned in the law shall be judged by the law;

D. [6] Who will render to every man according to his deeds:

D'. [11] For there is no respect of persons with God.

E. [7] To them who by patient continuance in well doing seek for glory and honour and immortality, eternal life:

E'. [10] But glory, honour, and peace, to every man that worketh good, to the Jew first, and also to the Gentile:

F. [8] But unto them that are contentious, and do not obey the truth, but obey unrighteousness, indignation and wrath,

F'. [9] Tribulation and anguish, upon every soul of man that doeth evil, of the Jew first, and also of the Gentile;

Correlations:

Judging others

2:1 Therefore thou art inexcusable, O man, whosoever thou art that judgest
2:3 And thinkest thou this, O man . . . that thou shalt escape the judgement of God?
1:16 In the day that God shall judge the secrets of men by Jesus Christ
14:4 Who art thou that judgest another man's servant?
14:10 But why does thou judge thy brother?
Or why dost thou set at nought thy brother?
For we shall all stand before the judgment seat of Christ.

Christ shall judge

2:6 Who will render to every man according to his deeds:
2:9 The Jew first, and also of the Gentile
2:10 The Jew first, and also the Gentile.

God's standard of judgement

2:11 For there is no respect of persons with God.
10:12 For there is no difference between the Jew and the Greek: for the same Lord over all is rich unto all that call upon him.
3:22 For there is no difference: 23 For all have sinned, and come short of the glory of God;
7:16 If then I do that which I would not, I consent unto the law that *it is* good.
7:18 For I know that in me (that is, in my flesh,) dwelleth no good thing: for to will is present with me; but *how* to perform that which is good I find not
7:19 For the good that I would I do not: but the evil which I would not, that I do.
7:21 I find then a law, that, when I would do good, evil is present with me.

Blessings

3:14 For when the Gentiles, which have not the law, do by nature the things contained in the law, these, having not the law, are a law unto themselves:

11:15 Which shew the work of the law written in their hearts,

27 For this *is* my covenant unto them, when I shall take away their sins.

2:7 To them who by patient continuance in well doing seek for glory and honour and immortality, eternal life:

2:10 But glory, honour, and peace, to every man that worketh good, to the Jew first, and also to the Gentile:

8:28 And we know that all things work together for good to them that love God, to them who are the called according to *his* purpose.

12:9 Abhor that which is evil; cleave to that which is good.

12:17 Recompense to no man evil for evil.

12:21 Be not overcome of evil, but overcome evil with good.

13:3 Rulers are not a terror to good works, but to the evil. Wilt thou then not be afraid of the power? Do that which is good, and thou shalt have praise of the same:

13:4 For he is the minister of God to thee for good. But if thou do that which is evil, be afraid; for he beareth not the sword in vain: for he is the minister of God, a revenger to *execute* wrath upon him that doeth evil.

The following illustrates one of Paul's techniques for building macro-systems. Three chiasma are made into one literary unit by extending the pattern of inversion of the central chiasmus through the adjacent chiasma.

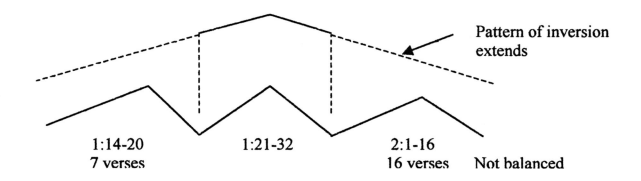

Pattern of inversion extends

1:14-20
7 verses

1:21-32

2:1-16
16 verses   Not balanced

Correlations
In the day when God shall judge the secrets of men
by Jesus Christ according to my gospel. 2:16
And unrighteousness of men. 1:18

A. ²·¹⁷ Behold, **thou art called a Jew**, and restest in the law, and makest thy **boast** of God,

B. ¹⁸ And knowest *his* will, and approvest the things that are more excellent, **being instructed out of the law**; ¹⁹ And art confident that thou thyself art a guide of the blind, light of them which are in darkness, ²⁰ **An instructor of the foolish, a teacher of babes,** which hast the form of knowledge and of the truth in the law.

> A.   Thou art called a Jew
>   B.   Being instructed out of the law
>   C.   Teachest not thyself?
>   D.   Breaking the law dishonourest thou God?
>   E.   The name of God is blasphemed
>   D'.   If thou be a breaker of the law
>   C'.   If the uncircumcision keep the righteousness of the law
>   B'.   Shall not uncircumcision . . . if it fulfil the law, judge thee
> A'.   For he is not a Jew: He is a Jew

C. ²¹ Thou therefore which teachest another, **teachest thou not thyself?** thou that preachest a man should not steal, dost thou steal? ²² Thou that sayest a man should not commit adultery, dost thou commit adultery thou that abhorrest idols, dost thou commit sacrilege?

D. [23] Thou that makest thy boast of the law, through **breaking the law dishonourest thou God?**

    E. [24] For **the name of God is blasphemed among the Gentiles through you,** as it is written.

D'. [25] For circumcision verily profiteth, if thou keep the law: but if thou be a **breaker of the law,** thy circumcision is made uncircumcision.

    C'. [26] Therefore if the uncircumcision **keep the righteousness of the law,** shall not his uncircumcision be counted for circumcision?

B'. [27] And shall not uncircumcision which is by nature, **if it fulfil the law,** judge thee, who by the letter and circumcision **dost transgress the law?**

A'. a. [28] For **he is not a Jew,** which is one **outwardly;**

    b. neither *is that* circumcision, which is **outward** in the flesh:

a'. [29] But **he *is* a Jew,** which is one **inwardly;**

    b'. and circumcision *is that* of the heart, **in the spirit,** *and* not in the letter whose **praise** *is* not of men, but of God.

The chiastic reading:

A. [2:17] Behold, thou art called a Jew, and restest in the law, and makest thy boast of God,

A'. [28] For he is not a Jew, which is one outwardly; neither is that circumcision, which is outward in the flesh: [29] But he is a Jew, which is one outwardly; and circumcision is that of the heart, in the spirit, and not in the letter whose praise is not of men, but of God.

B. [18] And knowest *his* will, and approvest the things that are more excellent, being instructed out of the law; [19] And art confident that thou thyself art a guide of the blind, light of them which are in darkness,

B'. [27] And shall not uncircumcision which is by nature, if it fulfil the law, judge thee, who by the letter and circumcision dost transgress the law?

C. ²¹ Thou therefore which teachest another, teachest thou not thyself? thou that preachest a man should not steal, dost thou steal? ²² Thou that sayest a man should not commit adultery, dost thou commit adultery thou that abhorrest idols, dost thou commit sacrilege?

C'. ²⁶ Therefore if the uncircumcision keep the righteousness of the law, shall not his uncircumcision be counted for circumcision?

D. ²³ Thou that makest thy boast of the law, through breaking the law dishonourest thou God?

D'. ²⁵ For circumcision verily profiteth, if thou keep the law: but if thou be a breaker of the law, thy circumcision is made uncircumcision.

E. ²⁴ For the name of God is blasphemed among the Gentiles through you, as it is written.

Correlations:

²·¹ Thou art called a Jew

²·²⁸ He is not a Jew which is one outwardly

²·²⁹ He is a Jew which is one inwardly

³·²⁹ Is he the God of the Jews only? Is he not also of the Gentiles?

⁴·⁹ Cometh this blessedness then upon the circumcision only, or upon the uncircumcision also?

⁹·⁶ For they are not all Israel, which are of Israel.

¹¹·²⁴ For if thou wert cut out of the olive tree which is wild by nature, and wert grafed contrary to nature into a good tree:

And shall not uncircumcision which is by nature, if it fulfil the law, judge thee, who by the letter and circumcision dost transgress the law?

⁸·³ For what the law could not do, in that it was weak through the flesh, God sending his own Son in the likeness of sinful flesh, and for sin, condemned sin in the flesh:

Boasting

[2:27] Makest thy boast of God

[2:29] Whose praise is not of men, but of God

[3:27] Where is boasting then? It is excluded

[4:1] For if Abraham were justified by works, he hath where of to glory, but not before God.

[11:18] Boast not against the branches.

[12:3] Not to think of himself more highly than he ought to think

The law

[2:23] Thou that makest thy boast of the law, though breaking the law dishonourest thou God?

[3:31] Do we then make void the law through faith? God forbid: yea, we establish the Law.

[4:14] For if they which are of the law be heirs, faith is made void, and the promise made of none effect:

[4:20] He staggered not at the promise of God through unbelief; but was strong in faith, giving glory to God;

[9:6] Not as though the word of God hath taken none effect.

[13:8] He that loveth another hath fulfilled the law.

Serving Christ

[2:29] And circumcision *is that* of the heart, in the spirit, *and* not in the letter whose praise *is* not of men, but of God.

[7:6] That we should serve in newness of spirit, and not *in* the oldness of the letter.

Romans 2:17–3:31 is an extended chiasmus,[24] that is made up of three smaller chiasma. This portion of Romans is the foundation of thought for 4:1–15:17.

2:14 and 15 state the theme of 2:17–29 in more detail than was stated in 1:32.

In this the religious seek to live by the rulebook, but ultimately are condemned by it. The proselyte was baptized, circumcised, and finally recognized when he offered up a

---

[24] Pg. 129

burnt offering, but none of this changes the inner man nor can it transform the convert into a saint.

This chiasmus has in view the failure of the religious experience, to produce righteousness in its membership. "Thou art called a Jew" and "he *is* a Jew, which is one inwardly," constitute the secondary emphasis, while "Dishonoring God," and "The name of God is blasphemed," constitute the primary emphasis. The theme of the first half is law, and circumcision that of the second half. In this passage, men sin against truth and its author by breaking the law. The Gentile who fulfils the law[25] shall judge those who call themselves Jews, but break the law. The reader might be wondering, what Gentiles keep the law? This passage correlates with,

> For what the law could not do, in that it was weak through the flesh, God sending his own Son in the likeness of sinful flesh, and for sin, condemned sin in the flesh: [4]That the righteousness of the law might be fulfilled in us who walk not after the flesh, but after the Spirit.[26]

The circumcision of the heart is not a new idea, but was required under law.

"Circumcise therefore the foreskin of your heart, and be no more stiffnecked."[27]

Israel failed to do this and remained stubborn, but as usual there is a provision under promise.

"And the LORD thy God will circumcise thine heart, and the heart of thy seed, to love the LORD thy God with all thine heart, and with all thy soul, that thou mayest live."[28]

This circumcision of the heart is something that God does when the sinner turns to God in repentance and faith.[29] God of course is the one who gave circumcision, the Ten Commandments, the priesthood, the temple and its service. The unsaved Jew failed to understand that these did not provide saving grace, but pointed the sinner to repentance and faith in the Messiah, i.e. the Christ.

---

[25] Romans 8:4, 13:8–10
[26] Romans 8:3–4
[27] Deuteronomy 10:16
[28] Deuteronomy 30:6
[29] Deuteronomy 30:2

Correlations
The Truth of the Gospel Held in Unrighteousness. 1:18
For he is not a Jew . . . but he is a Jew. 2:28–29

A. ³:¹ What advantage then hath the Jew? Or what profit *is there* of circumcision? ² Much every way: chiefly, because that unto them were committed the **oracles of God**.

> A.   The oracles of God
> B.   . . . God forbid
> B'. . . . God forbid
> A'. The truth of God

B. ³ For what if some did not believe? Shall their unbelief make the faith of God without effect? ⁴ **God forbid**: yea, **let God be true**, **but every man a liar**; as it is written, That thou mightest be justified in thy sayings, and mightest overcome when thou art judged.

B'. ⁵ But if our unrighteousness commend the righteousness of God, what shall we say? *Is God unrighteous who taketh vengeance?* (I speak as a man) ⁶ **God forbid**: for then how shall God judge the world?

A'. ⁷ For if **the truth of God** hath more abounded through my lie unto his glory; why yet am I also judged as a sinner? ⁸ An not *rather*, (as we be slanderously reported, and as some affirm that we say) Let us do evil, that good may come? whose damnation is just.

The chiastic reading:

A. ³:¹ What advantage then hath the Jew? Or what profit *is there* of circumcision? ² Much every way: chiefly, because that unto them were committed the oracles of God.

A'. ⁷ For if the truth of God hath more abounded through my lie unto his glory; why yet am I also judged as a sinner? ⁸ An not *rather*, (as we be slanderously reported, and as some affirm that we say,) Let us do evil, that good may come? whose damnation is just.

B. ³ For what if some did not believe? Shall their unbelief make the faith of God without effect? ⁴ God forbid: yea, let God be true, but every man a liar; as it is written, That thou mightest be justified in thy sayings, and mightest over-come when thou art judged.

B'. ⁵But if our unrighteousness commend the righteousness of God, what shall we say? *Is* God unrighteous who taketh vengeance? (I speak as a man) ⁶God forbid: for then how shall God judge the world?

Correlations

³:¹⁻² unto them were committed the oracles of God.

⁹:³⁻⁵ Who are Israelites; to whom *pertaineth* the adoption, and the glory, and the cov-enants, and the giving of the law, and the service of God, and the promises; Whose are the fathers, and of whom as concerning the flesh Christ came,

³:³ shall their unbelief make the faith of God without effect?

⁹:⁶ Not as though the word of God hath taken none effect.

³:⁵ Is God unrighteous who taketh vengeance?

⁹:¹⁴ Is there unrighteousness with God? God forbid.

³:⁷ as we be slanderously reported,

³:²⁰ that every mouth may be stopped

⁹:²⁰ who art thou that repliest against God?

Paul teaches that what is important with God is not the circumcision of the flesh but the circumcision of the heart, and having the law written on the heart rather than having it written on tablets of stone. The unbelieving Jew then asked certain questions that are intended to show what they see as the falsity of Paul's message. In the center section it is implied that if Paul's gospel is true, then God need not be faithful to those who fail, and that God would be unjust when he judges the world and lets guilty believers go unpun-ished. His answer, God forbid (may it never be), is a very strong rejection of their argu-ments. In this chapter there is a third "God forbid" in 3:31. The first two have to do with

God's righteousness and the third the righteousness of God's people. In this chiasmus the first and last elements have "the oracles of God" and "the truth of God" as their common idea.

There are four rhetorical questions in this section; the first (1–2) asks what advantage do the Jews have? After what has already been said, the unsaved Jew would expect the answer to be nothing, but the answer is God has delivered the Word of God to their care. Paul has already said concerning the gospel, "Which he had promised afore by his prophets in the Holy Scriptures."[30] Knowledge gives advantage, but the advantage is lost when knowledge is neglected or rejected.

The second rhetorical question (3–4) is, If man is unfaithful to God, does God have to remain faithful to man? In answering, Paul quotes from David's confession of sin after he had committed adultery and then killed Uriah in an attempt to escape the consequences of his sin.[31] God remained faithful to David even when David was unfaithful to God. The law did not give David the option of bringing a sin sacrifice,

> But if a man come presumptuously upon his neighbour, to slay him with guile; thou shalt take him from mine altar, that he may die. [32]

For this reason David does not bring a sacrifice,

> For thou desirest not sacrifice; else would I give *it:* thou delightest not in burnt offering. [17] The sacrifices of God *are* a broken spirit: a broken and a contrite heart, O God, thou wilt not despise.[33]

Because of God's promises, David finds forgiveness as he turns from his sin to trust in the living God.

"Just" and "righteous" are translations of the same Greek word. To help minimize confusion, every time some form of the word "just" appears, it will be expressed as "righteous" in brackets.

---

[30] Romans 1:2
[31] Psalms 51:4
[32] Exodus 21:14
[33] Psalms 51:16–17

The third rhetorical question (5–6) asks if this would make God unjust (not righteous) when he judges sinners. The legalistic person thinks that this would make God guilty of a double standard. The man who picked up sticks on the Sabbath day[34] and Achan who took for himself some of the spoil of Jericho[35] died without mercy, yet David, quoted here, gets away with murder. How can God treat sinners so differently, and not be guilty of having a double standard?[36] The answer is found in the other side of the inverted order.

> Whom God hath set forth *to be* a propitiation through faith in his blood, **to declare his righteousness** for the remission of sins that are past, through the forbearance of God; [26]**To declare,** *I say,* **at this time his righteousness:** that he might be **just (righteous),** and the **justifier (the one who declares righteous)** of him which believeth in Jesus.[37]

It is the offering of God's Son, as the sacrifice of atonement for past sins, that made it possible for God to forgive David, judge unbelievers, still be righteous, and the one who declares righteous those who believe. Judgment is handed out based on justice, but forgiveness is dispensed to sinners based on God's grace and mercy. God's grace is available to all that have faith in the atoning sacrifice of Jesus the Messiah (Christ). In the words of the Passover "when I see the blood, I will pass over."[38] That is not justice, but mercy and grace. Justice would kill all, because all are guilty, but those who believe are saved from God's wrath because God is gracious. In mercy we do not receive what we deserve, but when we do receive what we do not deserve, it is grace.

The fourth rhetorical question capitalizes on the fact that without sin we could not experience God's grace. The legalist reasons that according to Paul's gospel: grace is good and desirable, therefore sin must not be that bad; it is required to receive grace and mercy. Since grace is good and brings glory to God, they further assert that Paul's gospel teaches we should not be judged because of the good that comes. Paul answers this with, "God forbid." This would keep God from judging the world, but God will judge the world. The judgment of the world was set forth in 2:1–16. The closing statement of that section says,

---

[34] Numbers 15:32–36
[35] Joshua 7
[36] Romans 2:6,11
[37] Romans 3:25–26
[38] Exodus 12:13

In the day when God shall judge the secrets of men by Jesus Christ according to my gospel. [39]

The gospel does not exclude God's judgment of the world, but begins by declaring the certainty of it. There has been an inference that if Paul's gospel were true, then God would be deceptive, unjust, or not able to condemn the guilty. In verse eight there is no inference, but a bold, hostile accusation. Sinful man presumes to pass judgment on God's plan of redemption. In doing so they set themselves up as judge over God. "Their condemnation is just," not because they are the worst sinners, but because they have rejected God's plan of salvation. "They hold the truth of the gospel in unrighteousness."

Chapter four begins with the phrase "What shall we say then?" This phrase will be repeated six times in Romans, the last is in 9:30. Paul is contrasting the slanderous speech of chapter three with what should be said. Starting in 10:18, a new repetitive phrase begins: "I say then." This phrase appears five times. This is one side of another system that encompasses 4:1–15:13 (See pg. 208.)

Paul is concerned with those who are contentious and say not the truth. They hold the truth in unrighteousness. To them, "indignation and wrath." This extended chiasmus is concerned with the universal and total sinfulness of man (3:8–20).

Our Sinful Speech and God's Wrath: Extended Chiasmus (2)

(A.) **a.** [2:17] Makest thy **boast** in God [23] **boast** in the law
  b. [17] Thou art called a **Jew**
  c. [23, 27] Through breaking the **law**

(B.) **a.** [3:1] Given the **oracles of God**
  b. 1. [3] Will their lack of faith nullify **God's faithfulness**? NIV
    2. [5] Is God **unrighteous** who taketh vengeance?
    3. [6-7] Why yet am I also **judged as a sinner**?

---

[39] Romans 2:16

Correlations
1:18 Who hold the truth in unrighteousness

Chiasmus

(C.) **A.** [8] And not rather, (as we be slanderously reported, and as some affirm that we say,) Let us do evil, that good may come? Whose damnation is just.

(D.) **B.** [9] What then? are we better *than they?* No, in no wise: for we have before proved both Jews and Gentiles, that they are **all under sin;**

(E.) **C.** [10] As it is written, There is **none righteous,** no, not one:

(F.) **D.** [11] There is none that **understandeth,** there is none that **seeketh after God.**

(G.) **E.** [12] They are all **gone out of the way,** they are together become unprofitable;

(H.) **F.** there is **none that doeth good,** no, not one.

(I.) **G.** [13] Their **throat** *is* an open sepulchre; with their **tongues** they have used deceit;

(I'.) **G'.** The poison of asps *is* under their **lips:** [14] Whose **mouth** *is* full of cursing and bitterness:

(H'.) **F'.** [15] Their feet *are* **swift to shed blood:**

(G'.) **E'.** [16] Destruction and misery *are* **in their ways:**

(F'.) **D'.** [17] And the way of peace have **they not known:**

(E'.) **C'.** [18] There is **no fear of God** before their eyes.

(D'.) **B'.** [19] Now we know that what things soever the law saith, it saith to them who are **under the law:**

(C'.) **A'.** [20] **That every mouth may be stopped, and all the world may become guilty before God.**

(B'.) a'. ²¹ Righteousness . . . of God witnessed by **the law and the prophets**

b'. ²⁵ **Whom God hath set forth** to be a propitiation through faith in his blood

    1. **To declare his righteousness** for the remission of **sins that are past**, through the forbearance of God;

    2. ²⁶ **To declare,** *I say,* **at this time his righteousness that he might be** juc **Jesus.**

(A'.) a'. ²⁷ Where is **boasting** then?

b'. ²⁹ Is he the God of the **Jews** only?

c'. ³¹ Do we make void **the law** [40] through faith?

Correlations

³:⁵ *Is God unrighteous who taketh vengeance?*

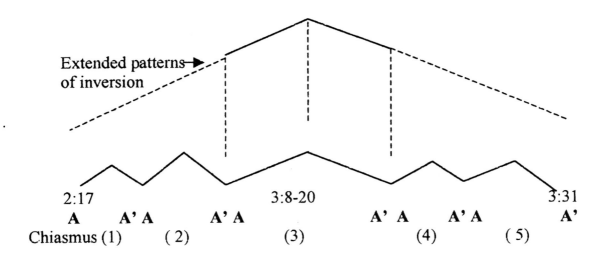

<hr>

[40] For Purpose of the Law, see Appendix Pg. 267–270

A. a. [3:21] **The righteousness of God** without the law is manifested, being **witnessed by the law and the prophets;**

> A. The righteousness of God . . . is made manifest
> B. Being justified . . . through the redemption
> B'. Whom God set forth to be a propitiation . . . through faith in his blood
> A'. To declare his righteousness

   b. [22] Even the **righteousness of God** *which is* **by faith of Jesus Christ** unto all and upon all them that believe: for there is no difference: [23] For **all have sinned**, and come short of the glory of God;

B. a. [24] **Being justified** [declared righteous] **freely by his grace**
   b. **through the redemption** that is in Christ Jesus:

B'. a'. [25] Whom God hath set forth *to be* **a propitiation**
    b'. **through faith in his blood,**

A'. a'. **To declare his righteousness** for the remission of **sins that are past,** through the forbearance of God;

    b'. [26] **To declare,** *I say,* **at this time his righteousness:** that he might be **just,** [righteous] and the **justifier** [one who declares righteous] **of him which believeth in Jesus.**

The chiastic reading:

A. a. [3:21] The righteousness of God without the law is manifested, being witnessed by the law and the prophets;

   b. [22] Even the righteousness of God *which is* by faith of Jesus Christ unto all and upon all them that believe: for there is no difference: [23]For all have sinned, and come short of the glory of God;

A'. a'. To declare his righteousness for the remission of sins that are past, through the forbearance of God;
    b'. [26] To declare, *I say,* at this time his righteousness: that he might be just, (righteous) and the justifier (one who declares righteous) of him which believeth in Jesus.

B. **a.** ²⁴Being justified [declared righteous] freely by his grace
b. through the redemption that is in Christ Jesus:

B'. **a'.** ²⁵Whom God hath set forth *to be* a propitiation
b'. through faith in his blood,

The above verses are part of E-TIP (2) and are the secondary emphasis for the extended chiasmus in 2:17–3:31. These verses are one side of the center section for E-TIP (2) and are part of the main emphases of the whole book. E-TIP (2) spans the whole of Romans.

As a note of interest, in 1742, J. A. Bengel suggested that Romans is written in chiasmus. He sought to demonstrate this with a section of Romans. Nils Lund tells us this about Bengel's work:

He arranges Rom. 3:9–6:12 in a series of seven sections, which are treated as being parallel in an inverted order, thus placing Faith (3:22) in the fourth, or central, section.[41]

Bengel's suggestion, while not the same as is being presented in this paper, must have been very close to what is the middle section of E-TIP (2). See pg. 133–135.

Correlations
2:17 Boasting.
2:21–28 Jews and Gentiles.
2:23–25 & 3:1–8 Breaking the law.

³:²⁷**Where *is* boasting then?** It is excluded. By what law? of works? Nay: but by the law of faith. ²⁸Therefore we conclude that **a man is justified** [declared righteous] **by faith** without the deeds of the law.

²⁹*Is he* **the God of the Jews only?** *Is he* not **also of the Gentiles?** Yes, of the Gentiles also: ³⁰Seeing *it is* one God, which shall justify [declare righteous] the circumcision by faith, and uncircumcision through faith.

³¹**Do we then make void the law through faith?** God forbid: yea, **we establish the law.**

---

[41] *Chiasmus in the New Testament*, Nils W. Lund, Pg. 36. Hendrickson Publishers, Peabody, Mass. Reprint 1992

The theme of 4:1–8:30 is "the righteousness of God is revealed." The primary topic of chapters four and five is:

Whom God hath set forth *to be* a propitiation through faith in his blood.[42]

Chapter four: to declare his righteousness for the remission of sins **that are past**, through the forbearance of God;

Chapter five: to declare, I say, at this time his righteousness: that he might be just, and the justifier of him which believeth in Jesus.

Chapter four presents salvation of Old Testament saints, and is organized around the three questions in 3:27–31. The three questions are the segue to the next extended chiasmus and form the center of E-TIP (2). Chapter five presents the salvation of present-day believers and is organized around being justified by faith and the blood. The basis for the inversion in E-TIP (2) and (3) is verses 25–26. The main theme of the coming section is:

[24] **Being justified** [declared righteous] **freely by his grace through the redemption** that is in *Christ Jesus*:

[25] *Whom* God hath set forth *to be* **a propitiation** [43] **through faith in his blood,**

(**This will be discussed according to the two declarations**)

1.   **To declare his righteousness** for the remission of **sins that are past**, through the forbearance of God;

2.   [26] **To declare,** *I say,* **at this time his righteousness**: that he might be **just,** [righteous} and the **justifier** [one who declares righteous] **of him which believeth in Jesus.**

In the following inverted order that encompasses the whole of Romans, the center section begins with verse 3:21, and ends at 5:21. Once it is established that God is righteous, then He can give to believers that which he has. As sovereign, He has the prerogatives of forgiveness and graciousness.

---

[42] Romans 3:25
[43] Propitiation, see appendix Pg. 273

E-TIP (2) 1:1–16:27

A. [1:1-7] Paul's gospel

  B. Called to be an apostle

    C. [8-10] Paul's prayer ministry

      D. [11-15] Paul's planned visit

        E. [16-20] Paul's confidence

          F. [21-32] Gentiles fail to give glory or to be thankful

            G. [2:1-3] Judging others

              H. [1-3] The judgment of God is according to truth

                I. [7-10] Principles of judgement and blessing; good and evil . . .

                  J. [16] God shall judge the secrets of men by Jesus Christ . . .

                    K. [13-15] Law written in the heart

                      L. [11] For there is no respect of persons with God [9-10] . . . to the Jew first, and also to the Gentile

                        M. [17] Call thyself a Jew [28] He is not a Jew, which is one outwardly He is a Jew, which is one inwardly

                          N. [27] . . . if it fulfil the law

                            O. [16-24] Jews breaking the law causes the name of God to be blasphemed

                            P. [24-29] Circumcision of the heart [a love relationship Deut. 30:6] [29] . . . in the spirit, and not in the letter;

Q. [3:8] Doing evil that good may come

R. [8–20] Sinful behavior

S. [21–26] Righteousness of God declared

 a. [25] For past sins
 b. [26] At this present time
 [27–31] Three questions

S'. [4:1–25] God's righteousness imputed

 a'. [for past sin] [organized around the three questions]
 b'. [5:1–11] (for present sin)

R'. [12–21] Sin nature

Q'. [6:1–12] Shall we continue in sin . . . [gospel] [13–23] Shall we sin [personal experience]

P'. [7:1–6] Marriage [Christ is the new husband, righteousness shall reign] [6] That we should serve in newness of spirit, and not *in* the oldness of the letter.

O'. [7–24] Saul tries to serve *in* the oldness of the letter; Saul breaks the law

N'. [8:4] Righteousness of the law fulfilled in us [by the Spirit]

M'. [9:3] My kinsmen according to the flesh; [6] They are not all Israel, which are of Israel; [8] The children of promise are counted for the seed

L'. [10:12] For there is no difference between the Jew and the Greek: for the same Lord over all is rich unto all that call upon him. [9:1–10:18] To the Jew first; [10:19–11:32] To the Gentile

K'. [11:27] This is my covenant

J'. [12:19–13:5] God-ordained powers

I'. [12:1–13:14] Good and evil

H'. [14:9–12] Christ shall judge

G'. [1–13] Judging your brother

F'. [15:1–13] Gentiles give glory and are thankful

E'. [14] Paul's confidence

D'. [22–29] Paul's visit

C'. [30–33] Paul's prayer request

B'. [16:7] Andronicus and Junia . . . who are of note among the apostles

A'. [25–27] Paul's gospel

The Righteousness of God was Imputed to Past Believers 4:1–5:21
A comparison between 3:27–31 and chapter four

A. [3:27] Where *is* **boasting** then? It is excluded. By what law? of works? Nay: but by the law of faith.

[28] Therefore we conclude that a man is **justified** [declared righteous] **by faith** without the deeds of the law.

A'. [4:1] What shall we say then that Abraham our father, as pertaining to the flesh, hath found? [2] For if Abraham were justified (declared righteous) by works, *he hath whereof to glory;* but not before God. [3] For what saith the scripture? *Abraham believed God,* and it was **counted unto him for righteousness.**

B. [3:29] *Is he* **the God of the Jews only?** *Is he* not also of the Gentiles? Yes, of the Gentiles also: [30] Seeing *it is* one God, which shall justify (declare righteous) the circumcision by faith, and uncircumcision through faith.

B'. [9] *Cometh* this blessedness then upon the circumcision *only,* or upon the uncircumcision also? For we say that faith was reckoned to Abraham for righteousness.

C. [31] **Do we then make void** the law through faith?

[31] God forbid: yea, **we establish the law.**

C'. [13] For the promise, that he should be the heir of the world, *was* not to Abraham, or to his seed, through the law, but through the righteousness of faith. [14] For if they which are of the law *be* heirs, **faith is made void, and the promise made of none effect:**

[20] He staggered not at the promise of God through unbelief; but was strong in faith, **giving glory to God;**

It should be obvious from the above that Paul is using the three questions at the end of chapter three to develop his thoughts in chapter four. The reader of scripture must be careful here, because these questions are not the topic of chapter four. The topic is God's righteousness in justifying those who believed, before the death of Christ.

As we begin looking at E-TIP (2), the reader will notice a change. Paul will often be using large sections as single units of thought. These units of thought are directly compared to their counterpart.

Verse 21–31 gives us the general theme of the coming section. That theme is "There is a righteousness that comes from God." Verses 29–31 introduce us to the coming extended chiasma. They are also the point of reflection for E-TIP (2). This means that this system has as its point of reflection, the transition between two extended chiasma.

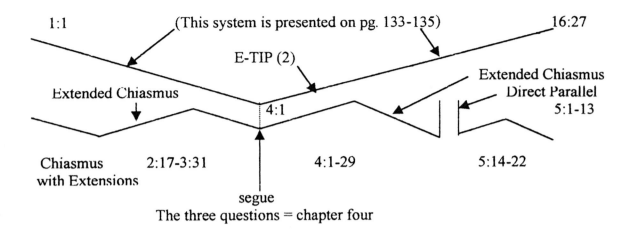

The righteousness that comes from God correlates with 4:1–5:13. Radiating outward the sinful behavior of 3:9–20 correlates with the old and new Adam of 5:12–21. The accusation of 3:8 correlates with the two "shall we sin because" statements of chapter six. Next, the discussion of who is a Jew in 2:29 correlates with "I speak to you who know the law," 7:1. This progression continues until 1:1 correlates with chapter sixteen.

This is a very large macro-system. It is symmetrical; fairly detailed but very unbalanced. Its center is the transition between two other systems. We will see both micro and macro examples of this type. From this point on, the complexity of Paul's presentation will increase until chapter ten. Individually, each system is clear, but the number of simultaneous systems increases.

III

The Righteousness of God Revealed by Faith 4:1–8:30

To Declare His Righteousness for the Remission of Sins that are Past 3:25

To illustrate this truth Paul chooses two sinners. The first is Abram, an uncircumcised idol-worshiping Gentile; the other is David, a Jewish adulterer and murderer. Abram, four hundred and twenty years before the law,[44] offers up sacrifices similar to those required by the law, sacrifices that could not take away sin.[45] David, who lives under the law, does not offer up a sacrifice.[46] Both men believe God, and God imputes the righteousness of the coming Christ to both. Abram illustrates salvation of the lost, but David illustrates what happens when a believer sins.

"For the law was given by Moses, *but* grace and truth came by Jesus Christ."[47]

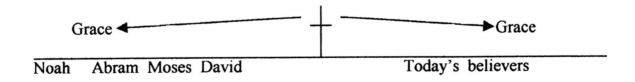

Grace ◄—————————————————|—————————————————► Grace

Noah   Abram Moses David   Today's believers

---

[44] Genesis 15
[45] Hebrews 10:1–3
[46] Psalm 51:16
[47] John 1:17

In this chapter, Abram and David, who lived before Christ, received grace because of the death of Christ. God had promised a Messiah who would die for their sins and they believed that promise.

The three questions from chapter three do supply a topic of discussion that will be used to develop this new thought. This new thought will be developed as two inverted orders. The first, 4:1–12, will address the first two questions. Verses 13–22 will address the last question to develop another truth. The English words *count*, *impute*, and *reckoned* are all translations of the same Greek word. Faith is the theme of the first half; it then shifts to the absence of circumcision. The conclusion (verses 7–8) is a quotation from Psalm 32. In this psalm, David confesses his sins of adultery and murder and finds himself blessed by God.

Correlations
3:27 Where is boasting?
3:29 *Is he* the God of the Jews only?
1:17 From faith to faith, the just shall live by faith

A. ⁴:¹ What shall we say then that **Abraham our father**, as pertaining to the flesh, hath found? ² For if Abraham were justified [declared righteous] by works, he hath *whereof* to glory [boast] but not before God.

> A. Abraham our father
> > B. It was counted unto him for righteousness
> > > C. To him that worketh is the reward not reckoned
> > > > D. Blessedness
> > > > > E. Blessed
> > > > > E'. Blessed
> > > > D'. Blessedness
> > > C'. How was it then reckoned
> > B'. That righteousness might be imputed unto them also
> A'. The father of circumcision; Our father Abraham

B. ³ For what saith the scripture? **Abraham believed** God, and it was **counted unto him for righteousness**.

C. ⁴ Now to him that worketh is the reward not **reckoned** [counted] of grace, but of debt. ⁵ But to him that worketh not, but believeth on him that justifieth [declares righteous] the ungodly, his faith is counted for righteousness.

D. ⁶Even as David also describeth the **blessedness** of the man, unto whom God imputeth [counted] righteousness without works,

    E. ⁷*Saying,* **Blessed** *are* they whose iniquities are forgiven, and whose sins are covered.

    E'. ⁸**Blessed** *is* the man to whom the Lord will not impute [count] sin.

D'. ⁹*Cometh* this **blessedness** then upon the circumcision *only,* or upon the uncircumcision also? for we say that faith was reckoned [counted] to Abraham for righteousness.

C'. ¹⁰How was it then **reckoned** [counted]? when he was in circumcision, or in uncircumcision? Not in circumcision, but in uncircumcision.

B'. ¹¹And he received the sign of circumcision, a seal of the righteousness of the faith which *he had yet* being uncircumcised: that he might be the father of all them that believe, though they be not circumcised; that **righteousness might be imputed** [counted] **unto them also:**

A'. ¹²And **the father of circumcision** to them who are not of the circumcision only, but who also walk in the steps of that faith of **our father Abraham**, which *he had* being *yet* uncircumcised.

The chiastic reading:

A. ⁴:¹What shall we say then that Abraham our father, as pertaining to the flesh, hath found? ²For if Abraham were justified (declared righteous) by works, he hath *whereof* to glory [boast] but not before God.

A'. ¹²And the father of circumcision to them who are not of the circumcision only, but who also walk in the steps of that faith of our father Abraham, which *he had* being *yet* uncircumcised.

B. ³For what saith the scripture? Abraham believed God, and it was counted unto him for righteousness.

B'. ¹¹And he received the sign of circumcision, a seal of the righteousness of the faith which *he had yet* being uncircumcised: that he might be the father of all them that believe, though they be not circumcised; that righteousness might be imputed [counted] unto them also:

C. [4] Now to him that worketh is the reward not reckoned [counted] of grace, but of debt. [5] But to him that worketh not, but believeth on him that justifieth [declares righteous] the ungodly, his faith is counted for righteousness.

C'. [10] How was it then reckoned [counted]? when he was in circumcision, or in uncircumcision? Not in circumcision, but in uncircumcision.

D. [6] Even as David also describeth the blessedness of the man, unto whom God imputeth [counted] righteousness without works,

D'. [9] *Cometh* this blessedness then upon the circumcision *only*, or upon the uncircumcision also? for we say that faith was reckoned [counted] to Abraham for righteousness.

E. [7] *Saying,* Blessed *are* they whose iniquities are forgiven, and whose sins are covered.

E'. [8] Blessed *is* the man to whom the Lord will not impute [count] sin.

The word for *count, reckon,* and *impute* was used in a couple of applications. One, when a person went to the bank and made a deposit, the banker would credit the account. When the banker recorded the amount of deposit, that amount was *counted* to this person's account. Second, when a person was brought before the court, the charges and the verdict would be recorded in the court records. The word for recording these things is this word that is translated *counted, reckoned* or *imputed.*

The sinner stands before the judge of all the earth. The verdict is guilty. The penalty is death. The lawyer (Christ) for the defendant pleads for mercy. This plea is based on the sacrifice of atonement. The judge issues a pardon. The court clerk records the pardon in the court records and the guilty sinner is now unconditionally forgiven. No matter how foolproof the case is against him, he is now beyond the reach of the law.

In the above passage the sinner is pardoned, and God's righteousness is *counted* to his account in heaven. He will never have sin recorded to his account again. This is because the blood of Christ covers all sin.

4:12 Who also walk in the steps of that faith of our father Abraham
3:31 Do we then make void the law through faith? God forbid: yea, we establish the law.

EXTENDED CHIASMUS (3) 4:13–25

(A.) [4:1-12] [Imputed righteousness]

Correlations
3:31 Do we then make void the law through faith?

Chiasmus

(B.) **A.** [4:13] **For the promise,**[48] **that he should be the heir of the world**, *was* not to Abraham, or to his seed, through **the law**, but through **the righteousness of faith**.

(C.) **B.** [14]For if they which are of the law *be* heirs, **faith is made void**, and **the promise made of none effect**: [15]Because the law worketh wrath: for where no law is, *there is* no transgression.

(D.) **C.** [16]**Therefore** *it is* of **faith**, that *it might be* by grace; to the end the promise might be sure to all the seed; not to that only which is of the law, but to that also which is of the **faith** of Abraham; who is the father of us all,

(E.) **D.** [17](As it is written, I have made thee **a father of many nations,**[49]) before him whom he believed, *even* God, who quickeneth the dead, and calleth those things which be not as though they were.

(E'.) **D'.** [18]Who against hope believed in hope, that he might become the **father of many nations**; according to that which was spoken, So shall thy seed be.

---

[48] Promise and Works. See Pg. 273
[49] Children of Abraham. See Appendix Pg. 272

(D'.) C'. [19]And being **not weak in faith**, he considered not his own body now dead, when he was about an hundred years old, neither yet the deadness of Sarah's womb:

(C'.) B'. [20]**He staggered not at the promise of God** through unbelief; but **was strong in faith**, giving glory to God;

(B'.) A'. [21]And being fully persuaded that, what he had **promised**, he was able also to perform. [22]And therefore **it was imputed** [counted] **to him for righteousness**.

(A'.) [23]Now it was not written for his sake alone, that it was **imputed** to him; [24]But for us also, to whom it shall be **imputed**, if we believe on him that raised up Jesus our Lord from the dead; [25]Who was delivered for our offences, and was raised again for our justification.

Segue: 22 . . . It was imputed to him for righteousness
         23 . . . That it was imputed to him

The chiastic reading:

A. [4:13] For the promise, that he should be the heir of the world, *was* not to Abraham, or to his seed, through the law, but through the righteousness of faith.

A'. [21] And being fully persuaded that, what he had **promised**, he was able also to perform. [22]And therefore it was imputed [counted] to him for righteousness.

B. [14]For if they which are of the law *be* heirs, faith is made void, and the promise made of none effect: [15]Because the law worketh wrath: for where no law is, *there is* no transgression.

B'. [20] He staggered **not** at the promise of God through unbelief; but was strong in faith, giving glory to God;

C. [16]Therefore *it is* of faith, that *it might be* by grace; to the end the promise might be sure to all the seed; not to that only which is of the law, but to that also which is of the faith of Abraham; who is the father of us all,

C'. [19] And being not weak in faith, he considered not his own body now dead, when he was about an hundred years old, neither yet the deadness of Sarah's womb:

D. [17] (As it is written, I have made thee a father of many nations,) before him whom he believed, *even* God, who quickeneth the dead, and calleth those things which be not as though they were.

D'. [18] Who against hope believed in hope, that he might become the father of many nations; according to that which was spoken, So shall thy seed be.

The center section contains the specific promise and the obstacles that faith had to overcome. Promise and faith, in a more general sense, are both in the extremes, and constitute the additional emphasis. The promise is the object of faith. When faith in God's promises is exercised, God gives grace. Not by works but by faith is the theme of the first half. The thought then shifts to Abram as an example.

Paul now takes two topics from verse twenty-five and presents them in inverse order.

TIP (1)

[25] Who was delivered for our offenses, and was raised again for our justification. [5:1–13] Justified by faith and the blood. [14–21] By one man's offences

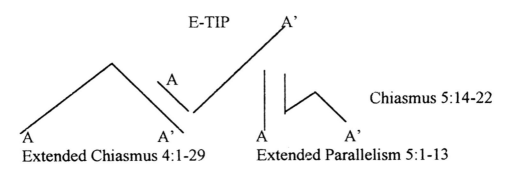

AT THIS TIME GOD DECLARED RIGHTEOUS THAT HE MAY BE JUST
AND THE JUSTIFIER OF THOSE WHO BELIEVE 5:1–8:30

What then? Are we better *than they?* No, in no wise: for we have before proved both Jews and Gentiles, that they are all under sin; [50]

---

[50] Romans 3:9

Correlations

^{5:1–11} Raised again for our justification

^{5:12–21} Delivered for our offences

A. ^{5:1} Therefore being **justified** [declared righteous] **by faith,**

A'. ^{5:9} Much more then, being now **justified** [declared righteous] **by his blood,**

B. we have **peace with God** through our Lord Jesus Christ:

B'. we shall be **saved from wrath** through him.

C. ² By whom also we have **access** by faith into this grace wherein we stand, and rejoice in hope of the glory of God.

C'. ¹⁰ For if, when we were enemies, we were **reconciled** to God by the death of his Son, much more, being reconciled, we shall be saved by his life.

D. ³ **And not only** *so,* **but we glory in tribulations** also: knowing that tribulation worketh patience; ⁴ And patience, experience; and experience, hope: ⁵ And hope maketh not ashamed; because the love of God is shed abroad in our hearts by the Holy Ghost which is given unto us.

D'. **And not only** *so,* **but we also joy in God through our Lord Jesus Christ,** by whom we have received the atonement.

E. ⁶ For when we were yet without strength, in due time **Christ died** for the **ungodly.** ⁷ For scarcely for a righteous man will one die: yet peradventure for a **good** man some would even dare to die. ⁸But God commendeth his love toward us, in that, **while we were yet sinners, Christ died for us.**

E'. ¹² Wherefore, as by one man sin entered into the world, and death by sin; and **so death passed upon all men,** for that all have sinned: ¹³For until the law sin was in the world: but sin is not imputed when there is no law.

In response to the exercise of faith in the blood of Christ, God as judge of all the earth considers the case of an ungodly sinner. The judge gives the righteousness of God's own Son to the sinner and with a declarative statement pronounces him righteous.

Segue:

5:12 So death passed upon all men. Nevertheless death reigned from Adam to Moses.

5:14 Neverthless death reigned from Adam to Moses

If righteous before God, then the blessings of 2:7 and 10 are his and the curse of 2:8–9 are not his. It is an act of grace on the part of the judge. The sinner is now at peace with his maker and need not fear his wrath. The believer can now enter into God's presence because a right relationship has been established between them. All of this is made possible, because Christ died for sinners past and present.

Correlations
5:11 By whom we have received the atonement
4:25 Delivered for our offenses

A. a. ¹⁴ Nevertheless **death reigned** from Adam to Moses, even over them that had not sinned after the similitude of Adam's transgression,

    b. who is the figure of him that was to come.

B. a. ¹⁵ But not as the offense, so also *is* the *free gift* [*charisma*]. For if through the **offense of one many** be dead,

    b. much more the grace [*charis*] of God, and **the gift** [*dorea*] **by grace** [*charis*], *which is* **by one man**, Jesus Christ, hath abounded unto many.

> A. Death reigned
>   . . . him that was to come
> B. Through the offence of one
>   Much more the grace
>   C. by one to condemnation
>   Many offences unto justification
>   D. Death reigned by one
>   Righteousness shall reign in life by one
>   C'. Judgment came upon all men to condemnation
>   The free gift came upon all men unto justification of life.
>   B'. By one man's disobedience
>   Grace did much more abound
> A'. Sin hath reigned unto death
>   Grace reign . . . unto eternal life by Jesus Christ

C. a. ¹⁶ And not as *it was* by one that sinned, *so is* the gift [*dorema*]: for the judgment *was* by one to **condemnation**,

    b. but the *free gift* [*charisma*] *is* of many offences unto **justification**.

  D. a. ¹⁷ For if by one man's offense **death reigned by one**;

    b. much more they which receive abundance of grace [*charis*] and of the gift of **righteousness shall reign** in life **by one** Jesus Christ.

C'. a'. ¹⁸ Therefore as by the offense of one *judgment came* upon all men to **condemnation**;

    b'. even so by the righteousness of one *the free gift* [*dorea*] *came* upon all men unto **justification** of life.

B'. a'. [19] For as by **one man's disobedience** many were **made sinners**, so **by the obedience of one** shall many be **made righteous.**

    b'. [20] Moreover the law entered, that the offense might abound. But where sin abounded, **grace** [*charis*] **did much more abound:**

A'. a'. [21] That as sin hath **reigned unto death,**

    b'. even so might **grace** [*charis*] **reign** through righteousness unto eternal life by **Jesus Christ our Lord.**[51]

The chiastic reading:

A. a. [14] Nevertheless death reigned from Adam to Moses, even over them that had not sinned after the similitude of Adam's transgression,

    b. who is the figure of him that was to come.

A'. a'. [21] That as sin hath **reigned unto death,**

    b'. even so might grace [*charis*] reign through righteousness unto eternal life by Jesus Christ our Lord.

B. a. [15] But not as the offense, so also *is* the *free gift* [*charisma*] For if through the offense of one many be dead,

    b. much more the grace [*charis*] of God, and the gift [*dorea*] by grace [*charis*], *which is* by one man, Jesus Christ, hath abounded unto many.

B'. a'. [19] For as by one man's disobedience many were made sinners, so by the obedience of one shall many be made righteous.

    b'. [20] Moreover the law entered, that the offense might abound. But where sin abounded, grace [*charis*] did much more abound:

C. a. [16] And not as *it was* by one that sinned, *so is* the gift [*dorema*]: for the judgment *was* by one to condemnation,

    b. but the *free gift* [*charisma*] is of many offenses unto justification.

C'. a'. [18] Therefore as by the offense of one *judgment came* upon all men to condemnation;

---

[51] Romans 5:12–21 is presented as chiasmus in, *Chiasmus in the Pauline Letters* by Ian Thompson; Sheffield Acadenic Press, Sheffield UK. 1997. Thompson's arrangement centers in verse 18.

b'. even so by the righteousness of one *the free gift* [*dorea*] *came* upon all men unto justification of life.

D. a. [17] For if by one man's offence death reigned by one;

   b. much more they which receive abundance of grace [*charis*] and of the gift of righteousness shall reign in life by one Jesus Christ.

In the previous chiasmus, the center section pits the reign of death against the reign of righteousness. Righteousness is associated with life and grace. In the extremes we have death reigns and grace reigns. The personification of death and grace helps illustrate the prevailing and far-reaching influence that these two have. In the Greek, the word *dora* refers to a gift similar to a birthday gift. The gift (*dora*) is usually given based on a relationship such as parents giving gifts to their children. [*Charis*] is a gift based solely on the nature of the giver. *Dora* emphasis, the gift, while [*Charis*], the giver. In this instance, God gives the gift (*Dora*) of salvation, because God is gracious, not because of a preexisting relationship.

Correlations

5:20 But where sin abounded, grace [*charis*] did much more abound
6:1 Shall we continue in sin, that grace may abound

5:20 Moreover the law entered, that the offense might abound
6:15 Shall we sin, because we are not under the law, but under grace?

5:21 That as sin hath reigned unto death even so might grace [*charis*] reign
7:1–6 Two husbands, Law and Grace

UNIVERSAL SIN NATURE

Before we continue it is important to note that there is another E-TIP. This one spans between 3:1 and 15:13, and its center is between chapters five and six. Here again, the transitional elements not only introduce the next chiasmus, but are also the point of reflection for another E-TIP.

Because this system takes four pages to present in abbreviated form, it will be difficult to compare paired parts. A is on page 150, and A' is on page 155. To make things easier, I have given a reference to another part of the document, where correlating parts are on the same page.

In the following system, A is presented as 3:25–4:20. It is possible that in the mind of Paul, A was 2:16–3:8. The reader will remember that the three questions at the end of chapter three correlate in both directions. They correlate back to 2:16–3:8 and ahead to chapter four. To maintain the pattern of inversion, 2:16–3:8 would be the choice that fits. When I compare these passages with A', I find that the most detailed correlation is with 3:23–4:20. I am not sure of the mind of Paul in this instance.

E-TIP (3)

A. (See pg. 227)

  a. ³:²⁵⁻²⁶ Whom God hath set forth *to be* a **propitiation through faith in his blood**, to declare his righteousness for the remission of sins that are past, through the forbearance of God; ²⁶ justifier of him which believeth in Jesus declare, *I say,* at this time his righteousness: that he might be just,

  b. ²⁵⁻²⁷ **Where *is* boasting then?** It is excluded. By what law? of works? Nay: but by the law of faith. ⁴:² if Abraham were justified by works, **he hath *whereof* to glory; but not before God.**

  c. ³:²⁹ *Is he* the God of the Jews only? *Is he* not also of the Gentiles? Yes, of the Gentiles also:
  ⁴:² **How was it then reckoned? When he was in circumcision, or in uncircumcision?** Not in circumcision, but in uncircumcision.

  d. ³:³¹ Do we then make void the law through faith? God forbid: yea, **we establish the law**. ⁴:¹⁰ For if they which are of the law *be* heirs, faith is made void, and the promise made of none effect:

  e. ¹⁹ And being not **weak in faith**, he considered not his own body now dead, when he was about an hundred years old, neither yet the deadness of Sarah's womb:

  f. ¹⁸ **Who against hope believed in hope,** that he might become the father of many nations; according to that which was spoken, So shall thy seed be.

g. [20]He staggered not at the promise of God through unbelief; but was **strong in faith**,

h. **giving glory to God**;

B. (See pg. 191)

a. [3:1-2]What advantage then hath the Jew? Or what profit *is there* of circumcision? [2]Much every way: chiefly, because that unto them were committed the **oracles of God**.

b. [3-4] For what if some did not believe? Shall their unbelief make **the faith of God without effect**? [4]God forbid: yea, let God be true, but every man a liar; as it is written, That thou mightest be justified in thy sayings, and mightest overcome when thou art judged.

c. [5] But if our unrighteousness commend the righteousness of God, what shall we say? *Is God unrighteous* who taketh vengeance? (I speak as a man) [6] God forbid: for then how shall God judge the world?

d. [22] Even the righteousness of God *which is* by **faith** of Jesus Christ unto all and upon all them that believe

e. [7-8] And not *rather,* (as we be **slanderously reported**, and as some affirm that we say,) Let us do evil, that good may come? whose damnation is just.

f. **for there is no difference**: [23] For all have sinned, and come short of the glory of God;

g. [24] Being justified freely by his **grace** through the redemption that is in Christ Jesus

h. [27] Where is boasting then? By what law? of works? Nay: but by the law of faith. [29-30] Is He God of Jews only? Is he not also of the Gentiles? Yes, of the Gentiles also:

j. [31] Do we make void the law through faith? God forbid: **we establish the law.**

k. [4:1] What shall we say then that Abraham our **father**, as pertaining to the flesh, hath found?

l. [21] He staggered not at the promise of God through unbelief; but was strong in faith, **giving glory to God**;

C. (See pg. 173)

    a. [5:1] we have **peace with God**

        1. [13-14] **heir**

        2. [16] **father of us all,**
           [17] **father of many nations**

        3. [18] **who against hope believed in hope**

        4. [20] was strong in faith, **giving glory to God;**

    b. [5:2] [we] rejoice in **hope of the glory**

    c. [3] we glory in **tribulation**

    d. [3] tribulation worketh **patience;**

    e. [4] patience, **experience;**

    f. [4] experience, **hope:**

    g. [6] hope maketh **not ashamed;**

    h. [6] because the **love of God** is shed abroad in our hearts

    i. [6] by **the Holy Ghost** which is given unto us.

    j. [12] by one man **sin entered into the world**

    k. [14-21] all points contrasting "Evil" and "Good": the old Adam and the new Adam

D.   a. [18] Therefore as by the offense of one *judgment came* upon all men to **condemnation;**

     b. even so by the righteousness of one *the free gift* [*dorea*] *came* upon all men unto **justification** of life.

E. [17] For if by one man's offense **death reigned by one**; much more they which receive abundance of grace [*charis*] and of the gift of **righteousness shall reign** in life by one' Jesus Christ.

F. [20] Moreover the **law entered, that the offense might abound.**

G. But where sin abounded, grace [*charis*] **did much more abound:**

G'. [6:1-14] Shall we continue in sin, that grace may abound? [14] For **sin shall not have dominion over you: for ye are not under the law, but under grace.**

F'. ⁶:¹⁵⁻²³ **Shall we sin, because we are not under the law**, but under grace? ²³ For the **wages of sin is death**; but **the gift** [*charis*] **of God** *is* **eternal life** through Jesus Christ our Lord.

E'. ⁷:¹⁻⁶ Marriage
 1. First husband, (Law and Death)
 2. Second husband, (Christ)

D'. ⁷:⁷ **What shall we say then?** *Is the law sin?* ⁹ but when the commandment came, sin revived, and **I died.** ¹² Wherefore the **law** *is* **holy**, and the commandment holy, and **just**, and **good.**

C'. a'. ⁸:⁶ To be spiritually minded is life and **peace**
 1. ¹⁷ and if children, then heirs; **heirs of God**, and joint heirs with Christ;
 2. ¹⁵ we cry, **Abba Father**
 3. ²⁴ For we are saved by **hope**
 4. ¹⁷ **glorified** together

b'. ¹⁷ that we may be also **glorified together.**

c'. ²² the whole creation groaneth and **travaileth in pain** together until now.

d'. ²⁵ But if we hope for that we see not, then do we **with patience wait for it.**

e'. ²⁸ all things **work together** for the good

f'. ²⁴ saved by **hope**

g'. ³⁰ them He also **glorified**

h'. ³⁷⁻³⁹ more than conquerors through **him that loved us.**

i'. ²⁶ the **Spirit** also helpeth our infirmities:

j'. ²⁰ the **creation was made subject to vanity**

k'. ¹⁻¹¹ all points contrasting "Evil" and "Good": the flesh and the spirit.

B'. a'. ⁹:³⁻⁵ Who are Israelites; to whom *pertaineth* **the adoption, and the glory, and the covenants, and the giving of the law, and the service** *of God*, **and the promises; Whose** *are* **the fathers**, and of whom as concerning the flesh Christ *came,* who is over all, God blessed for ever. Amen b'. [6]**Not as though the word of God hath taken none effect.** For they *are* not all Israel, which are of Israel:

c'. [14]What shall we say then? *Is there* **unrighteousness with God?** God forbid.

d'. [20]Nay but, O man, who art thou that **repliest against God?** Shall the thing formed say to him that formed *it,* Why hast thou made me thus?

e'. [32]Wherefore? Because *they sought it* not by **faith,** but as it were by the works of the law. For they stumbled at that stumblingstone; [10:6]But the righteousness which is of faith . . .

f'. [12]**For there is no difference** between the Jew and the Greek: for the same Lord over all is rich unto all that call upon him. For whosoever shall call upon the name of the Lord shall be saved

g'. [11:5-6]Even so then at this present time also there is a remnant according to the **election of grace.** [6]And if by **grace,** then *is it* no more of works: otherwise **grace** is no more **grace.** But if *it be* of works, then is it no more **grace:** otherwise work is no more work.

h'. [18]**Boast** not against the branches. But if thou **boast,** thou bearest not the root, but the root thee. [25]For I would not, brethren, that ye should be ignorant of this mystery, **lest ye should be wise in your own conceits** . . .

i'. [17-24]Natural and unnatural branches

j'. [11:27]For this *is* **my covenant** unto them, when I shall take away their sins.

k'. [11:28]As concerning the gospel, *they are* enemies for your sakes: but as touching the election, *they are* beloved for the **fathers'** sakes.

l'. [33-36]O the depth of the riches both of the wisdom and knowledge of God! How unsearchable *are* his judgments, and his ways past finding out! [34]For who hath known the mind of the Lord? Or who hath been his counsellor? [35]Or who hath first given to him, and it shall be recompensed unto him again? [36]For of him, and through him, and to him, *are* all things: **to whom** *be* **glory for ever.** Amen.

A'. **a'.** [12:1] I beseech you therefore, brethren, by the mercies of God, that ye **present your bodies a living sacrifice**, holy, acceptable unto God, *which is* your reasonable service. [2]And be not conformed to this world: but be ye transformed by the renewing of your mind, that ye may prove what is that good, and acceptable, and perfect, will of God.

    b'. [3]**For I say**, through the grace given unto me, to every man that is among you, **not to think** *of himself* **more highly than he ought to think**; but to think soberly, according as God hath dealt to every man the measure of faith.

    c'. [13:1] Let every soul be subject unto the higher powers. For there is no power but of God: **the powers that be are ordained of God. For he is the minister of God** to thee for good. But if thou do that which is evil, be afraid; for he beareth not the sword in vain: for **he is the minister of God**, a revenger to *execute* wrath upon him that doeth evil.

    d'. [8]Owe no man any thing, but to love one another: for **he that loveth another hath fulfilled the law.**

    e'. [14:1] Him that is **weak in the faith** receive ye, *but* not to doubtful disputations.

    f'. [15:4] For whatsoever things were written aforetime were written for our learning, that we **through patience and comfort of the scriptures might have hope.** [13] Now the **God of hope** fill you with all joy and peace in believing, **that ye may abound in hope**, through the power of the Holy Ghost.

    g'. [1]We then that are **strong** ought to bear the infirmities of the weak, and not to please ourselves.

    h'. [6]**That ye may with one mind** *and* **one mouth glorify God**, even the Father of our Lord Jesus Christ.

In the above system, Paul not comparing item to item, but one section to another section. This system will provide a third input to help develop the continuing message, and is one of the most detailed systems in Romans. One of its main characteristics is the contrasting of good and evil. Some examples of these contrasts are: in chapter six, the dominion of God vs. the dominion of sin, and servants of righteousness vs. servants of uncleanness, and in chapter seven, two husbands and two minds. In chapter eight, contrasts include the flesh vs. the spirit, and in chapters nine through eleven, two sons of Abraham (Isaac and Ishmael), two brothers (Jacob and Esau), two national leaders (Moses and Pharaoh), two pots (one of honor and one of dishonor), two people (Jews and Gentiles); and in chapter eleven, the goodness and severity of God, and two olive branches (wild and natural).

Section 9:1–11:36 and 12:1–15:17 are both organized around chapters three and four. This alone is enough to establish the fact, that chapters nine through eleven are not parenthetical, but an integral part of the whole of Romans.

Chapter six presents grace, sin, and the law. Grace is a good thing, but grace only comes to undeserving sinners. No matter how much sin, there is always more grace. This is true for unsaved persons like Abram who came to saving faith, and for saved individuals like David, who claim the promises of God concerning forgiveness. It is this teaching that prompted unsaved Jews to accuse Paul of teaching that believers should "do evil that good may come."[52] Those who make such accusations have left Paul's God out of their thinking. Without God they err. When an individual is saved by faith in God's promised Son, God gets involved in that individual's life to ensure that all of God's promises concerning believers are fulfilled. Grace is not a license to sin, but an assurance of ever-increasing holiness.[53]

Compare 3:4–8 and 6:1, 15

3:4 & 6 **God forbid:**	6:1 What shall we say then? **Shall we continue in sin**, that grace may abound? [2] **God forbid.**
3:8 And not *rather,* (as we be slanderously reported, and as some affirm that we say,) **Let us do evil, that good may come?** whose damnation is just.	6:15 What then? **Shall we sin**, because we are not under the law, but under grace? **God forbid.**

In chapter three, God deals with the accuser of the brethren. Every mouth is stopped and becomes guilty before the law.[54] In chapter six, the accusation is dealt with, and put to rest by the death, burial, and resurrection of Christ, i.e. the gospel.[55]

---

[52] Romans 3:8
[53] Romans 6:19
[54] Romans 3:19
[55] Sins of Ignorance vs. Intentioinal Sin, see Appendix Pg. 276–279

Correlations
3:8 As we be slanderously reported . . . Let us do evil, that good may come?
5:20 But where sin abounded, grace [*charis*] did much more abound.

A. ^{6:1} **What shall we say then? Shall we continue in sin, that grace may abound?**

² **God forbid. How shall we, that are dead to sin, live any longer therein?**

B. a. ³ Know ye not, that so many of us as were baptized into Jesus Christ were baptized into his death?

    b. ⁴ Therefore we are buried with him by baptism into death:

    b'. that like as Christ was **raised up from the dead** by the glory of the Father,

a'. even so we also should walk in newness of life.

C. ⁵ For if we have been planted together in the likeness of his death, we shall be also in the **likeness of his resurrection:**

    D. ⁶ Knowing this, that **our old man is crucified with him**, that the body of sin might be destroyed, that henceforth we should not serve sin.

      E. ⁷ For he that is **dead is freed from sin.**

        F. ⁸ Now if we be dead with Christ, we believe that **we shall also live with him:**

        F'. ⁹ Knowing that **Christ being raised from the dead dieth no more;**

A.   Dead to sin
    B.   Raised from the dead
      C.   The likeness of his resurrection
        D.   Our old man is crucified with him
          E.   He that is dead is freed from sin
            F.   We shall also live with him
            F'.   Christ being raised from the dead
          E'.   Death hath no more dominion over him
        D'.   He died unto sin once
      C'.   Alive unto God
    B'.   Alive from the dead
A'.   Sin shall not have dominion over you

       E'. **death hath no more dominion over him.**

     D'. [10] For **in that he died, he died unto sin once:** but in that he liveth, he liveth unto God.

    C'. [11] Likewise reckon ye also yourselves to be dead indeed unto sin, but **alive unto God through Jesus Christ our Lord.**

  B'. **a.** [12] Let not sin therefore **reign in your mortal body,** that ye should obey it in the lusts thereof.

    b. [13] Neither yield ye your members *as* instruments of unrighteousness unto sin:

    b'. but yield yourselves unto God, as those that are **alive from the dead,** and your members *as* instruments of righteousness unto God.

   a'. [14] For **sin shall not have dominion over you:**

A'. for ye are not under the law, but under grace.

The chiastic reading:

A. [6:1] **What shall we say then? Shall we continue in sin, that grace may abound?** [2] **God forbid.** How shall **we, that are dead to sin, live any longer therein?**

A'. for ye are not under the law, but under grace.

B. **a.** [3] Know ye not, that so many of us as were baptized into Jesus Christ were baptized into his death?

    b. [4] Therefore we are buried with him by baptism into death:
    b'. that like as Christ was **raised up from the dead** by the glory of the Father,

  a'. even so we also should walk in newness of life.

B'. a. [12] Let not sin therefore **reign in your mortal body,** that ye should obey it in the lusts thereof.

    b. [13] Neither yield ye your members *as* instruments of unrighteousness unto sin:
    b'. but yield yourselves unto God, as those that are **alive from the dead,** and your members *as* instruments of righteousness unto God.

  a'. [14] For **sin shall not have dominion over you:**

C. ⁵ For if we have been planted together in the likeness of his death, we shall be also in the likeness of his resurrection:

C'. ¹¹ Likewise reckon ye also yourselves to be dead indeed unto sin, but alive unto God through Jesus Christ our Lord.

D. ⁶ Knowing this, that our old man is crucified with him, that the body of sin might be destroyed, that henceforth we should not serve sin.

D'. ¹⁰ For in that he died, he died unto sin once: but in that he liveth, he liveth unto God.

E. ⁷ For he that is dead is freed from sin.

E'. Death hath no more dominion over him.

F. ⁸ Now if we be dead with Christ, we believe that we shall also live with him:

F'. ⁹ Knowing that Christ being raised from the dead dieth no more;

Paul takes elements from both E-TIP (2) and (3) to continue developing his presentation of the righteousness of God from TIP (1).

. . . Moreover the law entered, that the offence might abound. But where sin abounded, grace did much more abound:[56] death passed upon all men,[57] death reigned,[58] sin hath reigned unto death . . .[59]

And from E-TIP (2) comes the accusation and the answer (propitiation).

In 3:4 and 6, the righteousness of God is questioned, but in chapter six it is the righteousness of God's people that is in question. Shall the convert to Christ continue in sin, experiencing no change in lifestyle? Will grace become an excuse for sin?

This chiasmus is concerned with the reign of death,[60] and gives as an answer the death of Christ. The conclusion is "For he that is dead is freed from sin" and "death hath no more dominion over him." This rhymes with, "That as sin hath reigned unto death."[61]

---

[56] Romans 5:20

[57] Romans 5:12

[58] Romans 5:14, Romans 5:17

[59] Romans 5:21

[60] Romans 5:17

[61] Romans 5:21

In the extremes the believers are presented as being dead to sin and that sin no longer has dominion over them. The reader will be interested to know that converts to the Jewish faith went through a three-fold initiation rite, baptism, circumcision, and the offering of a blood sacrifice. The baptism was presided over by a priest. The convert would go into the water and be face down in a dead man's float. When the convert came up out of the water he was given a new (Jewish) name. This was his temple name that would be recorded in Jerusalem. From this point in time the authorities in the temple regarded the convert as being this new person. He was now considered to be no longer a Gentile, but a Jew.

In chapter four, the righteousness of Jesus Christ was placed to the believer's account; in this chapter, the death, burial, and resurrection are placed to the believer's account. The wages of sin is death. When the Judge of all the earth checks the books in the temple of heaven, He finds that the penalty has been paid. Believers share in the resurrection of Christ as well, allowing them to have a new life. It is as though the believer has died, but lives a new creature in Christ. In the court of heaven it is so.

Correlations

3:8 Let us do evil, that good may come

5:20 Moreover the law entered, that the offence might abound

For ye are not under the law, but under grace. 6:14

⁶:¹⁵ What then? **Shall we sin**, because we **are not under the law, but under grace?** God forbid.

A. ⁶:¹⁶ Know ye not, that to whom ye obey; whether of **sin unto death**, or of **obedience unto righteousness**?

B. ¹⁷ But God be thanked, that **ye were the servants of sin**, but ye have **obeyed from the heart** that form of doctrine which was delivered you. ¹⁸ **Being then made free from sin, ye became the servants of righteousness.**

A. his servants ye are to whom ye obey;
whether of sin unto death,
or of obedience unto righteousness
  B. Ye were servants of sin
  Ye became the servants of righteousness.
    C. ye have yielded your members servants to uncleanness and
    to iniquity unto iniquity;
    C'. even so now yield your members servants to righteousness unto holiness.
  B'. Ye were servants of sin . . .
  And become servants of God,
A'. The wages of sin is death . . .
The gift of God is eternal life . . .

C. [19] I speak after the manner of men because of the infirmity of your flesh: for as ye have **yielded your members servants to** uncleanness and to **iniquity unto iniquity**;

C'. even so now **yield your members servants to righteousness unto holiness.**

B'. [20] For when **ye were the servants of sin, ye were free from righteousness**. [21] What fruit had ye then in those things whereof ye are now ashamed? For the end of those things *is* death.

A' [22] But **now being made free from sin, and become servants to God,** ye have your fruit unto holiness, and the end everlasting life. [23] For the **wages of sin *is* death**; but **the gift of God *is* eternal life** through Jesus Christ our Lord.

The chiastic reading:

A. [6:16] Know ye not, that to whom ye yield yourselves servants to obey, his servants ye are to whom ye obey; whether of sin unto death, or of obedience unto righteousness?

A'. [22] But now being made free from sin, and become servants to God, ye have your fruit unto holiness, and the end everlasting life. [23] For wages of sin is death; but the gift of God is eternal life through Jesus Christ our Lord.

B. [17] But God be thanked, that ye were the servants of sin, but ye have obeyed from the heart that form of doctrine which was delivered you. [18] Being then made free from sin, ye became the servants of righteousness.

B'. [20] For when ye were the servants of sin, ye were free from righteousness. [21] What fruit had ye then in those things whereof ye are now ashamed? For the end of those things *is* death.

C. [19] I speak after the manner of men because of the infirmity of your flesh: for as ye have yielded your members servants to uncleanness and to iniquity unto iniquity;

C'. even so now yield your members servants to righteousness unto holiness.

In this section Paul continues to deal with the accusation from 3:8, but here the accusation says that conversion will actually result in increased sin. The legalist reasons that if the believer is not under the covenant of law, the believer will not do what is required but will do the forbidden. The legalist does not understand that law does not change the willful sinner into a law-abiding citizen. Also, grace does not change the law-abiding citizen into a willful sinner. On the contrary, law makes the sinner a lawbreaker, but servants of the Lord are the products of grace.

Paul will merge in the ideas of law and grace from 5:20. His conclusion is

[19] I speak after the manner of men because of the infirmity of your flesh: for as ye have **yielded** your members servants to uncleanness and to **iniquity unto iniquity**; even so now **yield** your members servants to **righteousness unto holiness**.

The idea of yielding to and being the servant of righteousness ties this argument to 5:17 where righteousness reigns. Paul will illustrate this with marriage. A' of the previous chiasmus closes with, "**for ye are not under the law, but under grace.**" This introduces the next chiasmus. The first half reminds the believers at Rome of their own experience in Christ. The second half reminds them of their life before becoming believers.

The extremes contrast sin and death with grace and eternal life. The two nearly identical statements in C and C' are typical of many centers.

Compare 5:21 with 6:15 and 6:23

[6:15] His servants ye are to whom ye obey; whether of **sin unto death,**	[6:23] For the **wages of sin** *is* **death**;
[6:15] or of **obedience unto righteousness?**	[5:21] That as **sin hath reigned unto death,**
[6:23] **the gift** [*charis*] **of God** *is* **eternal life** through Jesus Christ our Lord.	[5:21] even so might **grace** [*charis*] **reign** through righteousness **unto eternal life** by **Jesus Christ our Lord.**

In the covenant of the Law, Israel was under the pledge to "do all," and if they should fail, the LORD could do unto them as had been done to the sacrifice with whose blood they sealed the covenant. Believers are not under this covenant to do all or die, but the moral code contained in the law is a reflection of God's holy character. That code remains intact, but changes position. In the old covenant it was written on tablets of stone, but in the new covenant it is written on the tablets of the heart. This puts the Decalogue at the very heart of our relationship in the new covenant. We are not bound to do all or die, but our desire should be to do all. The Decalogue can be summarized by two commandments:

> Jesus said unto him, Thou shalt love the Lord thy God with all thy heart, and with all thy soul, and with all thy mind. [38] This is the first and great commandment. [39] And the second *is* like unto it, Thou shalt love thy neighbour as thyself. [40] On these two commandments hang all the law and the prophets.[62]

These two commandments do not replace the Ten Commandments but summarize them.

Compare 5:17 and 7:4

5:17 For if by one man's offense **death reigned** by one; much more they which receive abundance of grace and of the gift of **righteousness shall reign** in life by one, Jesus Christ.	7:4 Wherefore, my brethren, ye also are become dead to the **law** by the body of Christ; that ye should be **married to another**, *even* to him who is raised from the dead, that we should bring forth fruit unto God.

In the following system the first husband (law and death), is contrasted with the second husband (Christ and grace).

For the **wages of sin** *is* **death**; (first husband)
but **the gift of God** *is* **eternal life** through **Jesus Christ our Lord**. (second husband)

---

[62]Matthew 22:37–40

Extended Chiasmus (4)

(A.) [6:6] Knowing this, that **our old man is crucified with him**, [11] Likewise reckon ye also yourselves to be dead indeed unto sin, but **alive unto God through Jesus Christ our Lord.** [14] For **sin shall not have dominion over you**: for ye are not under the law, but under grace.

(B.) [17] But God be thanked, that **ye were the servants of sin**, but ye have obeyed from the heart that form of doctrine which was delivered you. [18] Being then made free from sin, ye became the servants of righteousness. [22] But **now being made free from sin, and become servants to God**, ye have your **fruit unto holiness**, and the end everlasting life.

Correlations
[5:17, 21] Grace/righteousness reigns
[2:29] Circumcision *is that* of the heart

Chiasmus

(C.) A. [7:1] Know ye not, brethren, (for I speak to them that know the law,) how that the **law hath dominion** over a man as long as he liveth?

(D.) B. [2] For the woman which hath an husband is bound by the law to *her* husband so long as he liveth; but **if the husband be dead, she is loosed from the law of *her* husband.**[63]

(E.) C. [3] So then if, while *her* husband liveth, **she be married to another man**, she shall be called an adulteress:

(E'.) C'. but if her husband be dead, she is free from that law; so that she is no adulteress, though **she be married to another man.**

---

[63] The Covenant of the Law as a Wedding Vow, See Appendix Pg. 279–281

(*D'.*) **B'.** [4] Wherefore, my brethren, **ye also are become dead to the law by the body of Christ**; that ye should be married to another, *even to* him who is raised from the dead, that we should bring forth fruit unto God.

(*C'.*) **A'.** [5] For when we were in the flesh, **the motions of sins, which were by the law**, did work in our members to bring forth fruit unto death. [6] **But now we are delivered from the law, that being dead wherein we were held**; that we should serve in newness of spirit, and not *in* the oldness of the letter.

(*B'.*) [9] but when the commandment came, sin revived, and **I died.** [11] For **sin, taking occasion by the commandment**, deceived me, and by it slew *me.*

(*A'.*) [17] Now then it is no more I that do it, but sin that dwelleth in me. [21] I find then a law, that, when I would do good, evil is present with me. O wretched man that I am! **Who shall deliver me from the body of this death?**

TIP (2)

That we should serve in newness spirit 7:6
and not in the oldness of the letter 7:6

not in the oldness of the letter 7:6
that we should serve in newness of spirit 8:1–30

The chiastic reading for 7:1–6:

8:30

7:6b   7:7

A. ⁷:¹ Know ye not, brethren, (for I speak to them that know the law,) how that the law hath dominion over a man as long as he liveth?

A'. ⁵ For when we were in the flesh, the motions of sins, which were by the law, did work in our members to bring forth fruit unto death. ⁶ But now we are delivered from the law, that being dead wherein we were held; that we should serve in newness of spirit, and not *in* the oldness of the letter.

B. ² For the woman which hath an husband is bound by the law to *her* husband so long as he liveth; but if the husband be dead, she is loosed from the law of *her* husband.

B'. ⁴ Wherefore, my brethren, ye also are become dead to the law by the body of Christ; that ye should be married to another, *even* to him who is raised from the dead, that we should bring forth fruit unto God.

C. ³ So then if, while *her* husband liveth, she be married to another man, she shall be called an adulteress:

C'. but if her husband be dead, she is free from that law; so that she is no adulteress, though she be married to another man.

The "we" refers to believers. "Not serving in the oldness of the letter" is the theme of the remainder of chapter seven and "serving in the newness of the spirit" is the theme of chapter eight. It has been often debated whether the following struggle took place before or after Saul's conversion. This section of Romans is dealing with how believers should serve the Lord and answers the accusation that Paul, and Christians in general, taught their followers to "sin that good (grace) may come." Only if this is the struggle of a believer with his own sin nature would it fit the context. The struggle of unbelievers is not the topic of discussion. Believers and willful sin was the concern of chapter six, but the believer and sins of ignorance are now in focus.

Compare (from E-TIP 2) pg. 133–135

N. circumcision *is that* of the heart, in the spirit, *and* not in the letter. 2:29

N'. that we should serve in newness of spirit, and not *in* the oldness of the letter. 7:6

Correlations
3:20 By the law is the knowledge of sin
7:6 Not serving in the oldness of the letter

5:13 For until the law sin was in the world: but sin is not imputed when there is no law.

A. ^{7:7} What shall we say then? *Is the law sin?* God forbid. Nay, I had not known sin, but by the law: for I had not known lust, except the law had said, Thou shalt not covet.

> A.   Is the law sin
> B.   Sin, taking occasion by the commandment
>   C.   Sin was dead
>   D.   I was alive
>   D'. I died
>   C'. The commandment . . . I found to be unto death
> B'. Sin taking occasion by the commandment
> A'. The law is holy . . . just and good

B. ⁸ But **sin, taking occasion by the commandment**, wrought in me all manner of concupiscence.

C. For without **the law sin** *was* **dead**.

D. ⁹ For **I was alive** without the law once:

D'. but when the commandment came, sin revived, and **I died**.

C'. ¹⁰ And **the commandment**, which *was ordained* to life, **I found *to be* unto death**.

B'. ¹¹ For **sin, taking occasion by the commandment**, deceived me, and by it slew *me*.

A'. ¹² Wherefore the **law** *is* **holy**, and the commandment holy, and **just**, and **good**.

The chiastic reading:

A. [7:7] Nay, I had not known sin, but by the law: for I had not known lust, except the law had said, Thou shalt not covet.

A'. [12]Wherefore the law *is* holy, and the commandment holy, and just, and good.

B. [8]But sin, taking occasion by the commandment, wrought in me all manner of concupiscence.

B'. [11]For sin, taking occasion by the commandment, deceived me, and by it slew *me*.

C. For without the law sin *was* dead.

C'. [10]And the commandment, which *was ordained* to life, I found *to be* unto death.

D. [9]For I was alive without the law once:

D'. but when the commandment came, sin revived, and I died.

Paul now speaks in the first person. He too is a Jew, and is faced with the very same dilemma. Saul of Tarsus is saved from his old life as a Pharisee; as a believer he tries very hard to keep the Law. The Law is holy, just and good, but in verse nine, the power of suggestion is all that is needed for him to sin. He is by nature sinful and condemned by the law to death.

When the rich young ruler called Jesus good, Jesus replied, "There is none good but God."[64] The Law is good, just, and holy because it is an expression of the character of God. The law was not needed for God to pass judgment, nor could it justify the sinner. Before the Covenant of Law, God judged sin: He destroyed the earth with a flood, and Sodom and Gomorrah with fire. Before the Law, the sinner was condemned, but all too often he failed to recognize this. God's glory is the measure, and the law reveals how far short of His glory we fall. This should make us aware of our sinful condition, and seek forgiveness through the promised Messiah (Christ).

Verses eight and eleven are nearly identical statements, but are too far apart to be the center. The center of the chiasmus will be halfway between these passages.

---

[64] Mark 10:17–18

The principles of works that provide the basis for judgment are presented in chapter two. These principles require the continual practice of good and the absence of evil for blessings. Anything short of this results in judgment. In Saul's early Christian experience, he wanted to meet these requirements of good and not evil, but found evil to be always with him and not good. The trinity of evil—the world, the flesh and the devil—would have us believe that all we have to do is say "no" to evil and "yes" to good. This is based on a denial of our sinful nature, which weights everything in the direction of evil. Even the most sincere decisions end up in defeat of good and victory for evil.

From E-TIP (2)

A comparison 2:7–10 and 7:13–24

2:7 To them who by patient continuance in well doing seek for glory and honour and immortality, eternal life:

8–9 But unto them that are contentious, and do not obey the truth, but obey unrighteousness, indignation and wrath,

9 Tribulation and anguish, upon every soul of man that doeth **evil**, of the Jew first, and also of the Gentile;

10 But glory, honour, and peace, to every man that **worketh good**, to the Jew first, and also to the Gentile:

7:13 . . . God forbid. But sin, that it might appear sin, working death in me by that which is **good**; that sin by the commandment might become exceeding sinful . . .

16 If then I do that which I would not, I consent unto the law that *it is* good. 17Now then it is no more I that do it, but sin that dwelleth in me . . .

18 For I know that in me (that is, in my flesh,) dwelleth no **good** thing: for to will is present with me; but *how* to perform that which is good I find not. 19 For the **good** that I would I do not: but the **evil** which I would not, that I do. 20 Now if I do that I would not, it is no more I that do it, but sin that dwelleth in me. 21 I find then a law, that, when I would do **good**, **evil** is present with me. 22 For I delight in the law of God after the inward man: 23 But I see another law in my members . . .

E-TIP (3) supplies us with this truth:

5:9 Much more then, being now justified by his blood, we shall be saved from wrath through him.

Correlations

2:23 Breaking the law dishonourest thou God?
5:18 Therefore as by the offense of one *judgment came* upon all men to condemnation.
7:6 That we should serve in newness of spirit, and not *in* the oldness of the letter.
7:12 Wherefore the law is holy, and the commandment holy, and just and good.

[7:13] Was then that which is good [the law] made death unto me? God forbid.

A. But sin, that it might appear sin, **working death in me** by that which is good; that **sin by the commandment might become exceeding sinful**.

> A. That sin by the commandment might become exceeding sinful
> B. I am carnal, sold under sin
> > C. For that which I do I allow not: it is no more I that do it, but sin that dwelleth in me
> > > D. I know that in me . . . dwelleth no good thing
> > C'. For the good that I would I do not: Now if I do that I would not, it is no more I that do it, but sin that dwelleth in me
> B'. When I would do good, evil is present with me
> A'. I delight in the law of God after the inward man

B. [14] For we know that the law is spiritual: but **I am carnal**, sold under sin.

C. [15] For that which I do I allow not: for what I would, that do I not; but what I hate, that do I. [16] If then I do that which I would not, I consent unto the law that *it is* **good**.

[17] Now then **it is no more I that do it, but sin that dwelleth in me**.

D. [18] For **I know that in me** (that is, in my flesh,) **dwelleth no good thing**: for to will is present with me; but *how* to perform that which is **good** I find not.

C'. [19] For the **good** that I would I do not: but the **evil** which I would not, that I do. [20] Now if I do that I would not, **it is no more I that do it**, **but sin that dwelleth in me**.

B'. [21] I find then a law, that, when I would do **good, evil is present with me**.

A'. [22] For **I delight in the law of God** after the inward man: [23] But I see another law in my members, warring against the law of my mind, and bringing me into captivity the law of sin which is in my members.

[24] O wretched man that I am! **who shall deliver me from the body of this death?** [25] **I thank God through Jesus Christ our Lord.** So then with the mind I myself serve the law of God; but with the flesh the law of sin.

The chiastic reading:

A. [7:13] But sin, that it might appear sin, working death in me by that which is good; that sin by the commandment might become exceeding sinful.

A'. [22] For I delight in the law of God after the inward man: [23] But I see another law in my members, warring against the law of my mind, and bringing me into captivity the law of sin which is in my members.

B. [14] For we know that the law is spiritual: but I am carnal, sold under sin.

B'. [21] I find then a law, that, when I would do good, evil is present with me.

C. [15] For that which I do I allow not: for what I would, that do I not; but what I hate, that do I. [16] If then I do that which I would not, I consent unto the law that *it is* good. [17] Now then it is no more I that do it, but sin that dwelleth in me.

C'. [19] For the good that I would I do not: but the evil which I would not, that I do. [20] Now if I do that I would not, it is no more I that do it, but sin that dwelleth in me.

D. [18] For I know that in me (that is, in my flesh,) dwelleth no good thing: for to will is present with me;[65] but how to perform that which is good I find not.

C and C' are nearly identical passages. They begin with similarly constructed statements that are very different from the rest of the chiasmus and both end with identical statements, "it is no more I that do it, but sin that dwelleth in me."

---

[65] *The Will of Man*, See Appendix Pg. 281–283

The words *good* and *evil* are from E-TIP (2)[66] as also Christ judging all mankind.[67] The concept of sin becoming exceedingly sinful comes from E-TIP (3).[68] In this passage the judge of all the earth delivers the sinner from judgment. A pardon protects the guilty from prosecution. The law cannot be used to prosecute the one who is pardoned, because he is beyond the reach of the law.

Paul acknowledged that it was wrong to covet, but then he coveted. He is therefore no better than the unbelievers of chapter two who judged others, but were guilty of the same things. According to the early part of chapter three, he is without excuse. He is condemned by the law, the very standard that he acknowledged being right. Due to the ministry of the Law, Paul of Tarsus concludes that he is totally evil. "In me dwells no good thing." Even when he decides to do what is good, (as God defines good in the Law), he fails. In the extremes of this chiasmus, Paul, convicted by the Law of coveting, cries out, "O wretched man that I am!" When he acknowledges that he is totally powerless and evil by nature, the Law has accomplished its ministry.

Until this point in the presentation, sin has reigned, but starting with Saul's call for help, the Holy Spirit will bring righteousness to reign. Because of the grace of God he who was convicted of coveting will be able to say,

> Yea doubtless, and I count all things *but* loss for the excellency of the knowledge of Christ Jesus my Lord: for whom I have suffered the loss of all things, and do count them *but* dung, that I may win Christ.[69]

The reader should note that the answer to Paul's dilemma is not in the exercise of his will. He has tried that and failed. The will is effective when it comes to doing evil, but when it comes to consistently doing *good*, it is totally powerless. He has tried everything in his power and failed. The answer is not in education. Paul was very well educated and knew what was expected of him. This is beyond his ability. The evil within him overpowers his cognitive decisions. He needs divine intervention. On his own, Paul is spiritually defeated, but having acknowledged this, he turns to Christ for help. Christ will

---

[66] Romans 2:7–10
[67] Romans 2:16
[68] Romans 5:20
[69] Philippians 3:8

deliver him from the dominion of his evil nature. "I thank God through Jesus Christ our Lord" is the answer. "So then with the mind [new nature][70] I myself serve the law of God; but with the flesh [old nature] the law of sin."

From E-TIP (3)

A comparison between 4:13–25, 5:1–6, and 8:1–39; see pg. 150–155.

C. a. [5:1] we have **peace with God**

1. [4:13-14] **heir**
2. [16] **father of us all**
   [17] **father of many nations**
3. [18] **who against hope believed in hope**
4. [20] **strong in faith, giving glory to God;**

b. [5:2] [we] rejoice in **hope of the glory**

c. [3] we glory in **tribulation**

d. [3] tribulation worketh **patience;**

e. [4] patience, **experience;**

f. [4] experience, **hope:**

g. [6] hope maketh **not ashamed;**

h. [6] because the **love of God** is shed abroad in our hearts

i. [6] by **the Holy Ghost** which is given unto us.

j. [12] by one man **sin entered into the world**

k. [14-21] All points contrasting the old Adam and the new Adam

C'. a'. [8:6] To be spiritually minded is life and **peace**

1. [17] and if children, then heirs; **heirs of God**, and joint heirs with Christ;
2. [15] we cry, **Abba, Father**
3. [24] For we are saved by **hope**
4. [17] **glorified** together

b'. [17] that we may be also **glorified together.**

c'. [22] the whole creation groaneth and **travaileth in pain** together until now.

d'. [25] But if we hope for that we see not, then do we **with patience wait for it.**

e'. [28] all things **work together** for the good

f'. [24] saved by **hope**

g'. [30] them He also **glorified**

h'. [37-39] more than conquerors through **him that loved us.**

i'. [26] Likewise the **Spirit** also helpeth our infirmities:

j'. [20] For the **creation was made subject to vanity**

k'. [1-11] All points contrasting the flesh and the Spirit

---

[70] Romans 7:25

Hope is what enabled Abraham to bring God glory. Glory was revealed in Abraham. Hope then leads this presentation into glory.

Correlations

7:6 Serving in the newness of the spirit

8:1 Delivered by Christ

5:17 Righteousness reigns

From E-TIP (2)

A comparison 2:7, 10 and 8:1–30

^{2:7} To them who by patient continuance in well doing seek for **glory** and **honour** and **immortality, eternal life:**

¹⁰ But **glory, honour,** and **peace,** to every man that worketh good, to the Jew first, and also to the Gentile:

^{8:6} [Life and peace] For to be carnally minded *is* death; but to be spiritually minded *is* **life and peace.**

¹⁵ [Honour] For ye have not received the spirit of bondage again to fear; but ye have received the Spirit of adoption, whereby we cry, Abba, Father.

¹⁷ And if children, then heirs; heirs of God, and joint-heirs with Christ; if so be that we suffer with *him,* that we may be also **glorified together.**

¹⁸ [Glory] For I reckon that the sufferings of this present time *are* not worthy *to be compared* with the **glory** which shall be revealed in us.

It is not surprising then that the conclusion of the following chiasmus involves life and peace, which are followed by honour and glory. The requirements for being blessed are met by the Holy Spirit. The first half presents two opposing persons, and the second half presents two very different results.

Until now E-TIP (3) has been doing an inversion. Paul now begins a series of direct comparisons as part of that system.

To be condemned is to die, and to live is to not be condemned. Condemnation is contrasted with life (verses 12–13). The flesh cannot please God, but the Holy Spirit is assigned the task of fulfilling the righteousness of the Law in the believer.

Correlations

2:15 Shew the work of the law written in their hearts
2:27 And shall not uncircumcision which is by nature, if it fulfil the law, judge thee
5:12–21 The old and new Adam
7:25 So then with the mind I myself serve the law of God;
but with the flesh the law of sin

A. a. [7:24] O wretched man that I am! **Who shall deliver me from the body of this death?**

b. I thank God through Jesus Christ our Lord.

b'. [25] So then with the mind I myself serve the law of God;

a'. but with the flesh the law of sin.

A.   The body of this death
　B.   No condemnation
　　C.   Free from the law of sin and death
　　　D.   For what the law could not do
　　　D'. The righteousness of the law fulfilled in us
　　C'. For they that are after the flesh do mind the things of the flesh
　B'. To be carnally minded is death
A'. Because the carnal mind is enmity against God

B. [8:1]*There is* therefore now **no condemnation** to them which are **in Christ Jesus**, . . .

C. [2] For the law of the **Spirit of life** in Christ Jesus hath made me **free from the law of sin and death**.

D. [3] **For what the law could not do**, in that it was weak through the flesh, God sending his own Son in the likeness of sinful flesh, and for sin, condemned sin in the flesh:

D'. [4] That the **righteousness of the law might be fulfilled in us** who walk not after the **flesh**, but after the **Spirit**.

C'. [5] For they that are after the **flesh do mind the things of the flesh**; but they that are after the **Spirit** the things of the **Spirit**.

B'. [6] For to be carnally minded **is death;but to be spiritually minded is life and peace.**

A'. **a.** [7]Because the carnal mind *is* **enmity against God:**

    b. for it is not subject to the law of God,
    b'. neither indeed can be.

  a'. [8]So then they that are in the flesh **cannot please God**

The chiastic reading:

A. **a.** [7:24] O wretched man that I am! Who shall deliver me from the body of this death?

    b. I thank God through Jesus Christ our Lord.
    b'. [7:25] So then with the mind I myself serve the law of God;

  a'. but with the flesh the law of sin.

A'. **a.** [7]Because the carnal mind *is* enmity against God:

    b. for it is not subject to the law of God,
    b' neither indeed can be.

  a'. [8]So then they that are in the flesh cannot please God

B. [8:1] *There is* therefore now no condemnation to them which are in Christ Jesus, . . .

B'. [6]For to be carnally minded is death; But to be spiritually minded is life and peace

C. [2]For the law of the Spirit of life in Christ Jesus hath made me free from the law of sin and death.

C'. [5]For they that are after the flesh do mind the things of the flesh; but they that are after the Spirit the things of the Spirit.

D. [3]For what the law could not do, in that it was weak through the flesh, God sending his own Son in the likeness of sinful flesh, and for sin, condemned sin in the flesh:

D'. [4]That the righteousness of the law might be fulfilled in us who walk not after the flesh, but after the Spirit.

  Segue: [8] So then they that are **in the flesh** cannot please God
    [9] But ye are not **in the flesh** but in the Spirit

Correlations
7:6 That we should serve in newness of spirit
An embedded chiasmus

A. a. [8:9] **But ye are not in the flesh** but **in the Spirit**, if so be that **the Spirit of God dwell in you.**

> A. The Spirit of God dwell in you
> B. Christ be in you
> A'. His Spirit dwelleth in you

b. Now if any man have **not the Spirit of Christ**, he is none of his.

B. [10] And if **Christ** *be* in you, the **body** *is* **dead because of sin**; but the **Spirit** *is* **life because of righteousness.**

A'. a'. [11] **But if the Spirit of him** that raised up Jesus from the dead **dwell in you**, he that raised up Christ from the dead

b'. shall also **quicken your mortal bodies** by his Spirit that **dwelleth in you.**[71]

The chiastic reading:

A. a. [8:9] But ye are not in the flesh but in the Spirit, if so be that the Spirit of God dwell in you.

b. Now if any man have not the Spirit of Christ, he is none of his.

A'. a'. [11] But if the Spirit of him that raised up Jesus from the dead dwell in you, he that raised up Christ from the dead

b'. shall also quicken your mortal bodies by his Spirit that dwelleth in you

B. [10] And if Christ *be* in you, the body *is* dead because of sin; but the Spirit *is* life because of righteousness.

---

[71] Romans 8:9–11 is presented as chiasmus in *The Shape of Biblical Language* by John Breck, pg. 252. St. Vladimir's Seminary Press. Crestwood, New York 1994

Extended Chiasmus (5)

Correlations

2:29 But he *is* a Jew, which is one inwardly; and circumcision *is that* of the heart

7:25 Quicken [give life to] your mortal bodies by his Spirit that dwelleth in you

(A.) [8:1-11] The Holy Spirit's ministry produces righteousness.

   (B.) A. [12] Therefore, brethren, we are debtors, not to the flesh, to live after the flesh. [13] For if ye live after the flesh, ye shall die: but if ye through the Spirit do **mortify the deeds of the body**, ye shall live.

      (C.) B. [14] For as many as are **led by the Spirit of God**, they are the **sons of God**.

         (D.) C. [15] For ye have **not received the spirit of bondage** again to fear;

         (D'.) C'. but **ye have received the Spirit of adoption**, whereby we cry, Abba, Father.

      (C'.) B'. [16] The **Spirit itself beareth witness** with our spirit, that we are the children of God:

   (B'.) A'. [17] And if children, then heirs; heirs of God, and joint-heirs with Christ; if so be that we **suffer with** *him,* that we may be also **glorified together**. [72]

(A'.) The Holy Spirit's ministry of prayer produces good.

The chiastic reading for 8:12–17:

A. [8:12] Therefore, brethren, we are debtors, not to the flesh, to live after the flesh. [13] For if ye live after the flesh, ye shall die: but if ye through the Spirit do mortify the deeds of the body, ye shall live.

A'. [17] And if children, then heirs; heirs of God, and joint-heirs with Christ; if so be that we suffer with *him,* that we may be also glorified together.

---

[72] Romans 8:1–17 is presented as chiasmus in *The Shape of Biblical Language,* by John Breck, pg. 253, St. Vladimir's Seminary Press. Crestwood, New York. 1994

B. [14] For as many as are led by the Spirit of God, they are the sons of God.

B'. [16] The Spirit itself beareth witness with our spirit, that we are the children of God:

C. [15] For ye have not received the spirit of bondage again to fear;

C'. but ye have received the Spirit of adoption, whereby we cry, Abba, Father.

> We **suffer with** *him*, [8:18–30]
> that we may be also **glorified together**. [8:31–39]

There is a rabbinical principle here: "The night cometh before the day." There are many applications. The travail of childbirth comes before the joy of giving birth to a child. There will be a time of trouble; such as the world has never known before the millennium. In 8:18, suffering comes before glory.

Do we then make void the law through faith? God forbid: yea, we establish the law. [73]

According to the principles of judgement, set forth in chapter two, there are certain blessings that come when the righteousness of the law is produced in us.

Correlations
8:17 We suffer with *him*

A. [8:18] For **I reckon** that the sufferings of this present time *are* not worthy *to be compared* with the **glory** which shall be revealed **in us**.

B. [19] For **the earnest expectation of the creature** waiteth for the manifestation of the sons of God.

A.	The glory which shall be revealed
	B. The earnest expectation of the creation
	C. Subject to vanity
	C'. Subjected the same in hope
	B'. The creature itself also shall be delivered
A'.	The glorious liberty of the children of God

C. [20] For the creature was made **subject to vanity**, not willingly,

---

[73] Romans 3:31

C'. but by reason of him who hath
subjected *the same* **in hope,**

B'. [21] Because the **creature itself also shall be delivered** from the bondage of corruption

A'. into the **glorious liberty** of the **children of God.**

The chiastic reading:

A. [8:18] For I reckon that the sufferings of this present time *are* not worthy *to be compared* with the glory which shall be revealed in us.

A'. into the glorious liberty of the children of God.

B. [19] For the earnest expectation of the creature waiteth for the manifestation of the sons of God.

B'. [21] Because the creature itself also shall be delivered from the bondage of corruption

C. [20] For the creature was made subject to vanity, not willingly,

C'. but by reason of him who hath subjected *the same* in hope,

A. [22] For **we know** that the whole creation groaneth and travaileth in pain together until now.

> A. We know
>   B. Have the firstfruits of the Spirit
>   C. We . . . groan
>   D. Saved by hope
>   D'. We hope for that we see not
>   C'. Maketh intercession . . . with groanings
>   B'. The mind of the Spirit
> A'. We know

B. [23] And not only *they*, but ourselves also, which **have the firstfruits of the Spirit,**

C. even we ourselves **groan** within ourselves, waiting for the adoption, *to wit,* the redemption of our body.

D. [24] For we are saved by **hope:** but **hope** that is seen is not **hope:** for what a man seeth, why doth he yet **hope** for?

D'. [25] But if we **hope** for that we see not, *then* do we with patience wait for *it.*

C'. [26] Likewise the Spirit also helpeth our infirmities: for we know not what we should pray for as we ought: but the Spirit itself maketh intercession for us with **groanings** which cannot be uttered.

B'. [27] And he that searcheth the hearts **knoweth what** *is* **the mind of the Spirit,** because he maketh intercession for the saints **according to** *the will of* **God.**

A'. [28] And **we know** that all things work together for **good** to them that love God, to them who are the called according to *his* purpose. [29] For whom he did foreknow, he also did predestinate *to be* conformed to the image of his Son, that he might be the firstborn among many brethren. [30] Moreover whom he did predestinate, them he also called: and whom he called, them he also justified: and whom he justified, **them he also glorified.**

The chiastic reading:

A. [22] For we know that the whole creation groaneth and travaileth in pain together until now.

A'. [28] And we know that all things work together for good to them that love God, to them who are the called according to *his* purpose. [29] For whom he did foreknow, he also did predestinate *to be* conformed to the image of his Son, that he might be the firstborn among many brethren.

B. [23] And not only *they,* but ourselves also, which have the firstfruits of the Spirit,

B'. [27] And he that searcheth the hearts knoweth what *is* the mind of the Spirit, because he maketh intercession for the saints according to *the will of* God. [30] Moreover whom he did predestinate, them he also called: and whom he called, them he also justified: and whom he justified, them he also glorified.

C. even we ourselves groan within ourselves, waiting for the adoption, *to wit,* the redemption of our body.

C'. [26] Likewise the Spirit also helpeth our infirmities: for we know not what we should pray for as we ought: but the Spirit itself maketh intercession for us with groanings which cannot be uttered.

D. [24] For we are saved by hope: but hope that is seen is not hope: for what a man seeth, why doth he yet hope for?

D'. [25] But if we hope for that we see not, *then* do we with patience wait for *it*.

We have confidence in God, and [hope] that he will carry out his plan for us. That plan is defined in verses 29–30.

In chapter one, the Gentiles knew God, but glorified Him not as God. In this chiasmus we know God and He glorifies us.[74] In chapter one, sin depraved man, and now all of creation. The believer and the Holy Spirit groan because creation lost its former glory when sin entered the world. In a fallen world, the believer confronts the trials of life with the hope of the glory of God.[75] Hope here refers to a strong confidence in God and can be viewed as faith strengthened by spiritual maturity. Previously, Abraham's hope determined his conduct.[76]

> [4:18] Who against **hope** believed in **hope**, that he might become the father of many nations; according to that which was spoken, So shall thy seed be. [19] And being not weak in faith, he considered not his own body now dead, when he was about an hundred years old, neither yet the deadness of Sarah's womb: [20] He staggered not at the promise of God through unbelief; but was strong in faith, giving **glory** to God; [21] And **being fully persuaded that, what he had promised, he was able also to perform.** [22] And therefore it was imputed to him for righteousness.[77]

Hope resulted in a behavior that brings glory to God. Glory is what God was deprived of in chapter one.

Starting with 8:1, the general theme has been serving in the newness of the spirit, which defeats the flesh. Serving in the spirit ends with the glorification of the believer. Suffering is presented as essential for glorification, which is key to the defeat of the flesh. Tribulation is so important that we glory in it. It produces a series of changes to our inner person. The result is, "The love of God is shed abroad in our hearts by the Holy

---

[74] Romans 8:17
[75] Romans 5:2
[76] Romans 4:18
[77] Romans 4:18–22

Ghost which is given unto us."[78] In chapter eight, "we know that the whole creation groaneth and travaileth in pain together until now."

The good of 8:28 is the good of 2:10, which is the basis of God's blessing. It is the good that Paul admitted lacking when he said:

For **I know that in me** (that is, in my flesh,) **dwelleth no good thing**: for to will is present with me; but *how* to perform that which is **good** I find not.[79]

It is not good, as the flesh defines good, because the flesh does not define "travaileth in pain"[80] as good. The mind of the Spirit says;

Before I was afflicted I went astray: but now I have kept thy word . . .
It is **good** for me that I have been afflicted; that I might learn thy statutes.[81]

In this fallen world, all things work out for this righteous good, because God the Father takes action in response to the Holy Spirit's prayer. God's five-fold answer ends with the believer being glorified. Being glorified is the product of suffering, the prayer of the Holy Spirit, and the intervention of God the father.[82] The good of 2:10 and 8:28 is now to be realized. This five-fold response in 8:29–30 is God's plan for glorification and is stated in the past tense. God the Father has already made provision for the believer to be glorified, so that in the mind of God it is an accomplished fact.

There is another reason for these five words to be stated in the past tense. In the next section there will be many illustrations of Old Testament saints (saints of the past). The past tense tells us that God has dealt this way with his elect throughout history. The five rhetorical questions that follow in chapter eight are in the present tense, and tell us what practical blessing are ours as a result of God's intervention. They are stated in the present tense and tell us that God continues to deal with his people in the same way. The reader will remember that chapter four dealt with justification of past sinners. Starting with chapter five, justification of present sinners was the topic of discussion. These two sets of five are pivotal in this section.

---

[78] Romans 5:5
[79] Romans 7:18
[80] Romans 8:22
[81] Psalms 119:67 and 71
[82] Romans 8:29–30

Correlations
8:31–39 All things work together for the good
9:1–5 To them who love God
9:6–13 To them that are called
9:14–30 According to his purpose

Five Word TIP (4)

2:10 But **glory**, honour, and peace, to every man that worketh good, to the Jew first, and also to the Gentile:

8:18 For I reckon that the sufferings of this present time *are* not worthy *to be compared* with the **glory** which shall be revealed in us.

8:30 Moreover
whom he did **predestinate**, them he also **called**:
and whom he **called**, them he also **justified**:
and whom he **justified**, them he also **glorified**.

A comparison: 2:10 with 8:18 and 9:1–11:36

God's program for glory

A. [8:31–39] Pardoned

   B. [9:6–13] Family tree

      C. [14–24] **Election**

         D. [25–29] **Called**

           E. [30–33] **Justified**

              F. [10:1–10] Not ashamed

           E'. [11–13] **Justified**

D'. [13–21] **Called**

C'. [11:1–12] **Election**

B'. [13–32] Olive tree

A'. [33–36] Mercy

The three topics: election, called, and justified appear in order in chapter nine, and in inverse order in chapters ten and eleven. In the context of inversion this implies that the family tree and the olive tree correlate and represent foreknowledge, and being "Not ashamed,"[83] equals being glorified. This is the center section:

> For I am **not ashamed** of the gospel of Christ: for it is the power of God unto salvation
> to every one that believeth; to the Jew first, and also to the Greek.[84]

The five words from 8:29–30 provide a twofold outline for chapters 9–11, and the extended chiasmus (8:30–11:36) provides the detail.[85] The five words are the reason "all things work together for the good, for those who love God and are called according to His purpose." The five-word chiasmus (above) is an expanded explanation of why 8:28 is true.

This section has both the blessings and cursing of God. The cursing, like the judgment of Pharaoh and Hosea's son "Judged," rhymes with:

> Wherefore **God also gave them up** to uncleanness through the lusts of their own hearts,
> to dishonour their own bodies between themselves:

> For this cause **God gave them up** unto vile affections: for even their women did change
> the natural use into that which is against nature: [86]

The Five Words

These five truths are the reason that 8:28 is true.

---

[83] Romans 1:16

[84] Romans 1:16

[85] Pg 105–108

[86] Romans 1:24, 26

In E-TIP (2), glory is to be revealed in us. The five words give us God's plan for glorifying the believer in this life, and they become a major theme starting in chapter nine.

Foreknow: The Greek word for *knowledge* used here never refers to intellectual knowledge, but to knowledge gained through experience. The Jews used this word for a personal, intimate relationship as well. It is in this latter sense that Paul uses this term here. The prefix *fore* indicates knowing by experience beforehand and conveys the thought of engagement.

Predestinate: To mark out beforehand. Those who receive His mark are to be conformed to the image of his Son. This Christlikeness is what glorifies the believer. It should be noted that with firstfruits, the father would take his son, and mark out a section of his field while the crop was still immature and growing. The harvest from that section would be their firstfruits offering. We are the firstfruits of Christ, and we were marked out beforehand.

Called: This has two usages, to invite or answer, and to name. The LORD calls us by name and we respond by calling on the name of the LORD.

Justified: Declared righteous. As an act of mercy, we are forgiven and as an act of grace, we are given the righteousness of Christ.

Glorified: To honor, or to praise. As the LORD praised Job.

TIP systems four, five, and six exist simultaneously. They therefore have some characteristics of extended transitional system and in some ways resemble a transitional system. This probably means that the criteria for distinguishing between the two types needs some adjustment. I doubt if they break the rule used by Paul, but the rule used in this paper probably does not match what Paul had.

In the section that we are about to begin there is so much happening simultaneously that I have a difficult time following everything and presenting it. I will do my best but ask for your patience and understanding.

IV

I Am Not Ashamed of the Gospel of Christ for It Is the Power of God Unto Salvation 1:16

But Israel shall be saved in the LORD with an everlasting salvation: Ye shall not be ashamed nor confounded world without end.[87]

Correlations

2:29 Whose praise is not of men, but of God

8:17 That we may be also glorified together

8:31–10:10 Transitional System (5)

God answers the prayer of the Holy Spirit

FOUR BLESSINGS FOR BELIEVERS 8:31–39
TIP (4) 8:31–39

8:31 What shall we then say to these things?

A. If God *be* for us, who *can be* against us? [32] He that spared not his own Son, but delivered him up for us all, how shall he not with him also freely give us all things?

B. [33] Who shall lay any thing to the charge of God's elect? It is God that justifieth.

---

[87] Isaiah 45:17

C. [34] Who *is* he that condemneth? *It is* Christ that died, yea rather, that is risen again, who is even at the right hand of God, who also maketh intercession for us.

    D. [35] Who shall separate us from the love of Christ? *Shall* tribulation, or distress, or persecution, or famine, or nakedness, or peril, or sword?

    D'. [9:1–13] God's love

  C'. [1–13] Could Israel be condemned

 B'. [25–29] Who could bring an accusation against

A'. [30–33] A gift [see 5:14–21]

In 4:23–25, the redemptive experience of Abraham is applied to present-day believers. Now the redemptive experience returns to Old Testament saints.

A. [8:35] Who shall **separate us from the love of Christ?**

    B. *shall* tribulation, or distress, or persecution, or famine, or nakedness, or peril, or sword? [36] As it is written,
For thy sake we are killed all the day long; we are accounted as sheep for the slaughter.

A.	Who shall separate us from the love of Christ?
B.	Shall tribulation, or distress . . .
	C. We are more than conquerors . . .
B'.	For I am persuaded, that neither death, nor life . . .
A'.	Shall be able to separate us from the love of God

      C. [37] Nay, in all these things **we are more than conquerors** through him that **loved** us.

  B'. [38] For I am persuaded, that neither death, nor life, nor angels, nor principalities, nor powers, nor things present, nor things to come, [39] Nor height, nor depth, nor any other creature,

A'. shall be able to **separate us from the love of God,** which is in Christ Jesus our Lord.

This system has a list in both **B** and **B'** resulting in a balanced system. The love of Christ and the love of God correlate, demonstrating that Christ's love is God's love. God's love for Israel will be expressed through Paul in chapter nine. The main theme is in verse thirty-seven.

The chiastic reading:

A. $^{8:35}$Who shall separate us from the love of Christ?

A'. shall be able to separate us from the love of God, which is in Christ Jesus our Lord.

B. *shall* tribulation, or distress, or persecution, or famine, or nakedness, or peril, or sword? ^{36}As it is written, For thy sake we are killed all the day long; we are accounted as sheep for the slaughter.

B'. ^{38}For I am persuaded, that neither death, nor life, nor angels, nor principalities, nor powers, nor things present, nor things to come, ^{39}Nor height, nor depth, nor any other creature,

C. ^{37}Nay, in all these things we are more than conquerors through him that loved us.

Correlations
5:5 The love of God in Christ Jesus is shed abroad through Paul

$^{9:1}$ **I say** the truth in Christ, I lie not, my conscience also bearing me witness in the Holy Ghost, ^{2}That I have great heaviness and continual sorrow in my heart. ^{3}For I could wish that myself were accursed from Christ for my brethren, my kinsmen according to the flesh: ^{4}Who are Israelites; to whom *pertaineth* the adoption, and the glory, and the covenants, and the giving of the law, and the service *of God,* and the promises; ^{5}Whose *are* the fathers, and of whom as concerning the flesh Christ *came,* who is over all, God blessed for ever. Amen.

ADVANTAGES FOR ISRAEL
TIP (5) 9:4–29

A. [9:4] Who are Israelites; to whom *pertaineth* the adoption, and the glory,

  B. a. And the covenants, and the giving of the law,
     b. And the service *of God,* and the promises;

    C. [5] Whose *are* the fathers, and of whom as concerning the flesh Christ *came,* Who is over all, God blessed for ever. Amen

    C'. [6–13] Abraham, Isaac and Jacob

  B'. a. [14–18] Moses (when receiving the law)
      b. [19–24] Clay pots

A'. [25–29] Hosea and his children

[5] Whose are the fathers, and of whom as concerning the flesh Christ came, [9:6–13]
who is over all, [9:14–11:12]
God blessed for ever. Amen [11:13–32]

The following correlation is from E-TIP (3), **B** an **B'**. It will actually correlate with 9:1–15:13. This correlation is presented in two segments. The first is as follows:

[3:25] To declare his righteousness for the remission of sins that are past, through the forbearance of God . . .

A comparison between 3:1–4:25 and 9:1–11:36
For a more complete presentation see pg. 150–155.

B.		B'.	
a.	[3:1-2] unto them were committed the **oracles of God.**	a'.	[9:3-5] Who are Israelites; to whom *pertaineth* the adoption, and the glory, and the covenants, and the giving of the law, and the service *of God*, and the promises; Whose *are* the fathers, and of whom as concerning the flesh Christ *came,*
b.	[3-4] shall their unbelief make **the faith of God without effect?**	b'.	[6] **Not as though the word of God hath taken none effect.**
c.	[5] *Is God unrighteous* who taketh vengeance?	c'.	[14] *Is there* **unrighteousness** with God? God forbid.
d.	[7-8] as we be **slanderously reported**, [20] that every mouth may be stopped	d'.	[20] who art thou that **repliest against God?**
e.	[22] the righteousness of God *which is* by **faith**	e'.	[32] Because *they sought it* not by **faith,** [10:6] But the righteousness which is of faith . . .
f.	for **there is no difference**: [23] For all have sinned, and come short of the glory of God;	f'.	[10:12-13] For **there is no difference** between the Jew and the Greek:
g.	[23] Being justified freely by his **grace:**	g'.	[11:5-6] the **election of grace.**
h.	[27-28] Where is **boasting?**	h'.	[18] **Boast** not against the branches
i.	[29-30] God of Jews only?	i'.	[17-24] Natural and unnatural branches
j.	[31] We establish the law	j'.	[27] For this *is* my covenant unto them, when I shall **take away their sins.**
k.	[4:1] Abraham our **father**	k'.	[28] *they are* beloved for the **fathers'** sakes.
l.	[20] was strong in faith, **giving glory to God;**	l'.	[33-36] to whom *be* **glory for ever.**

The objections to God's involvement in chapter nine are the same objections raised earlier to the gospel of Christ.[88] These objections are to no avail; God is now for

---

[88] Romans 3:1–8

believers.[89] The accuser of the brethren is foiled by a complete pardon,[90] and even if he could bring an accusation, it is Christ who died who is the judge.[91] We believers are "more than conquerors through him that loves us."[92] God the Father loves us for his Son's sake.

The first segment of this correlation with **B** and **B'** of E-TIP (3) (pg. 150–155) is concerned with God's righteousness in regards to his dealings with Israel.

The second correlation (**A** and **A'**) is concerned with God's dealing with present-day believers.[93] These are based on God's twofold declaration of his righteousness in Romans 3:25–26.

The advantages enumerated in verses four and five, rhyme with the advantages given to Israel according to chapter three and verse one and two.[94] These advantages have come to them, because God loves them for the Father's sake. Chapter eight ended with a strong emphasis on God's love, and chapter nine begins with a demonstration of that love as it is expressed through Paul to Israel. Paul's stating that he wished himself "accursed from Christ for his kinsmen according to the flesh," links this passage to an Old Testament event in which Moses does the same thing.[95] Because of Israel's sin, worshipping the golden calf, they were all condemned to death by the Law. Moses offered to die in their place.

Moses understands that Israel is condemned justly, and expresses love for them. This is commendable, but he does not understand that one sinner can not die for another. An acceptable substitute would have to be sinless.

As Moses loved Israel, who had rebelled against God, rejecting his message and killing his prophets, so Paul loves Israel even though the unsaved Jews continually rejected Paul's message. They even stoned and left him for dead at Lystra. They were "loved for the fathers, sakes."[96] Nothing could separate them from his love.

---

[89] Romans 8:31
[90] Romans 8:33
[91] Romans 8:34
[92] Romans 8:37
[93] Pg. 150
[94] Pg. 127–128
[95] Exodus 32:32
[96] Romans 11:28

If this is true, why is it that some Israelites are saved and others lost? Has God set aside his Word? Has he broken his promises to Israel?

Correlations
2:9–10 To the Jew first
2:28–29 For he is not a Jew, . . . which is one outward . . .
But he is a Jew, which is one inwardly
9:6–13 God's promise and his love
8:30 Foreknow, 8:35–39 Love, and 9:4 the Covenants
9:5 Whom as concerning the flesh Christ *came*

A. [9:6] Not as though the word of God hath taken none effect. **For they** *are* **not all Israel, which are of Israel:**

B. [7] **Neither,** because they are the seed of Abraham, *are they* all **children:** but, In **Isaac** shall thy seed be **called.**

> A. They are not all Israel, which are of Israel
> B. In Isaac shall thy seed be called
> C. The children of the flesh, . . . are not the children of God
> D. The children of promise
> D'. The word of promise
> C'. Even by our father Isaac
> B'. Purpose of God according to election
> A'. Jacob have I loved, but Esau have I hated

C. [8] That is, They which are the **children of the flesh,** these *are* not the children of God:

D. but the **children of the promise** are counted for the seed.

D'. [9] For this *is* the **word of promise,** At this time will I come, and **Sarah** shall have a son.

C'. [10] And not only *this;* but when **Rebecca** also had conceived by one, *even* by **our father Isaac;**

B'. [11] (For *the children* being not yet born, neither having done any **good or evil,** that the purpose of God according to election might stand, not of works, but of him that **calleth;**) [12] It was said unto her, The elder shall serve the younger.

A'. [13]As it is written, **Jacob have I loved, but Esau have I hated.**

The chiastic reading:

A.   [9:6] Not as though the word of God hath taken none effect. For they *are* not all Israel, which are of Israel:

A'.   [13] As it is written, Jacob have I loved, but Esau have I hated.

B.   [7] Neither, because they are the seed of Abraham, *are they* all children: but, In Isaac shall thy seed be called.

B'.   [11] (For *the children* being not yet born, neither having done any good or evil, that the purpose of God according to election might stand, not of works, but of him that calleth;) [12] It was said unto her, The elder shall serve the younger.

C.   [8] That is, They which are the children of the flesh, these *are* not the children of God:

C'.   [10] And not only *this;* but when Rebecca also had conceived by one, *even* by our father Isaac;

D.   but the children of the promise are counted for the seed.

D'.   [9] For this *is* the word of promise, At this time will I come, and Sarah shall have a son.

The flesh objects to God making this choice, rather than the choice being made by man. Israel's advantage was that she had the Word of God. The promises of the Word of God are the main theme of the above chiasmus, the word being in both extremes and in the middle section; the first half focuses on Abraham's two sons and the second half on Rebecca's two sons. God made a promise to Abraham. Isaac was chosen even before he was born, because God will keep his promise. God did not need to choose Ishmael to fulfill his promise. God's choice of Rebecca's children is interesting. Paul emphasizes that the choice was made before they were born, and before they had done any good or evil.

According to chapter two, good and evil conduct is the basis for God's blessing or cursing, but this eliminates behavior as the motive for God's choosing. Like grace this choice is conditioned on some aspect of God's character. The exact nature of that character is one of God's best-kept secrets. The statement "Jacob have I loved, but Esau have I hated" is made at the very end of the Old Testament [97] and looks back over time at what has transpired since God said in Genesis: "The elder shall serve the younger."

Some would say, because of God's foreknowledge he knew what these boys would be like, and based his decision on their future behavior. This brings works back as the basis for God's decision. This explanation is not consistent with what has been said:

> For *the children* being not yet born, neither having done any good or evil, that the purpose of God according to election might stand, not of works, but of him that calleth; [98]

It is also not consistent with the meaning of foreknowledge, because the word for *knowledge* in foreknowledge is never used of intellectual knowledge. Thirdly, it is not consistent with what comes in the next section.

The following question is natural from the flesh's point of view. If foreknowledge is the correct explanation for the previous section, then the answer to the following question should be, "No, God is not unrighteous. God knew what was going to happen and acted accordingly." This is not the answer given.

Correlations
3:9 Are we better than they?
8:30 To the Jew first (continued), Election, Calling
8:33 Who can bring an accusation?
8:34 Who condemns?
9:13 Jacob have I loved, but Esau have I hated

[9:14] *Is there* unrighteousness with God? God forbid.

For he saith to Moses,

A. I will have mercy on whom I will have mercy, and I will have compassion on whom I will have compassion.

> A.   I will have mercy
>   B.   It is not of him that willeth
>   B'.   For this purpose have I raised thee up
> A'.   On whom he will have mercy

---

[97] Malachi 1:2
[98] Romans 9:11

B.   [16]So then *it is* not of him that willeth, nor of him that runneth, but of God that sheweth mercy.

B'.   [17]For the scripture saith unto Pharaoh, Even for this same purpose have I raised thee up, that I might shew my power in thee, and that my name might be declared throughout all the earth.

A'.   [18]Therefore hath **he mercy on whom he will** *have mercy,* and whom he will he hardeneth.

The chiastic reading:

A. I will have mercy on whom I will have mercy, and I will have compassion on whom I will have compassion.

A'.   [18]Therefore hath he mercy on whom he will *have mercy,* and whom he will he hardeneth.

B.   [16]So then *it is* not of him that willeth, nor of him that runneth, but of God that sheweth mercy.

B'.   [17]For the scripture saith unto Pharaoh, Even for this same purpose have I raised thee up, that I might shew my power in thee, and that my name might be declared throughout all the earth.

Many people are bothered by what Paul has just said.

After Israel sinned in worshiping the golden calf of Egypt, we read

[9]And the LORD said unto Moses, I have seen this people, and, behold, it *is* a stiffnecked people: [10]Now therefore let me alone, that my wrath may wax hot against them, and that I may consume them: and I will make of thee a great nation. [99]

Moses knew that according to the law, God could destroy Israel. Moses also knew that God made a promise to the fathers, and appeals to God, claiming that promise. God spares the nation, but because of the sin some of the people died. Moses is perplexed. He understood why some died, for the wages of sin is death and they were sinners, but he

---

[99] Exodus 32:9–10

doesn't understand why some lived. Those who lived, like Aaron, (who made the golden calf) were just as guilty of sin as those who died. Moses seeks to understand this by getting to know God better. God's answer is:

> And he said, I will make all my goodness pass before thee, and I will proclaim the name of the LORD before thee; and will be gracious to whom I will be gracious, and will shew mercy on whom I will shew mercy.[100]

The other part of the answer is God's dealings with Pharaoh. When Moses first came with the message, "Let my people go," this message was delivered to Pharaoh:

> For I will at this time send all my plagues upon thine heart, and upon thy servants, and upon thy people; that thou mayest know that *there is* none like me in all the earth. [15]For now I will stretch out my hand, that I may smite thee and thy people with pestilence; and thou shalt be cut off from the earth. [16]And in very deed for this *cause* have I raised thee up, for to shew *in* thee my power; and that my name may be declared throughout all the earth.[101]

The flesh objects, stating that Pharaoh first hardened his own heart, but I would remind the reader that when the message of deliverance was first given to Israel, they did not believe.

> And Moses spake so unto the children of Israel: but they hearkened not unto Moses for anguish of spirit, and for cruel bondage.[102]

> But they rebelled against me, and would not hearken unto me: they did not every man cast away the abominations of their eyes, neither did they forsake the idols of Egypt: then I said, I will pour out my fury upon them to accomplish my anger against them in the midst of the land of Egypt. [9]But I wrought **for my name's sake**, that it should not be polluted before the heathen, among whom they *were,* in whose sight I made myself known unto them, in bringing them forth out of the land of Egypt.[103]

Both hardened their hearts in sin, but God deals differently with the two of them, because of the covenant of promise.

---

[100] Exodus 33:19
[101] Exodus 9:14–16
[102] Exodus 6:9
[103] Ezekiel 20:8–9

And he said unto Abram, Know of a surety that thy seed shall be a stranger in a land *that is* not theirs, and shall serve them; and they shall afflict them four hundred years;[104] But in the fourth generation they shall come hither again: for the iniquity of the Amorites *is* not yet full.[105]

God will keep his promises even though it means that he saves the guilty. God also gave a promise to Abram concerning the Egyptians:

> And also that nation, whom they shall serve, **will I judge**: and afterward shall they come out with great substance.[106]

Israel, Pharaoh, and Egypt all hardened their hearts, but God showed mercy to Israel, in spite of their hard hearts. He did this because of the word of promise given to the fathers,[107] and He judged Egypt, because of their sin in keeping with His promise to Abram. The Egyptians deserved judgment, but the Israelites did not deserve salvation. God responded to Israel's hard heart with acts of love.

> The LORD hath appeared of old unto me, *saying,* Yea, I have loved thee with an everlasting love: therefore with loving kindness have I drawn thee.[108]

He responded to Egypt's hard heart by further hardening its heart, just as He gave up the sinners in Romans 1 The children of Israel were no better than the Egyptians and the Egyptians were no worse than the children of Israel. What God promised He does, and He does what He promised. The judgment theme is received from E-TIP (2), chapter 2:11–16. This theme is reccurring in chapters 9–11.

God has given us many promises concerning salvation. The sinner who claims such promises by faith will find himself on the favored ground of God's salvation.

> So then *it is* not of him that willeth, nor of him that runneth, but of God that sheweth mercy. [109]

---

[104] Genesis 15:13
[105] Genesis 15:16
[106] Genesis 15:14
[107] Exodus 6:1–7
[108] Jeremiah 31:3
[109] Romans 9:16

With these things being true, the flesh naturally raises the next objection. The reader should note that the objections raised in chapter three came from the unsaved, but in this chapter we read, "Thou wilt say then unto me." Here the same objections come from within the church and like the world, the flesh objects to God's judgment. If the flesh can not maintain its sovereignty by setting God aside, then it will blame God, i.e. "God made me do it." Fallen man has the audacity to rail on God, setting himself up as judge over God and his plan of salvation. The flesh says:

9:19 . . . **Why doth he yet find fault**? For who hath resisted his will?

The Word of God answers:

20 Nay but, O man, who art thou that repliest against God? Shall the thing formed say to him that formed *it,* Why hast thou made me thus?

21 Hath not the potter power over the clay, of the same lump to make one vessel unto honour, and another unto dishonour?

In the above passage, the vessels of honor are those that God delivered when he judged Israel after Israel built the golden calf. The vessels of dishonor are the condemned, including Pharaoh and the Egyptians.

Correlations

4:12 and 17–18 Abraham the father of many nations (Gentiles)
3:29 But he *is* a Jew, which is one inwardly
9:18 He mercy [hath] on whom he will *have mercy,* and whom he will he hardeneth

A. 9:22 *What* if God, willing to shew *his* wrath, and to make his power known, endured with much **long-suffering** the **vessels of wrath fitted to destruction:**

B. 23 And that he might make known the riches of his glory on the **vessels of mercy,** which he had afore prepared unto glory,

A. Vessels of destruction
  B. Vessels of mercy
    C. Whom he called
      D. I will call them my people
    C'. A remnant shall be saved
  B'. Not my people . . . called the children of the living God
A'. Been as Sodom, and been made like unto Gomorrah

C. [24] Even us, **whom he hath called**, not of the Jews only, but also of the Gentiles?

> D. [25]As he saith also in Osee, **I will call them my people, which were not my people**; and **her beloved, which was not beloved.**

C'. [27] Esaias also crieth concerning Israel, Though the number of the children of Israel be as the sand of the sea, **a remnant shall be saved:**

B'. [26] And it shall come to pass, *that* in the place where it was said unto them, Ye *are* not my people; there shall they be **called the children of the living God.**

A'. [28] For **he will finish the work**, and cut *it* short in righteousness: because a short work will the Lord make upon the earth. [29] And as Esaias said before, Except the Lord of Sabaoth had left us a seed, **we had been as Sodom, and been made like unto Gomorrah.**

The chiastic reading:

A. [9:22] *What* if God, willing to shew *his* wrath, and to make his power known, endured with much longsuffering the vessels of wrath fitted to destruction:

A'. [28] For he will finish the work, and cut *it* short in righteousness: because a short work will the Lord make upon the earth. [29]And as Esaias said before, Except the Lord of Sabaoth had left us a seed, we had been as Sodom, and been made like unto Gomorrah.

B. [23]And that he might make known the riches of his glory on the vessels of mercy, which he had afore prepared unto glory,

B'. [27] Esaias also crieth concerning Israel, Though the number of the children of Israel be as the sand of the sea, a remnant shall be saved:

C. [24] Even us, whom he hath called, not of the Jews only, but also of the Gentiles?

C'. [26] And it shall come to pass, *that* in the place where it was said unto them, Ye *are* not my people; there shall they be called the children of the living God.

D. [25] As he saith also in Osee, I will call them my people, which were not my people;
and her beloved, which was not beloved.

God has a purpose, a plan, and a program. In keeping with these, He gives prophecies and promises. All confirm that there are two kinds of sinners; lost sinners and saved sinners. Sinners either do what seems right to them, or they place their faith in Jesus and allow him to direct their paths. The LORD'S message to Moses was:

And the LORD passed by before him, and proclaimed, The LORD, The LORD God, merciful and gracious, longsuffering, and abundant in goodness and truth, [7]Keeping mercy for thousands, forgiving iniquity and transgression and sin, and that will by no means clear *the guilty;* visiting the iniquity of the fathers upon the children, and upon the children's children, unto the third and to the fourth *generation.*[110]

There is still forgiveness with the LORD, and for those who fail to claim salvation, all that remains is the certainty of judgment day.

In Paul's day clay jars were used for many purposes. They were used for storing dry goods and water, etc., or for when a person had to relieve himself. There were vessels of honor and vessels of dishonor. The same clay is used to make both, and it is the potter's prerogative to choose. The clay cannot complain or blame the potter.

In the chiastic system of verses 22–29, the first half sets forth God's mercy and patient waiting for the sinner to respond to his offer. The second half of this chiasmus illustrates this with the family of Hosea the prophet. Hosea marries a harlot, who will bear three children. Hosea is the father of the first and names (calls) this son "Judged," because God will judge the house of Israel.[111] She then has two children out of wedlock. The first of these (a little girl) is called "Not Beloved," and the second (a boy) is called "Not My People."[112] "Not My People" probably had a non-Jewish father. Hosea's wife leaves him for life in the street. She becomes destitute and eventually is placed in the slave market to be auctioned for non-payment of debt.

---

[110] Exodus 34:6–7
[111] Hosea 1:2–5
[112] Hosea 1:6,9

Hosea is instructed by the LORD to love her again.[113] He goes to the slave market and pays the price for her and the children.[114] She becomes his wife again, and Hosea adopts the two children born out of wedlock as his own. When he adopts them he renames them. The Gentile who was "Not My People" becomes "My People" and the Jew who was "Not Beloved" becomes "Beloved." "Judged," Hosea's own flesh and blood, remains "Judged."

In the book of Hosea, God uses Hosea's wife to illustrate Israel's spiritual condition, as the unfaithful wife of Jehovah. In Romans, Paul uses the illegitimate children to illustrate the church (Jew and Gentile), and Hosea's natural son to illustrate lost Israel.

In the first half of 9:22–29, the clay vessels could not change; they were what they were. In the second half "Judged" remains "Judged," a vessel of wrath fitted to destruction as God destroyed Sodom and Gomorrah, but "Not Beloved," and "Not My People" were vessels of dishonor fitted for destruction, and they became vessels of honor prepared for glory. These changes argue against a fatalistic viewpoint.

Correlations
2:11 For there is no respect of persons with God
9:29 Except the Lord of Sabaoth had left us a seed

A. [9:30] That the Gentiles, **which followed not after righteousness,**

    B. **have attained** to righteousness,

        C. **even the righteousness which is of faith.**

A'. [31] But Israel, **which followed after the law of righteousness,**

    B'. **hath not attained** to the law of righteousness.

        C'. [32] Wherefore? Because *they **sought it** not by faith*, but as it were by the works of the law. For they stumbled at that stumblingstone. [33] As it is written, Behold, I lay in Sion a stumblingstone and rock of offence: and whosoever believeth on him shall not be ashamed.

---

[113] Hosea 3:1
[114] Hosea 3:1–3

The double prime (") indicates contrast.

^{10:1} Brethren, my heart's desire and prayer to God for Israel is, that they might be saved. ² For I bear them record that they have a zeal of God, but not according to knowledge.

Correlations
3:22 The righteousness of God *which is* by faith of Jesus Christ
unto all and upon all them that believe

A. ^{10:3} For they being ignorant of **God's righteousness,**

> B. and going about to establish **their own righteousness,**

>> C. ⁴ have not submitted themselves unto **the righteousness of God.**

A.	God's righteousness	
	B.	Their own righteousness
		C. The righteousness of God
		C'. Christ is the end of the law for righteousness
	B'.	The righteousness which is of the law
A'.	The righteousness which is of faith	

>> C'. **For Christ *is* the end of the law for righteousness** to every one that believeth.

> B'. ⁵ For Moses describeth the **righteousness which is of the law,** That the man which doeth those things shall live by them.

A'. ⁶ **But the righteousness which is of faith** speaketh on this wise,

The chiastic reading:

A. ^{10:3} For they being ignorant of God's righteousness

A'. ⁶ But the righteousness which is of faith speaketh on this wise,

B. and going about to establish their own righteousness,

B'. ⁵ For Moses describeth the righteousness which is of the law, That the man which doeth those things shall live by them.

C. [4] have not submitted themselves unto the righteousness of God.

C'. For Christ *is* the end of the law for righteousness to every one that believeth.

Correlations

3:26 The justifier [one who declares righteous] of him
which believeth in Jesus

A. [10:6] **Say not in thine heart**, Who shall ascend into heaven? (that is, to bring Christ down *from above)* [7] Or, Who shall descend into the deep? (that is, to bring up Christ again from the dead.)

> A. Say not in thine heart
> B. Confess with thy mouth
> C. Believe in thine heart
> C'. With the heart man believeth
> B'. With the mouth confession is made
> A'. The scripture saith

B. [8] But what saith it? The word is nigh thee, *even* in thy mouth, and in thy heart: that is, the word of faith, which we preach; [9] That if thou shalt **confess with thy mouth** the Lord Jesus,

C. and shalt believe in thine **heart** that God hath raised him from the dead, thou shalt be saved.

C'. [10] For with the **heart** man believeth unto **righteousness**;

B'. and **with the mouth confession** is made unto salvation.

A'. [11] For **the scripture saith**, Whosoever believeth on him shall not be ashamed. [12] For there is no difference between the Jew and the Greek: for the same Lord over all is rich unto all that call upon him. [13] For whosoever shall **call upon the name of the Lord shall be saved. How then shall they call** on him in whom they have not believed?

The chiastic reading:

A. ^{10:6} Say not in thine heart, Who shall ascend into heaven? (that is, to bring Christ down *from above*) ⁷ Or, Who shall descend into the deep? (that is, to bring up Christ again from the dead.)

A'. ¹¹ For the scripture saith, Whosoever believeth on him shall not be ashamed. ¹² For there is no difference between the Jew and the Greek: for the same Lord over all is rich unto all that call upon him. ¹³ For whosoever shall call upon the name of the Lord shall be saved.

B. ⁸ But what saith it? The word is nigh thee, *even* in thy mouth, and in thy heart: that is, the word of faith, which we preach; ⁹ That if thou shalt confess with thy mouth the Lord Jesus,

B'. and with the mouth confession is made unto salvation

C. and shalt believe in thine heart that God hath raised him from the dead, thou shalt be saved.

C'. ¹⁰ For with the heart man believeth unto righteousness;

^{10:14} How then shall they call on him in whom they have not believed?

A. and how shall they believe in him of whom they have not heard?

B. and how shall they hear without a preacher?

C. ¹⁵ And how shall they preach, except they be sent? As it is written, How beautiful are the feet of them that preach the gospel of peace, and bring glad tidings of good things!

A'. ¹⁶ But they have not all obeyed the gospel. For Esaias saith, Lord, who hath believed our report? ¹⁷ So then faith *cometh* by hearing, and hearing by the word of God.

B'. ¹⁸ But I say, Have they not heard? Yes verily, their sound went into all the earth, and their words unto the ends of the world.

C'. ¹⁹ But I say, Did not Israel know?

First **Moses** saith, I will provoke you to jealousy by *them that are* no people, *and* by a foolish nation I will anger you.

[20] But **Esaias** is very bold, and saith, I was found of them that sought me not; I was made manifest unto them that asked not after me. [21] But to Israel he saith, All day long I have stretched forth my hands unto a disobedient and gainsaying people.

In the first half of the following extended chiasmus, the emphasis is on Israel's efforts in establishing their own righteousness according to the law. Words like *followed, sought, zeal, establish* and *not submitted*, tell the story. The second half emphasizes in calling out to God in faith. Words like *confess* and *call* tell the story. The reader will remember that in chapter three, incorrect speech was an issue, here the correct verbal response that comes from a believing heart is the answer. Not my God, becomes my God, and the God that was not loved, becomes loved.

Promise requires faith, and faith requires knowledge of the promise. Essential to this is the proclamation of the message of salvation. More often than not those who hear reject the message, but for those who believe the promise, there is salvation. "For whosoever shall call upon the name of the Lord shall be saved."[115]

The main theme, correct speech among believers, is a continuation of the theme of extended chiasmus (2). The main theme of that passage is the incorrect speech of unbelievers.

EXTENDED CHIASMUS (6)
AN ATYPICAL SYSTEM 4:1–12:8

(A.) [4:1] **What shall we say then** that Abraham our father, as pertaining to the flesh, hath found? . . . He hath *whereof* **to glory**; but not before God.

  (B.) a. 6:1 **What shall we say then**? Shall we continue in sin, that grace may abound? [2] **God forbid**; [death, burial and resurrection]

---

[115] Romans 1:13

b. [15] What then? Shall we sin, because we are not under the law, but under grace? **God forbid.** [19] . . . Even so now **yield** your members servants to **righteousness unto holiness.**

(C.) [7:7] **What shall we say then?** *Is* the law sin? **God forbid.** [Paul covets, but God does not reject him]

(D.) [8:31] **What shall we then say** to these things? If God *be* for us, who *can be* against us? . . . What can separate us from the love of God?

(E.) [9:14] **What shall we say then?** *Is there* unrighteousness with God? God forbid.

(F.) [30] **What shall we say then?** That the Gentiles, which followed not after righteousness, have attained to righteousness, even the righteousness which is of faith. [10:1] Brethren, my heart's desire and prayer to God for Israel is, that they might be saved.

Chiasmus 10:5–13 [116]

(G.) A. [5] For Moses **describeth the righteousness of the law,** [6] **But the righteousness which is of faith speaketh** on this wise . . .

(H.) B. [9] if thou shalt **confess** with thy mouth the Lord Jesus

(I.) C. and shalt believe in thine **heart** that God hath raised him from the dead, thou shalt be saved.

(I'.) C'. [10] For with the **heart** man believeth unto righteousness,

(H'.) B'. and with the mouth **confession** is made unto salvation.

(G'.) A'. [13] For whosoever shall **call upon the name of the Lord** shall be saved.

---

[116] Romans 10:6–12 is listed as chiasmus in *The Shape of Biblical Language,* by John Breck, pg. 54, St. Vladimir's Seminary Press. Crestwood, New York. 1994

(F'.) 9:1 I **say** the truth in Christ, I lie not, 3 For I could wish that
myself were accursed from Christ for my brethren, my kinsmen according to the flesh

(E'.) 10:18 **But I say**, Have they not heard?

(D'.) 19 **But I say**, Did not Israel know?

(C'.) 11:1 I **say then**, Hath God cast away his people? **God forbid**

(B'.) 11 I **say then**, Have they stumbled that they should fall? **God forbid:**

(A'.) 12:3 **For I say**, through the grace given unto me, to every man that is among you,
not to think *of himself* **more highly than he ought to think**; but to think soberly,
according as God hath dealt to every man the measure of faith.

The above system is atypical for two reasons. One: the first "I say" comes before the
last "What shall we say then," and it is hard to see how (E) and (D) correlate with (E')
and (D'). It is not hard to see the correlation between the other sets such as "glory" in 4:1
and "not to think of himself more highly than he ought to think" 1:3, but no such
relationship is apparent with these other two sets of correlation.

The many, "What shall we say than," and the many, "I say then," form an extended
chiasmus, centered in chapter ten. What unbelievers said in the beginning of chapter
three is contrasted with what believers should say. The believer's speech is not always
what it should be.

9:19 Thou wilt say then unto me, **Why doth he yet find fault?** For who hath resisted his will?

The Word of God answers. 20Nay but, O man, who art thou that repliest against God?

The believers, faith is the reason for their speech. In the second half, [hope] confidence in what God has said results in Paul's speech being in absolute agreement with God.

Extended Chiasmus (7) 8:35–11:36

Correlations
8:29–30 Five words

(A.) [8:35-39] Praise for God's love

(B.) [9:1-13] God love Israel through Paul

(C.) [9] The word of promise

(D.) [13] Jacob and Esau

(E.) [15-18] Moses and Pharaoh (God's mercy and God's hardening of hearts)

(F.) [21] Two types of clay pots

(G.) [23-24] Riches of His glory

(H.) [25-29] Hosea and his children

a. [25-27] His adopted children "a remnant shall be saved"
b. [28-29] His natural child

(I.) [30] That **the Gentiles**, which followed not after righteousness, **have attained to righteousness**, even the righteousness which is of faith. [31] But **Israel**, which followed after the law of righteousness, **hath not attained to the law of righteousness**. [32] Wherefore? Because *they sought it* not **by faith**, but as it were by the works of the law. For they stumbled at that stumblingstone;

Chiasmus

(J.) A. [33] As it is w ten, Behold, I lay in Sion a stumblingstone and rock of offence: and **whosoever believeth on him shall not be ashamed**.

(K.) B. [10:1] Brethren, my heart's desire and prayer to God for Israel is, **that they might be saved**.

(L.) C. [2] For I bear them record that they have a zeal of God, but **not according to knowledge**. [3] For they being ignorant of

God's righteousness, and going about to establish their own righteousness, have not submitted themselves unto the righteousness of God.

(M) **D.** [4]For **Christ** *is* the end of the law for righteousness to every one that believeth.

(N.) **E.** [5]For Moses describeth the **righteousness which is of the law**, That the man which doeth those things shall live by them.

(N'.) **E'.** [6]But the **righteousness which is of faith** speaketh on this wise,

(M'.) **D'.** Say not in thine heart, Who shall ascend into heaven? (that is, to bring **Christ** down *from above*) [7]Or, Who shall descend into the deep? (that is, to bring up **Christ** again from the dead.)

(L'.) **C'.** [8]But what saith it? The word is nigh thee, *even* in thy mouth, and in thy heart: that is, **the word of faith**, which we preach;

(K'.) **B'.** [9]That if thou shalt confess with thy mouth the Lord Jesus and shalt believe in thine heart that God hath raised him from the dead, **thou shalt be saved.** [10]For **with the heart man believeth unto righteousness**; and with the mouth confession is made unto salvation.

(J'.) A'. [11] For the scripture saith, **Whosoever believeth on him shall not be ashamed**.

(I'.) [12] For **there is no difference between the Jew and the Greek**: for the same Lord over all is rich unto all that call upon him. [13] **For whosoever shall call upon the name of the Lord shall be saved**.

a. [14] How then shall they call on him in whom they have **not believed**? But I say, Did not Israel know? First Moses saith, I will provoke you to jealousy by *them that are* no people, *and* by a foolish nation I will anger you.

b. and how shall they believe in him of whom they have **not heard**?

c. and how shall they hear without a **preacher**? [15] And how shall they preach, except they be **sent**? As it is written, How beautiful are the feet of them that **preach the gospel of peace**, and bring glad tidings of good things!

a'. [16] But they have not all obeyed the gospel. For Esaias saith, Lord, **who hath believed our report**?

b'. [17] So then faith *cometh* by **hearing**, and **hearing** by the word of God.

c'. [18] But **I say**, Have they not **heard**? Yes verily, their sound went into all the earth, and their words unto the ends of the world.

(H'.)   a. [11:5] There is a remnant

b. [8-10] Judged

(G'.) [12] Riches of the Gentiles

(F'.) [16-21] Wild and natural branches

(E'.) [22] Behold the goodness and severity of God

(D'.) [25] Blindness in part

(C'.) [26] This is my covenant

(B'.) [28] Israel is loved for the fathers' sakes

(A'.) [29-36] Praise for God's mercy

The chiastic reading:

A.   [9:33] As it is written, Behold, I lay in Sion a stumblingstone and rock of offence: and whosoever believeth on him shall not be ashamed.

A'. [11] For the scripture saith, Whosoever believeth on him shall not be ashamed.

B.   [10:1] Brethren, my heart's desire and prayer to God for Israel is, that they might be saved.

B'. [9] That if thou shalt confess with thy mouth the Lord Jesus and shalt believe in thine heart that God hath raised him from the dead, thou shalt be saved. [10] For with the heart man believeth unto righteousness; and with the mouth confession is made unto salvation.

C.   [2] For I bear them record that they have a zeal of God, but not according to knowledge. [3] For they being ignorant of God's righteousness, and going about to establish their own righteousness, have not submitted themselves unto the righteousness of God.

C'. [8] But what saith it? The word is nigh thee, *even* in thy mouth, and in thy heart: that is, the word of faith, which we preach;

D.   [4] For Christ *is* the end of the law for righteousness to every one that believeth.

D'. Say not in thine heart, Who shall ascend into heaven? (that is, to bring Christ down *from above*.) [7] Or, Who shall descend into the deep? (that is, to bring up Christ again from the dead.)

E. [5]For Moses describeth the righteousness which is of the law, That the man which doeth those things shall live by them.

E'. [6]But the righteousness which is of faith speaketh on this wise,

The dual quotes in **K** and **K'** help the reader find the center. In "What shall we say then?" (9:14–9:29), Paul discussed predestination and calling. In this final "What shall we say then?" (9:30–10:20) Paul presents justification and glorification. The reader will no doubt notice that the word *glorified* does not appear in this section, and may wonder why. With inverted parallelism it is not necessary for the same word to be used, only that the same thought be presented. The English words *boasting* and *glory* are both translations of the same Greek word (*doxa*). If we were to lists opposites, we would have to list *ashamed* as one possibility, and if we put the negative "not" in front of it, we would effectively be saying *glory* or *glorified*. Why would Paul do this? This section is presenting the power of God unto salvation.

For I am not ashamed of the gospel of Christ: for it is the power of God unto salvation to every one that believeth; to the Jew first, and also to the Greek.[117]

Being not ashamed is a result of believing faith maturing into hope.

And hope maketh not ashamed; because the love of God is shed abroad in our hearts by the Holy Ghost which is given unto us.[118]

The glorification of the believer under the new covenant was promised.

Incline your ear, and come unto me: hear, and your soul shall live; and I will make an everlasting covenant with you, *even* the sure mercies of David. [4]Behold, I have given him *for* a witness to the people, a leader and commander to the people. [5]Behold, thou shalt call a nation *that* thou knowest not, and nations *that* knew not thee shall run unto thee because of the LORD thy God, and for the Holy One of Israel; **for he hath glorified thee.**[119]

---

[117] Romans 1:16
[118] Romans 5:5
[119] Isaiah 55:3–5

The sure mercies of David[120] came because of God's promise to David concerning the kingdom. God always does what he says. Since God promised, we should not be surprised that this is what he does. Glorification of the believer is the topic of discussion for this section. In the last section[121] Paul presented "the Power of God"; in this section,[122] "unto salvation" and "I am not ashamed of the Gospel." He also presents "everyone who believeth" and "to the Jew first and also to the Greek."

Correlations
9:30–33 Israel hath not attained
8:30 Election
2:9–10 To the Greek
9:29 We had been as Sodom, and been made like unto Gomorrah

A. [10:19]But I say, Did not Israel know? First Moses saith, I will **provoke you to jealousy by** *them that are* **no people,** *and* by a foolish nation I will anger you.
[20] But Esaias is very bold, and saith, I was found of them that sought me not; I was made manifest unto them that asked not after me. [21] But to Israel he saith, All day long I have stretched forth my hands unto a disobedient and gainsaying people.

B. [11:1] **I say then, Hath God cast away his people? God forbid.** For I also am an Israelite, of the seed of Abraham, *of* the tribe of Benjamin. [2] God hath not cast away his people which he foreknew.

> A. I will provoke you to jealousy by them that are no people
> B. Hath God cast away his people? God forbid
>   C. Maketh intercession to God against Israel
>   D. The election of grace
>   E. If by grace . . . then it is no more of works
>   E'. If by works . . . then it is no more of grace
>   D'. The election hath obtained it
>   C'. David said, Let their table be a snare
> B'. Have they stumbled that they should fall?
> A'. Salvation is come to the Gentiles, for to provoke them to jealousy

---

[120] Psalms 89:28–37 in appendix, Pg. 275
[121] Romans 9:14–29
[122] Romans 9:30–10:13

C. Wot ye not **what the scripture saith of Elias? How he maketh intercession to God against Israel**, saying, [3] Lord, they have killed thy prophets, and digged down thine altars; and I am left alone, and they seek my life.

   D. [4] But what saith the answer of God unto him? I have reserved to myself seven thousand men, who have not bowed the knee to *the image of* Baal. [5] Even so then at this present time also **there is a remnant according to the election of grace**.

      E. [6] And if **by grace**, then *is it* no more **of works**: otherwise **grace** is no more **grace**.

      E'. But if *it be* of **works**, then is it no more **grace**: otherwise **work** is no more **work**.

   D'. [7] What then? Israel hath not obtained that which he seeketh for; but **the election hath obtained it**, and the rest were blinded

C'. [8] (**According as it is written**, God hath given them the spirit of slumber, eyes that they should not see, and ears that they should not hear;) unto this day. [9] And **David saith**, Let their table be made a snare, and a trap, and a stumblingblock, and a recompence unto them: [10] Let their eyes be darkened, that they may not see, and bow down their back alway.

B'. [11] I say then, **Have they stumbled that they should fall? God forbid:**

A'. but *rather* through their fall salvation *is come* unto the Gentiles, **for to provoke them to jealousy**. [12] Now if the fall of them *be* the riches of the world, and the diminishing of them the riches of the Gentiles; how much more their fulness?

Segue:

[12] Now if the fall of them *be* the riches of the world, [11:14–18]
and the diminishing of them the riches of the Gentiles; [11:19–24]
how much more their fulness? [11:25–32]

The chiastic reading:

A. [10:19] But I say, Did not Israel know? First Moses saith, I will provoke you to jealousy by them that are no people, and by a foolish nation I will anger you. [20] But Esaias is very bold, and saith, I was found of them that sought me not; I was made manifest unto them that asked not after me. [21] But to Israel he saith, All day long I have stretched forth my hands unto a disobedient and gainsaying people.

A'. but *rather* through their fall salvation *is come* unto the Gentiles, for to provoke them to jealousy. [12] Now if the fall of them *be* the riches of the world, and the diminishing of them the riches of the Gentiles; how much more their fulness?

B. [11:1] I say then, Hath God cast away his people? God forbid. For I also am an Israelite, of the seed of Abraham, *of* the tribe of Benjamin. [2] God hath not cast away his people which he foreknew.

B'. [11] I say then, Have they stumbled that they should fall? God forbid:

C. Wot ye not what the scripture saith of Elias? How he maketh intercession to God against Israel, saying, [3] Lord, they have killed thy prophets, and digged down thine altars; and I am left alone, and they seek my life.

C'. [8] (According as it is written, God hath given them the spirit of slumber, eyes that they should not see, and ears that they should not hear;) unto this day. [9] And David saith, Let their table be made a snare, and a trap, and a stumblingblock, and a recompence unto them: [10] Let their eyes be darkened, that they may not see, and bow down their back alway.

D. [4] But what saith the answer of God unto him? I have reserved to myself seven thousand men, who have not bowed the knee to *the image of* Baal. [5] Even so then at this present time also there is a remnant according to the election of grace.

D'. [7] What then? Israel hath not obtained that which he seeketh for; but the election hath obtained it, and the rest were blinded

E. [6] And if by grace, then *is it* no more of works: otherwise grace is no more grace.

E'. But if *it be* of works, then is it no more grace: otherwise work is no more work.

"Provoke to jealousy" is in both extremes. This is a quote from the song of Moses.[123]

Memorized by every Jewish child, this passage was divided into six parts, and a portion of it was sung every Sabbath morning as a part of the Sabbath day worship service. The main theme of this song is God's judgment of Israel's sin. The same construction of E and E', and the repetitive use of the words *grace* and *works* make it easy to identify the center.

The center section of 10:19–11:12 is stressing that grace and works are not the same, and do not mix. Elias (Elijah) was a prophet to the northern kingdom (Samaria). Samaria had a kingly line that was not of the house of David,[124] and priests that were not Levites.[125] They built two golden calves which they called Jehovah and worshiped them.[126] It is to these people, who were in full rebellion against the LORD, that Elijah was sent. These people had rejected and perverted the Word of God. If God ever had reason to cast away His people Israel it was here, but to do so would result in God breaking His promise.

Elijah was obedient to God's calling, but after a while he became discouraged with what appeared to him to be an exercise in futility. If God had not intervened, Elijah's assessment would have been right, but God had been working without the knowledge of Elijah. How far does God go in saving individuals as he has promised? He does whatever is needed to fulfill his promise. As a result of God's working, seven thousand men responded to the message, and were trusting in the LORD.

The first half focuses on Elijah's complaint to God, and the second half on election (God's choice, not man's). The center section focuses on works and grace as they relate to election. The term "election of grace," ties these two concepts together. Grace is given solely because of the nature of God, and has nothing to do with the one receiving it. When God works on behalf of sinful men, the one receiving God's forgiveness or help in time of need experiences grace, but when viewed from the throne of God, the same event is seen as election. I have concluded that election and grace are one and the same, the difference being where they are viewed from. When viewed from the throne of God it is election, but when viewed from human experience it is grace. To accept grace, but reject election is to reject God's involvement, which is necessary for grace to be experienced.

---

[123] Deuteronomy 32:21
[124] 1 Kings 11:26
[125] 1 Kings 13:31
[126] 1 Kings 12:28

For if they which are of the law *be* heirs, faith is made void, and the promise made of none effect:[127]

Correlations
To the Greek (continued)
11:12 Now if the fall of them be the riches of the world
9:30–33 The Gentiles have attained
8:30 Foreknowledge

[11:11]**I say then**, Have they stumbled that they should fall? God forbid: but *rather* through their fall salvation *is come* unto the Gentiles, for to provoke them to jealousy. [12] Now if the fall of them *be* the riches of the world, and the diminishing of them the riches of the Gentiles; how much more their fulness? [13] For **I speak** to you Gentiles, inasmuch as I am the apostle of the Gentiles, I magnify mine office:

A. [14]If by any means **I may provoke to emulation** *[jealousy] them which are* my flesh, and might save some of them.

A.	I may provoke to emulation
	B. The casting away of them
	C. If the firstfruit be holy, the lump is also holy
	C'. If the root be holy, so are the branches
	B'. If some of the branches be broken off
A'.	Boast not against the branches

B. For if the **casting away** of them *be* the reconciling of the world, what *shall* the receiving *of them be,* but life from the dead?

C. [16] For if the firstfruit[128] *be* **holy**, the lump *is* also **holy**:

C'. and if the root *be* holy, so *are* the branches.

B'. [17] And if some of the **branches be broken off**, and thou, being a wild olive tree, wert graffed in among them, and with them partakest of the root and fatness of the olive tree;

---

[127] Romans 4:14
[128] Firstfruits. See Appendix Pg. 283–284.

A'. [18]**Boast not against the branches**. But if thou boast, thou bearest not the root, but the root thee.

The chiastic reading:

A. [14]If by any means I may provoke to emulation *[jealousy] them which are* my flesh, and might save some of them.

A'. [18]Boast not against the branches. But if thou boast, thou bearest not the root, but the root thee.

B. For if the casting away of them *be* the reconciling of the world, what *shall* the receiving *of them be,* but life from the dead?

B'. [17]And if some of the branches be broken off, and thou, being a wild olive tree, wert graffed in among them, and with them partakest of the root and fatness of the olive tree;

C. [16]For if the firstfruit *be* holy, the lump *is* also holy:

C'. and if the root *be* holy, so *are* the branches.

Correlations
To the Greek (continued)
11:12 The diminishing of them the riches of the Gentiles

[11:19]**Thou wilt say then,**

A. The branches were broken off, **that I might be graffed in**. [20]Well; because of unbelief they were broken off, and **thou standest by faith**. Be not highminded, but fear:

B. [21]For **if God spared not the natural branches**, *take heed* lest he also spare not thee.

A. That I might be graffed in
　　B. If God spared not the natural branches
　　　　C. On them which fell,
　　　　C'. If thou continue in his goodness
　　B'. If they abide not still in unbelief, shall be graffed in
A'. Wert graffed contrary to nature into a good olive tree

C. [22] Behold therefore the **goodness and severity of God**: on them which fell, **severity**; but toward thee, **goodness**,

C'. if thou continue in *his* **goodness**: otherwise **thou also shalt be cut off.**

B'. [23] And they also, **if they abide not still in unbelief, shall be graffed in: for God is able to graff them in again.**

A'. [24] For if thou wert cut out of the olive tree which is wild by nature, and **wert graffed contrary to nature into a good olive tree:**[129] how much more shall these, which be the natural *branches,* be graffed into their own olive tree?

The chiastic reading:

A. The branches were broken off, that I might be graffed in. [20] Well; because of unbelief they were broken off, and thou standest by faith. Be not highminded, but fear:

A'. [24] For if thou wert cut out of the olive tree which is wild by nature, and wert graffed contrary to nature into a good olive tree: how much more shall these, which be the natural *branches,* be graffed into their own olive tree?

B. [21] For if God spared not the natural branches, *take heed* lest he also spare not thee.

B'. [23] And they also, if they abide not still in unbelief, shall be graffed in: for God is able to graff them in again.

C. [22] Behold therefore the goodness and severity of God: on them which fell, severity; but toward thee, goodness,

C'. if thou continue in *his* goodness: otherwise thou also shalt be cut off.

The first half of this chiasmus emphasizes the severity of God in removing the unbelieving Jew from His plan of redemption, and includes warnings to the Gentile. God has given the Gentile unprecedented favor since the death of Christ. As more and more of those who call themselves Christian live in unbelief and live like the world around them, there is less spiritual impact on society. The failure of religion that was presented in chapter two has become the failure of the professing church, and the name of God is

---

[129] The Olive Tree, See Pg. 284

blasphemed among the Gentiles.[130] When sinners come to saving faith, saving faith delivers them from their life of sin.[131]

Israel fell spiritually, and if she were to spiritually stay down forever, she would make God a liar. Since God cannot lie, Israel cannot stay spiritually down. God will provoke her to get up by saving Gentiles. When the Gentiles enjoy the blessings promised to Abraham and Israel does not, Israel should get jealous and respond to God's call.

Correlations
2:15 Which shew the work of the law written in their hearts
11:12 How much more their fulness?
9:30–31 Israel shall attain
9:5 God blessed for ever Amen

[11:25] For I would not, brethren, that ye should be ignorant of this mystery

A. lest ye should be wise in your own conceits;[132] **that blindness in part is happened to Israel**, until the fulness of the Gentiles be come in.[133]

B. [26] And so **all Israel shall be saved**: as it is written, There shall come out of Sion the Deliverer, and shall turn away ungodliness from Jacob:[134]

> A. That blindness in part is happened to Israel
> B. So all Israel shall be saved
> C. This is my covenant unto them
> C'. As touching election
> B'. That through your mercy they also may obtain mercy
> A'. For God hath concluded them all in unbelief, that he might have mercy upon all

C. [27] For **this is my covenant unto them**, when I shall take away their sins.

C'. [28] As concerning the gospel, *they are* enemies for your sakes: but **as touching the election**, *they are* **beloved for the fathers' sakes**. [29] For the gifts and calling of God *are* without repentance

---

[130] Romans 2:24
[131] Romans 3:31, 6:15–23
[132] Romans 3:27–28
[133] Romans 3:29–30
[134] Romans 3:31

B'. [30] For as ye in times past have not believed God, yet have now obtained mercy through their unbelief: [31] Even so have these also now not believed, **that through your mercy they also may obtain mercy.**

A'. [32] For God hath concluded them all in unbelief, that he might have mercy upon all.

The chiastic reading:

A. lest ye should be wise in your own conceits; that blindness in part is happened to Israel, until the fulness of the Gentiles be come in.

A'. [32] For God hath concluded them all in unbelief, that he might have mercy upon all.

B. [26] And so all Israel shall be saved: as it is written, There shall come out of Sion the Deliverer, and shall turn away ungodliness from Jacob:

B'. [30] For as ye in times past have not believed God, yet have now obtained mercy through their unbelief: [31]Even so have these also now not believed, that through your mercy they also may obtain mercy.

C. [27] For this *is* my covenant unto them, when I shall take away their sins.

C'. [28] As concerning the gospel, *they are* enemies for your sakes: but as touching the election, *they are* beloved for the fathers' sakes. [29] For the gifts and calling of God *are* without repentance

The first half of this chiasmus is concerned with the temporary and partial spiritual blindness that Israel is experiencing. The second half emphasizes the mercy of God that comes because of failure. All fail so that God can now show mercy to all. The center section teaches that when God is through with the Gentiles, a deliverer will come and take away Israel's sins. One of the main points of Romans is that the gospel leads to obedience.[135]

[11:33] O the depth of the riches both of the wisdom and knowledge of God! How unsearchable *are* his judgments, and his ways past finding out! [34] For who hath known the mind of the Lord? Or who hath been his counsellor? [35] Or who hath first given to

---

[135] Romans 1:5, 16:26

him, and it shall be recompensed unto him again? [36] For of him, and through him, and to him, *are* all things: to whom *be* glory for ever. Amen.

Nils W. Lund provides us with the following arrangement of the above verses:

O the depth of the *riches*,
   and of the *wisdom*,
      And of the *knowledge of God*!
         How unsearchable his judgments,
           And past tracing out his ways!
         For who *hath known* the mind of the Lord?
      Or who hath been his *counsellor*?
   Or who hath first given to him,
And it shall be recompensed unto him again?
For of him, and through him, and unto him, are all things.
To him be the glory for ever. Amen. [136]

In Romans 9–11, Paul has given the believer many reasons to hope in God, and thereby bring glory to God. There is a concern on Paul's heart. Paul's concern is that the Christian life will degenerate to the level of Judaism in Paul's day. He warns, do not boast against the branches. In the next section (Romans 12–15:13) Paul calls believers to a life that is entirely above nature. The living sacrifice is not normal. There is a strong emphasis on our inner thought life.

Think not more highly of yourself than you ought,
Despise not him that eateth,
and judge not another man's servant.

These are examples of Paul's admonitions. Paul's concern is that if believers do not present themselves as living sacrifices, they will, by default, be on a downward path that leads to this very low level of Christian living and the flesh will reign.

---

[136] *Chiasmus in the New Testament*, by Nils W. Lund, Pg. 222 Hendrickson. Peabody, Mass. Reprint 1992

V

Called to Be Saints

Correlations

1:7 To all that be in Rome, beloved of God, called *to be* saints

1:7 Grace to you and peace from God our Father, and the Lord Jesus Christ

11:32 For God hath concluded them all in unbelief,

that he might have mercy upon all

A. [12:1] I beseech you therefore, brethren, by the mercies of God **that ye present your bodies a living sacrifice,** [137] **holy, acceptable unto God,** *which is* your reasonable service.

> A. Present your bodies a living sacrifice
> B. Be not conformed
> B'. Be ye transformed
> A'. That ye may prove what is that good

B. [2] And **be not conformed** to this world:

B'. but **be ye transformed** by the renewing of your mind,

A'. **that ye may prove what is that good, and acceptable, and perfect, will of God.**

---

[137] Living Sacrifices, See Appendix. Pg. 285–288

The chiastic reading:

A. [12:1] I beseech you therefore, brethren, by the mercies of God that ye present your bodies a living sacrifice, holy, acceptable unto God, *which is* your reasonable service.

A'. that ye may prove what is that good, and acceptable, and perfect, will of God.

B. [2] And be not conformed to this world:

B'. but be ye transformed by the renewing of your mind,

TIP (6)

Proving the will of God

a. [12:3–18] Proving the good will of God
b. [12:19–13:7] Proving the acceptable will of God
c. [13:8–15:13] Proving the perfect will of God

From E-TIP (3)

[3:25–26] Whom God hath set forth *to be* a **propitiation through faith in his blood, to declare his righteousness** for the remission of sins that are past, through the forbearance of God; [26] **To declare**, *I say*, at this time **his righteousness**: that he might be just, and the justifier of him which believeth in Jesus.

[12:1–2] I beseech you therefore, brethren, by the mercies of God, that ye **present your bodies a living sacrifice**, holy, acceptable unto God, *which is* your reasonable service. [2] And be not conformed to this world: but be ye transformed by the renewing of your mind, **that ye may prove what is that good, and acceptable, and perfect, will of God.**

The following correlation is from E-TIP (3). The main theme is:

3:26 **To declare,** *I say,* **at this time his righteousness:** that he might be **just,** [righteous] and the **justifier** [one who declares righteous] **of him which believeth in Jesus.**

From E-TIP (3)

For a more complete presentation see pg. 150–155.

A.		A.'	
a.	3:25–26 Whom God hath set forth *to be* a **pro-pitiation through faith in his blood**	**a'.**	12:1-2 that ye **present your bodies a living sacrifice**
b.	25 **Where** *is* **boasting then? It is excluded.**	**b'.**	3 **For I say,** . . . **not to think** *of himself* **more highly than he ought to think;**
c.	29 *Is he* **the God of the Jews only?**	**c'.**	13:1 **For there is no power but of God: the powers that be are ordained of God.**
d.	31 **God forbid: yea, we establish the law.**	**d'.**	8 **for he that loveth another hath fulfilled the law.**
e.	4:19 And being not **weak in faith**	**e'.**	14:1 Him that is **weak in the faith** receive ye,
f.	19 **Who against hope believed in hope,**	**f'.**	15:4 that we **through patience and comfort of the scriptures might have hope.**
g.	20 but was **strong in faith,**	**g'.**	1 We then that are **strong**
h.	**giving glory to God;**	**h'.**	6 **That ye may with one mind** *and* **one mouth glorify God,**

The above comparison from (3) is concerned with God's righteousness in His dealings with those who believe at this present time. This righteousness is declared because,

8:32He that spared not his own Son, but delivered him up for us all, how shall he not with him also freely give us all things?

A comparison 8:31–39 and 12:1–13:10

8:32 He that spared not his own Son, but delivered him up for us all,

How shall he not with him also freely **give us all things**?

33 Who shall lay any thing to the charge of God's elect? *It is* God that justifieth.

35 Who shall separate us from the **love of Christ**?

12:1 I beseech you therefore, brethren, by the mercies of God, **that ye present your bodies a living sacrifice, holy, acceptable unto God**, *which is* your reasonable service.

3 **For I say**, through the **grace given unto me**,
6 Having then gifts differing according to **the grace that is given to us**,

19 Dearly beloved, avenge not yourselves, but *rather* give place unto wrath

13:1 Let every soul be subject unto the higher powers. For there is no power but of God: the **powers that be are ordained of God**.

10 **love** *is* **the fulfilling of the law**.

From E-TIP (2)

A comparison 2:7–10 and 12:1–13:14

2:7 To them who by patient continuance in well doing seek for glory and honour and immorality, eternal life: But unto them that are contentious and do not obey the truth, but obey unrighteousness, indignation and wrath, 9 Tribulation and anguish, upon every soul of man that **doeth evil**, of the Jew first, and also of the Gentile; 10 But glory, honour, and peace, to every man that **worketh good**, to the Jew first, and also to the Gentile:

12:9 *Let* love be without dissimulation. Abhor that which is **evil**; cleave to that which is **good**. 17 Recompense to no man **evil** for **evil**. Provide things honest in the sight of all men. 21 Be not overcome of **evil**, but overcome **evil** with **good**. 13:3 For rulers are not a terror to **good** works, but to the **evil**. Wilt thou then not be afraid of the power? Do that which is **good**, and thou shalt have praise of the same: 4 For he is the minister of God to thee for **good**. But if thou do that which is **evil**, be afraid; for he beareth not the sword in vain: for he is the minister of God, a revenger to *execute* wrath upon him that doeth **evil**.

In the following passage, believers are given gifts of ministry for the good of the body.

A. [12:3] **For I say**, through the **grace given unto me**, to every man that is among you, not to **think** *of himself* more highly than he ought to **think**; but to **think soberly**, according as God hath dealt to every man the measure of faith

A.	Grace given unto me
B.	We have many members
B'.	We being many
A'.	The grace that is given to us

B. [4] For **as we have many members in one body**, and all members have not the same office:

B'. [5] **So we**, *being* **many**, **are one body in Christ**, and every one members one of another.

A'. [6] Having then gifts differing according to **the grace that is given to us**, whether prophecy, *let us prophesy* according to the proportion of faith;[138] [7] Or ministry, *let us wait* on *our* ministering: or he that teacheth, on teaching; [8] Or he that exhorteth, on exhortation: he that giveth, *let him do it* with simplicity; he that ruleth, with diligence; he that sheweth mercy, with cheerfulness.

The chiastic reading:

A. [12:3] For I say, through the grace given unto me, to every man that is among you, not to think *of himself* more highly than he ought to think; but to think soberly, according as God hath dealt to every man the measure of faith

A'. [6] Having then gifts differing according to the grace that is given to us, whether prophecy, *let us prophesy* according to the proportion of faith . . .

B. [4] For as we have many members in one body, and all members have not the same office:

B'. [5] So we, *being* many, are one body in Christ, and every one members one of another.

---

[138] *Grace* verse, 3 and 6, and *gifts*, verse 6, are translations of the same Greek word (*chris*).

In chapters three and four the emphasis was on behavior, especially our speech, i.e. "boasting." In this chapter the emphasis is on the mind. It is what we think that is important and determines behavior.

Spiritual pride is a real danger in the family of God. We forget who we are and take credit for what belongs to God. Spiritual gifts are meant to be a blessing, but can become a stumbling block, when we worship the gift rather than the giver of gifts. When this happens the child of God falls into the same trap that the Gentiles did in chapter one, when they worshiped creation rather than the creator.

We have received gifts for ministry. Gifts according to grace. Gifts were given, not because we are worthy, for we are no better than the condemned. Gifts, because God is gracious. For his son's sake, he gives gifts. He gives gifts for the advancement of the kingdom of God. The gifts are not for our profit, but for the profit of the body of Christ.

The gifts that God has given are a trust. We are entrusted with them and are to invest them for the advancement of the kingdom of God.

> As every man hath received the gift, even so minister the same one to another, as good stewards of the manifold grace of God.[139]

The world says "pay me," and the flesh says "amen," but as members of the body, we are to function because we are members of the body.

A. [12:9] *Let* **love be without dissimulation**. Abhor that which is evil; cleave to that which is good.

   B. [10] *Be* **kindly affectioned one to another with brotherly love**; in honour preferring one another; [11] Not slothful in business; fervent in spirit; serving the Lord;

      C. [12] **Rejoicing in hope**; patient in tribulation; continuing instant in prayer;

         D. [13] **Distributing to the necessity** of saints; given to hospitality.

         D'. [14] **Bless them which persecute you**: bless, and curse not.

      C'. [15] **Rejoice with them that do rejoice**, and weep with them that weep.

---

[139] 1 Peter 4:10

B'. [16] *Be* **of the same mind one toward another.** Mind not high things, but condescend to men of low estate. Be not wise in your own conceits.

A'. [17] **Recompense to no man evil for evil.** Provide things honest in the sight of all men. [18] If it be possible, as much as lieth in you, live peaceably with all men.

The chiastic reading:

A. [12:9] Let love be without dissimulation. Abhor that which is evil; cleave to that which is good.

A'. [17] Recompense to no man evil for evil. Provide things honest in the sight of all men. [18] If it be possible, as much as lieth in you, live peaceably with all men.

B. [10] *Be* kindly affectioned one to another with brotherly love; in honour preferring one another; [11]Not slothful in business; fervent in spirit; serving the Lord;

B'. [16] *Be* of the same mind one toward another. Mind not high things, but condescend to men of low estate. Be not wise in your own conceits.

C. [12] Rejoicing in hope; patient in tribulation; continuing instant in prayer;

C'. [15] Rejoice with them that do rejoice, and weep with them that weep.

D. [13] Distributing to the necessity of saints; given to hospitality.

D'. [14] Bless them which persecute you: bless, and curse not.

TIP (7)

A'. [12:19–13:7] **Recompense to no man evil for evil**

A. [13:8–10] *Let* **love be without dissimulation**

B'. [14:1–13] *Be* **of the same mind one toward another**

B. [14–23] *Be* **kindly affectioned one to another with brotherly love**

C'. [15:1–4] **Rejoice with them that do rejoice**

C. ⁵⁻¹⁴ **Rejoicing in hope**

D. ¹⁵⁻²⁹ **Distributing to the necessity of the saints**

D'. ³⁰⁻³³ **Bless them which persecute you**

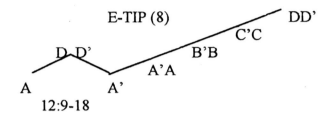

This last TIP is one of a kind in Romans, in that it reflects from both ends towards the center.

God has given to the believer everything. All that we are and have belongs to him. Having received from the hand of God, he would have us to be givers. Having received grace He would have us to be gracious.

2:7–10 from E-TIP (2)

To them who by patient continuance in well doing seek for glory and honour and immortality, eternal life: ⁸But unto them that are contentious, and do not obey the truth, but obey unrighteousness, indignation and wrath, ⁹ Tribulation and anguish, upon every soul of man that **doeth evil**, of the Jew first, and also of the Gentile; ¹⁰ But glory, honour, and peace, to every man that **worketh good**, to the Jew first, and also to the Gentile:

Correlations
12:17–18 Recompense to no man evil for evil

A. ¹⁹ Dearly beloved, **avenge not yourselves,**

   B. but *rather* give place unto wrath: for is written,

      C. ²⁰ Therefore if thine enemy hunger, feed him;

      C'. if he thirst, give him drink:

B'. for in so doing thou shalt heap coals of fire on his head·

A'. ²¹ Be not overcome of **evil**, but overcome evil with **good**.

A.   Avenge not yourselves
B.   Give place unto wrath
C.   Feed him
C'. Give him drink
B'. Heap coals of fire on his head
A'. Overcome evil with good

The chiastic reading:

A. ¹⁹ Dearly beloved, avenge not yourselves,

A'. ²¹ Be not overcome of evil, but overcome evil with good

B. but *rather* give place unto wrath: for is written,

B'. for in so doing thou shalt heap coals of fire on his head·

C. ²⁰ Therefore if thine enemy hunger, feed him;

C'. if he thirst, give him drink:

Correlations

2:16 . . . God shall judge the secrets of men by Jesus Christ according to my gospel

2:25 If thou be a breaker of the law

A. ¹³:¹ Let every soul **be subject** unto the higher powers.

A.   Be subject to the higher powers
B.   The powers that be are ordained of God
C.   Rulers are not a terror to good works
B'. He is the minister of God
A'. Ye must needs be subject

B. For there is no power but of God: the **powers that be a r e ordained of God.** ² Whoso-ever therefore resisteth the power, **resisteth the ordinance of God:** and they that resist shall receive to them selves damnation.

C. ³ **For rulers are not a terror to good works, but to the evil.** Wilt thou then not be afraid of the power? Do that which is **good**, and thou shalt have praise of the same:

B'. a.   [4]For **he is the minister of God** to thee for **good**.

  b.   But if thou do that which is **evil**, be afraid;
  b'.   for he beareth not the sword in vain:

 a'.   for **he is the minister of God, a revenger to** *execute* **wrath upon him that doeth evil.**

A'.   [5]Wherefore *ye* must needs **be subject**, not only for wrath, but also for conscience sake.

The chiastic reading:

A.   [13:1]Let every soul be subject unto the higher powers.

A'.   [5]Wherefore *ye* must needs be subject, not only for wrath, but also for conscience sake.

B. a.   For there is no power but of God:
       the powers that be are ordained of God.

  b.   [2]Whosoever therefore resisteth the power,
  b'.   resisteth the ordinance of God:

 a'.   and they that resist shall receive to themselves damnation.

B'. a.   [4]For he is the minister of God to thee for good.

  b.   But if thou do that which is evil, be afraid;
  b'.   for he beareth not the sword in vain:

 a'.   for he is the minister of God, a revenger to *execute* wrath upon him that doeth evil.

C.   [3]For rulers are not a terror to good works, but to the evil. Wilt thou then not be afraid of the power? Do that which is good, and thou shalt have praise of the same:

God in His mercy has withheld judgment on us. He would now have us to be merciful.

3:29–30 from E-TIP (3)

Is he the God of the Jews only? *Is he* not also of the Gentiles? Yes, of the Gentiles also: ³⁰ Seeing *it is* one God, which shall justify the circumcision by faith, and uncircumcision through faith.

A. ¹³˙⁶ For this cause pay ye tribute also:

    B. for they are God's ministers, attending continually upon this very thing.
    B'. ⁷ Render therefore to all their dues:

A'. tribute to whom tribute *is due;* custom to whom custom; fear to whom fear; honour to whom honour.

3:31 from E-TIP (3)

Do we then make void the law through faith? God forbid: yea, we establish the law.

Correlations
2:17–29 Jewish religious experience (continued), Gentiles fulfill the law
12:9 Let love be without dissimulation

A. ¹³˙⁸ Owe no man any thing, but to **love one another**: for he that **loveth another hath fulfilled the law.**

    B. ⁹ For this, **Thou shalt not** commit adultery, **Thou shalt not** kill, **Thou shalt not** steal, **Thou shalt not bear** false witness, **Thou shalt not** covet; and

    B'. if *there be* any other commandment, it is briefly comprehended in this saying, namely, **Thou shalt love thy neighbour as thyself.**

A'. ¹⁰ **Love** worketh no ill to his neighbour: therefore **love *is* the fulfilling of the law.**

A.	He that loveth another hath fulfilled the law
B.	Thou shalt not
B'.	Thou shalt love thy neighbour as thyself
A'.	Love is the fulfilling of the law

The chiastic reading:

A. ^{13:8} Owe no man any thing, but to love one another: for he that loveth another hath fulfilled the law.

A'. ¹⁰ Love worketh no ill to his neighbour: therefore love *is* the fulfilling of the law.

B. ⁹ For this, Thou shalt not commit adultery, Thou shalt not kill, Thou shalt not steal, Thou shalt not bear false witness, Thou shalt not covet; and

B'. if *there be* any other commandment, it is briefly comprehended in this saying, namely, Thou shalt love thy neighbour as thyself.

Correlations

2:19 . . . a guide of the blind, light of them which are in darkness

12:9 Abhor that which is evil; cleave to that which is good

^{13:11} And that, knowing the **time**,

A. that now *it is* high **time** to awake out of sleep:

    B. for now *is* our salvation **nearer** than when we believed.

A'. ¹² **The night is far spent,**

    B'. **the day is at hand:**

A. let us therefore cast off the **works of darkness,**

    B. and let us **put on the armour of light.**

        C. ¹³ **Let us** walk honestly, as in the **day;**

        C". not in rioting and drunkenness, **not** in chambering and wantonness, **not** in strife and envying.

    B'. ¹⁴ But **put ye on the Lord Jesus Christ,**

> A. Cast off the works of darkness
>   B. Put on the armour of light
>   C. Walk honestly
>   C'. Not in . . .
>   B'. Put on the Lord Jesus Christ
> A'. Make no provision for the flesh

A'. and make not provision for **the flesh**, to *fulfil* the **lusts** *thereof.*

The chiastic reading:

A. let us therefore cast off the works of darkness,

A'. and make not provision for the flesh, to *fulfil* the lusts *thereof.*

B. and let us put on the armour of light.

B'. [14] But put ye on the Lord Jesus Christ,

C. [13] Let us walk honestly, as in the day;

C'. not in rioting and drunkenness, not in chambering and wantonness, not in strife and envying.

Will those who name the name of Christ fall into the dark abyss of chapter one: sexual sin, backbiting, faultfinding, strife, etc., or will they be conformed to the image of Christ? When the values of the Lord Jesus Christ become our values, the goodness of Jesus will manifest itself through us. This is not possible without first coming to know Jesus as Savior.

Clothing is figurative of righteousness. Putting on Christ represents a righteousness that comes from God, a righteousness that brings glory to God.

From E-TIP (2)

13:12 . . . **let us** therefore cast off the **works of darkness,** 13 . . . not in rioting and drunkenness, not in chambering and wantonness, not in strife and envying. maliciousness; **full** of envy, murder, debate, deceit, malignity; whisperers,

1:28 And even as they **did not like to retain God in** *their* **knowledge,** God gave them over to a reprobate mind, to do those things which are not convenient; 29 Being **filled** with all unrighteousness, fornication, wickedness, covetousness, 30 Backbiters, haters of God, despiteful, proud, boasters, inventors of evil things, disobedient to parents, 31 **Without** understanding, covenantbr-eakers, **without** natural affection, implacable, unmerciful: 32 **Who knowing the judgment of God,** that they which commit such things are worthy of death, not only do the same, but have pleasure in them that do them.

A comparison2:1–3 and 14:1–13

2:1 Therefore thou art inexcusable, O man, whosoever thou art that **judgest:** for wherein thou **judgest another,** thou condemnest thyself; for **thou that judgest** doest the same things. 2 But we are sure that the judgment of God is according to truth against them which commit such things. 3 And thinkest thou this, **O man, that judgest** them which do such things, and doest the same, that thou shalt **escape the judgment of God?**

14:4 Who art thou that **judgest another** man's servant? to his own master he standeth or falleth. Yea, he shall be holden up: for God is able to make him stand . . . 9 For to this end Christ both died, and rose, and revived, that he might be Lord both of the dead and living. 13 **Let us not therefore judge one another** any more: but **judge** this rather, that no man put a stumblingblock or an occasion to fall in *his* brother's way.

The name Satan means *accuser.* Those who accuse the brethren do the work of Satan. When the believer does wrong, Christ is their advocate before the throne of God. Those who defend and support the brethren do the work of Christ. In chapter two the faultfinders were guilty of the very thing they accused others of. When we stand before the judgment seat of Christ and give an account, will we lose our reward because we are guilty of the very things we have accused others of?

Correlations

2:1 Therefore thou art inexcusable, O man, whosoever thou art that judgest

12:16 Be of the same mind one toward another

A. a. [14:1] Him that is weak in the faith receive ye, *but* not to doubtful disputations. [2] For one believeth that he may eat all things: another, who is weak, eateth herbs.

b. [3] **Let not him that eateth despise** him that eateth not; and let not him which eateth not judge him that eateth: for God hath received him.

> A. Receive him that is weak in the faith
> Despise not him that eateth
> B. Who art thou that judgest another man's servant?
> C. Regarding unto the Lord
> Eating unto the Lord
> C'. For none of us liveth to himself
> Whether we die or live we are the Lord's
> B'. But why dost thou judge thy brother?
> A'. So then every one of us shall give account of himself to God

B. a. **Who art thou that judgest another man's servant?** to his own master he standeth or falleth.

b. Yea, he shall be holden up: for God is able to make him stand. [5] One man esteemeth one day above another: another esteemeth every day *alike*. Let every man be fully persuaded in his own mind.

C. a. [6] He that regardeth the day, regardeth *it* unto the Lord; and he that regardeth not the day, to the Lord he doth not regard *it*.

b. He that eateth, eateth to the Lord, for he giveth God thanks; and he that eateth not, to the Lord he eateth not, and giveth God thanks

C'. a'. [7] For none of us liveth to himself, and no man dieth to himself. [8] For whether we live, we live unto the Lord;

b'. and whether we die, we die unto the Lord whether we live therefore, or die, we are the Lord's.

B'. a'. [9] For to this end Christ both died, and rose, and revived, **that he might be Lord** both of the dead and living.

b'. [10] **But why dost thou judge thy brother?** or why dost thou set at nought thy brother? for we shall all **stand before the judgment seat of Christ.**

A'. [11] For it is written,

    a'. *As* I live, saith the Lord, every knee shall bow to me, and every tongue shall confess to God. [12] **So then every one of us shall give account of himself to God.**

    b'. [13] Let us not therefore judge one another any more: but judge this rather, that no man put a stumblingblock or an occasion to fall in *his* brother's way

The chiastic reading:

A. a. Him that is weak in the faith receive ye, *but* not to doubtful disputations. [2] For one believeth that he may eat all things: another, who is weak, eateth herbs.

    b. [3] Let not him that eateth despise him that eateth not; and let not him which eateth not judge him that eateth: for God hath received him.

A'. [11] For it is written,

    a'. *As* I live, saith the Lord, every knee shall bow to me, and every tongue shall confess to God. [12] So then every one of us shall give account of himself to God.

    b'. [13] Let us not therefore judge one another any more: but judge this rather, that no man put a stumblingblock or an occasion to fall in *his* brother's way.

B. a. [4] Who art thou that judgest another man's servant? to his own master he standeth or falleth.

    b. Yea, he shall be holden up: for God is able to make him stand. [5] One man esteemeth one day above another: another esteemeth every day *alike*. Let every man be fully persuaded in his own mind.

B'. [9] For to this end Christ both died, and rose, and revived,

    a'. that he might be Lord both of the dead and living.

    b'. [10] But why dost thou judge thy brother? or why dost thou set at nought thy brother? for we shall all stand before the judgment seat of Christ

C. a. [6] He that regardeth the day, regardeth *it* unto the Lord; and he that regardeth not the day, to the Lord he doth not regard *it*.

    b. He that eateth, eateth to the Lord, for he giveth God thanks; and he that eateth not, to the Lord he eateth not, and giveth God thanks.

C'. a'. For none of us liveth to himself, and no man dieth to himself.
     ⁸For whether we live, we live unto the Lord;
  b'. and whether we die, we die unto the Lord
    whether we live therefore, or die, we are the Lord's.

We come to him as sinners, condemned, unclean and he receives us. Who are we then, to reject those who Christ has accepted? The tendency to find fault with our brothers and sisters in Christ comes from pride. When a person thinks he is better then others, he soon makes himself the standard, and becomes critical of those who differ from himself. The standard is God and we all fall short. The believer is to patiently help others rise toward that standard, while humbly acknowledging that he too falls short. Since Christ has accepted us, ought not we to accept others? The word *despise* emphasizes that the root problem is an incorrect attitude. If we despise someone who Christ loves with an everlasting love, something is wrong.

The Lordship of Christ is the central theme of this section. When we judge others we usurp the authority of Christ.

Correlations
1:21–32 Contrast with the reprobate mind
12:10 Be kindly affectioned one to another with brotherly love

A. ¹⁴:¹⁴ I know, and am persuaded by the Lord Jesus, **that** *there* **is nothing unclean of itself**: but to him that esteemeth any thing to be unclean, to him *it is* unclean.

B. ¹⁵ But if thy brother be grieved with *thy* meat, now walkest thou not charitably. **Destroy not him with thy meat**, for whom Christ died.

A. There is nothing unclean of itself
  B. Destroy not him with thy meat
    C. Let not your good be evil spoken of
      D. Let us . . . follow after the things which make for peace
      D'. It is evil for that man who eateth with offence
    C'. It is good neither to eat flesh . . . Whereby thy brother stumbleth
  B'. Happy is he that condemneth not himself
A'. For whatsoever is not of faith is sin

C. [16] **Let not then your good be evil spoken of**: [17] For the kingdom of God is not meat and drink; but righteousness, and peace, and joy in the Holy Ghost.

    D. [18] For he that in these things serveth Christ *is* acceptable to God, and approved of men. [19] **Let us therefore follow after the things which make for peace**, and things wherewith one may edify another.

    D'. [20] For meat destroy not the work of God. All things indeed *are* pure; but *it is* **evil for that man who eateth with offence**.

C'. [21] *It is* **good neither to eat flesh, nor to drink wine, nor** *any thing* **whereby thy brother stumbleth**, or is offended, or is made weak.

B'. [22] Hast thou faith? have *it* to thyself before God. Happy *is* he that **condemneth not himself** in that thing which he alloweth.

A'. [23] And he that doubteth is damned if he eat, because *he eateth* not of faith: **for whatsoever** *is* **not of faith is sin.**

The chiastic reading:

A. [14:14] I know, and am persuaded by the Lord Jesus, that *there is* nothing unclean of itself: but to him that esteemeth any thing to be unclean, to him *it is* unclean.

A'. [23] And he that doubteth is damned if he eat, because *he eateth* not of faith: for whatsoever *is* not of faith is sin.

B. [15] But if thy brother be grieved with *thy* meat, now walkest thou not charitably. Destroy not him with thy meat, for whom Christ died.

B'. [22] Hast thou faith? have *it* to thyself before God. Happy *is* he that condemneth not himself in that thing which he alloweth.

C. [16] Let not then your good be evil spoken of: [17] For the kingdom of God is not meat and drink; but righteousness, and peace, and joy in the Holy Ghost.

C'. [21] *It is* good neither to eat flesh, nor to drink wine, nor *any thing* whereby thy brother stumbleth, or is offended, or is made weak.

D. [18] For he that in these things serveth Christ *is* acceptable to God, and approved of men. [19] Let us therefore follow after the things which make for peace, and things wherewith one may edify another.

D'. [20] For meat destroy not the work of God. All things indeed *are* pure; but *it is* evil for that man who eateth with offence.

In chapter three Paul describes sinful man by saying, "The way of peace have they not known." In contrast to that, believers are to follow after peace.

Correlations
1:21–32 Contrast with the reprobate mind
12:15 Rejoice with them that do rejoice

A. [15:1] **We then that are strong** ought to bear the infirmities of the weak, and not to please ourselves.

> A. We . . . ought to bear the infirmities of the weak
> B. Let every one of us please his neighbour
> B'. Christ pleased not himself
> A'. The reproaches . . . fell o n me

B. [2] **Let every one of us please** *his* **neighbour** for *his* good to edification.

B'. [3] For even **Christ pleased not himself**;

A'. but, as it is written, The **reproaches of them that reproached thee fell on me**.

The chiastic reading:

A. [15:1] We then that are strong ought to bear the infirmities of the weak, and not to please ourselves.

A'. but, as it is written, The reproaches of them that reproached thee fell on me.

B. [2] Let every one of us please *his* neighbour for *his* good to edification.

B'. [3] For even Christ pleased not himself;

From E-TIP (2), [1:21] Because that, when they knew God, they glorified him not as God, neither were thankful; but became vain in their imaginations, and their foolish heart was darkened.

From E-TIP (3), [4:18] Who against hope believed in hope, that he might become the father of many nations; according to that which was spoken, So shall thy seed be.

Correlations
1:21 Gentiles did not glorify God
12:12 Rejoicing in hope

A. [15:4] For whatsoever things were written aforetime were written for our learning, that we through patience and comfort of the scriptures might have **hope**. [5] Now the God of patience and consolation grant you to **be likeminded one toward another** according to Christ Jesus:

> A.   Be likeminded one toward the another
> B.   That ye may glorify God
> C.   Receive ye one another
> C'. Jesus Christ was a minister . . . to confirm the promises
> B'. That the Gentiles might glorify God
> A'. I . . . am persuaded . . . that ye also are full of goodness

B.   [6] That ye may with one **mind** *and* one **mouth glorify God**, even the Father of our Lord Jesus Christ.

C.   [7] Wherefore receive ye one another, **as Christ also received us to the glory of God.**

C'. [8] Now **I say that Jesus Christ was a minister** of the circumcision for the truth of God, **to confirm the promises** *made* **unto the fathers:**

B'. [9] And that the Gentiles **might glorify God** for *his* mercy; as it is written, For this cause I will confess to thee among the Gentiles, and sing unto thy name. [10] And again he saith, **Rejoice**, ye Gentiles, with his people. [11] And again, **Praise** the Lord, all ye Gentiles; and **laud him**, all ye people. [12] And again, Esaias saith, There shall be a root of Jesse, and he that shall rise to reign over the Gentiles; in him shall the Gentiles **trust**.

A'. [13] Now the God of hope fill you with all joy and peace in believing, that ye may abound in hope, through the power of the Holy Ghost. [14] And I myself also am persuaded of you, my brethren, that ye also are full of goodness, filled with all knowledge, able also to admonish one another.

The chiastic reading:

A. [15:4] For whatsoever things were written aforetime were written for our learning, that we through patience and comfort of the scriptures might have hope. [5] Now the God of patience and consolation grant you to be likeminded one toward another according to Christ Jesus:

A'. [13] Now the God of hope fill you with all joy and peace in believing, that ye may abound in hope, through the power of the Holy Ghost. [14] And I myself also am persuaded of you, my brethren, that ye also are full of goodness, filled with all knowledge, able also to admonish one another.

B. [6] That ye may with one mind *and* one mouth glorify God, even the Father of our Lord Jesus Christ.

B'. [9] And that the Gentiles might glorify God for *his* mercy; as it is written, For this cause I will confess to thee among the Gentiles, and sing unto thy name. [10] And again he saith, Rejoice, ye Gentiles, with his people. [11] And again, Praise the Lord, all ye Gentiles; and laud him, all ye people. [12] And again, Esaias saith, There shall be a root of Jesse, and he that shall rise to reign over the Gentiles; in him shall the Gentiles trust.

C. [7] Wherefore receive ye one another, as Christ also received us to the glory of God.

C'. [8] Now I say that Jesus Christ was a minister of the circumcision for the truth of God, to confirm the promises *made* unto the fathers:

When Abram had hope, he gave glory to God, The apostle Paul wants the believers at Rome to have hope so that they will give glory to God.

Correlations
1:14 I am debtor both to the Greeks, and to the Barbarians; both to
the wise, and to the unwise
12:13 Distributing to the necessity of the saints
1:1 Paul, a servant of Jesus Christ, called *to be* an apostle,
separated unto the gospel of God

A. ^{15:15} Nevertheless, brethren, I have written the more boldly unto you in some sort, as putting you in mind, because of **the grace that is given to me of God,**

> A. The grace given to me of God
> B. That I should be the minister
> B'. Ministering the gospel of God
> A'. I may glory through Jesus Christ

B. ¹⁶ **That I should be the minister of Jesus Christ** to the **Gentiles,**

B'. **ministering the gospel of God,** that the offering up of the **Gentiles** might be acceptable, being sanctified by the Holy Ghost.

A'. ¹⁷ I have therefore whereof **I may glory through Jesus Christ** in those things which pertain to God.

The chiastic reading:

A. ^{15:15} Nevertheless, brethren, I have written the more boldly unto you in some sort, as putting you in mind, because of the grace that is given to me of God,

A'. ¹⁷ I have therefore whereof I may glory through Jesus Christ in those things which pertain to God.

B. ¹⁶ That I should be the minister of Jesus Christ to the Gentiles,

B'. ministering the gospel of God, that the offering up of the Gentiles might be acceptable, being sanctified by the Holy Ghost.

Correlations
1:14 I am a debtor (continued)

A. ^{15:18} For I will not dare to speak of any of those things which Christ hath not wrought by me, **to make the Gentiles obedient, by word and deed,**

> A. To make the Gentiles obedient
> B. I have full preached the gospel of Christ
> B'. I strived to preach the gospel
> A'. That have not heard shall understand

    B. ¹⁹ Through mighty signs and wonders, by the power of the Spirit of God; so that from Jerusalem, and round about unto Illyricum, **I have fully preached the gospel of Christ.**

    B'. ²⁰ Yea, so have **I strived to preach the gospel,** not where Christ was named, lest I should build upon another man's foundation:

A'. ²¹ But as it is written, **To whom he was not spoken** of, they shall see: **and they that have not heard shall understand.**

The chiastic reading:

A. ^{15:18} For I will not dare to speak of any of those things which Christ hath not wrought by me, to make the Gentiles obedient, by word and deed,

A'. ²¹ But as it is written, To whom he was not spoken of, they shall see: and they that have not heard shall understand.

B. ¹⁹ Through mighty signs and wonders, by the power of the Spirit of God; so that from Jerusalem, and round about unto Illyricum, I have fully preached the gospel of Christ.

B'. ²⁰ Yea, so have I strived to preach the gospel, not where Christ was named, lest I should build upon another man's foundation:

Correlations
1:8–13 Paul's desire to come
1:15 So, as much as in me is, I am ready to preach the gospel to you that are at Rome also

A. $^{15:22}$ For which cause also I have been much hindered from **coming** to you. ^{23}But now having no more place in these parts, and having a great desire these many years to **come** unto you;

> A. Desire . . . to come unto you
>> B. *when* I take my journey unto Spain, I will come to you
>>> C. It hath pleased them . . .
>>> C'. I that pleased them verily
>> B'. I will come by you into Spain
> A'. When I come unto you

B. ^{24}Whensoever I take my journey into **Spain**, I will come to you: for I trust to see you in my journey, and to be brought on my way thitherward by you, if first I be somewhat filled with your *company*.

C. ^{25}But now I go unto Jerusalem to minister unto the saints. ^{26}For **it hath pleased** them of Macedonia and Achaia to make a certain contribution for the poor saints which are at Jerusalem.

C'. ^{27}**It hath pleased** them verily; and their debtors they are. For if the Gentiles have been made partakers of their spiritual things, their duty is also to minister unto them in carnal things.

B'. ^{28}When therefore I have performed this, and have sealed to them this fruit, I will come by you into **Spain**.

A'. ^{29}And I am sure that, when I **come** unto you, I shall **come** in the fulness of the blessing of the gospel of Christ.

The chiastic reading:

A. $^{15:22}$ For which cause also I have been much hindered from coming to you. ^{23}But now having no more place in these parts, and having a great desire these many years to come unto you;

A'. ^{29}And I am sure that, when I come unto you, I shall come in the fulness of the blessing of the gospel of Christ.

B. ^{24}Whensoever I take my journey into Spain, I will come to you: for I trust to see you in my journey, and to be brought on my way thitherward by you, if first I be somewhat filled with your *company*.

B'. ^{28}When therefore I have performed this, and have sealed to them this fruit, I will come by you into Spain.

C. ²⁵ But now I go unto Jerusalem to minister unto the saints. ²⁶ For it hath pleased them of Macedonia and Achaia to make a certain contribution for the poor saints which are at Jerusalem.

C'. ²⁷ It hath pleased them verily; and their debtors they are. For if the Gentiles have been made partakers of their spiritual things, their duty is also to minister unto them in carnal things.

Correlations
1:12 That I may be comforted together with you
12:4 Bless them which persecute you

A. ^{15:30} **Now** I beseech you, brethren, for the Lord Jesus Christ's sake, and for the love of the Spirit, that ye strive together with me in *your* prayers to God for me;

    B. ³¹ **That I may** be delivered from them that do not believe in Judaea; and that my service which *I have* for Jerusalem may be accepted of the saints;

    B'. ³² **That I may** come unto you with joy by the will of God, and may with you be refreshed.

A'. ³³ **Now** the God of peace *be* with you all. Amen.

The chiastic reading:

A. ^{15:30} Now I beseech you, brethren, for the Lord Jesus Christ's sake, and for the love of the Spirit, that ye strive together with me in *your* prayers to God for me;

A'. ³³ Now the God of peace *be* with you all. Amen.

B. ³¹ That I may be delivered from them that do not believe in Judaea; and that my service which *I have* for Jerusalem may be accepted of the saints;

B'. ³² That I may come unto you with joy by the will of God, and may with you be refreshed.

Paul is taking an offering to Jerusalem for the poor. The believers there have heard and believed false reports concerning him. Because they have believed these reports, they are opposed to Paul. When Paul arrived at Jerusalem, James was concerned for Paul's safety. Paul had timed his trip to be at Jerusalem for Pentecost. Pentecost was the anniversary of their receiving the Law, which was written on tablets of stone by God himself. Their zeal for the law would be at its zenith. Their zeal for the law and their hostility towards Paul did not prevent Paul from meeting their needs.[140]

Believers at Rome are Servants

Correlations
1:1 Paul, a servant
1:7 To all that be in Rome

[16:1] I commend unto you Phebe our sister, which is a servant of the church which is at Cenchrea: [2] That ye receive her in the Lord, as becometh saints, and that ye assist her in whatsoever business she hath need of you: for she hath been a succourer of many, and of myself also. [3] Greet Priscilla and Aquila my helpers in Christ Jesus: [4] Who have for my life laid down their own necks: unto whom not only I give thanks, but also all the churches of the Gentiles. [5] Likewise *greet* the church that is in their house. Salute my wellbeloved Epaenetus, who is the firstfruits of Achaia unto Christ. [6] Greet Mary, who bestowed much labour on us. [7] Salute Andronicus and Junia, my kinsmen, and my fellowprisoners, who are of note among the apostles, who also were in Christ before me. [8] Greet Amplias my beloved in the Lord. [9] Salute Urbane, our helper in Christ, and Stachys my beloved. [10] Salute Apelles approved in Christ. Salute them which are of Aristobulus' *household*. [11] Salute Herodion my kinsman. Greet them that be of the *household* of Narcissus, which are in the Lord. [12] Salute Tryphena and Tryphosa, who labour in the Lord. Salute the beloved Persis, which laboured much in the Lord. [13] Salute Rufus chosen in the Lord, and his mother and mine. [14] Salute Asyncritus, Phlegon, Hermas, Patrobas, Hermes, and the brethren which are with them. [15] Salute Philologus, and Julia, Nereus, and his sister, and Olympas, and all the saints which are with them. [16] Salute one another with an holy kiss. The churches of Christ salute you.

[17] Now I beseech you, brethren, mark them which cause divisions and offences contrary to the doctrine which ye have learned; and avoid them. [18] For they that are such serve not our Lord Jesus Christ, but their own belly; and by good words and fair speeches

---

[140] Acts 21:18–22

deceive the hearts of the simple. [19] For your obedience is come abroad unto all *men*. I am glad therefore on your behalf: but yet I would have you wise unto that which is good, and simple concerning evil. [20] And the God of peace shall bruise Satan under your feet shortly. The grace of our Lord Jesus Christ *be* with you. Amen.

[21] Timotheus my workfellow, and Lucius, and Jason, and Sosipater, my kinsmen, salute you. [22] I Tertius, who wrote *this* epistle, salute you in the Lord. [23] Gaius mine host, and of the whole church, saluteth you. Erastus the chamberlain of the city saluteth you, and Quartus a brother. [24] The grace of our Lord Jesus Christ *be* with you all. Amen.

A.   [1:1] Paul, a **servant** . . .

   B.   [9] . . . That without ceasing I make mention of you always **in my prayers** . . .

      C.   [10–11] Making request, if by any means now at length I might have a prosperous **journey** by the will of God to **come unto you**. For I long to see you . . .

         D.   [8–16] Paul's ministry

            E.   [21] They **glorified him not** neither were **thankful**

               F.   [2:1–16] Gentiles **find fault** with one another

                  G.   [3] And thinkest thou this, O man, . . . that thou shalt **escape the judgment of God?**

                  G'.   [14:10] we shall all stand before the **judgment seat of Christ**

               F'.   [1–13] Believers **find fault** with one another

            E'.   [15:1] in him shall the Gentiles **trust**; [9] that the Gentiles might **glorify God**

         D'.   [14–33] Paul's ministry

      C'.   [24] Whensoever I take my **journey** into Spain, **I will come to you** . . .

   B'.   [30] Now I beseech you, brethren . . . that ye strive together with me in **your prayers** . . .

A'.   [16:1–21] Believers at Rome are **servants**

The first shall be last and the last first.

A. [1:1] . . . separated unto the **gospel** of God,

B. [3] . . . concerning **his son** . . .

C. [3-4] . . . which was made of the **seed of David** according to the flesh; **declared**

D. [2] Which he had **promised afore by his prophets in the holy scriptures,**

E. **for obedience to the faith among all nations**

F. [5] . . . **for his name**

A'. [16:25] . . . to stablish you according to my **gospel,**

B'. and the preaching of **Jesus Christ, to be the son of God** with power, . . . by the **resurrection from the dead:**

C'. [25] . . . according to the **revelation of the mystery,** which was kept secret since the world began,

D'. [26] But now is **made manifest, and by the scriptures of the prophets,**

E'. [26] . . . made known **to all nations for the obedience of faith:**

F'. [27] **To God only wise, be glory** through Jesus Christ for ever. Amen.

Correlations
1:1–7 The Gospel

A. [16:25] **Now to him** that is of power to stablish you according to my gospel, and the preaching of Jesus Christ,

  B. **according to the revelation of the mystery,** which was kept secret since the world began, [26] But now is made manifest, and by the scriptures of the prophets,

  B'. **according to the commandment of the everlasting God,** made known to all nations for the obedience of faith:

A'. [27] **To God only wise,** *be* glory through Jesus Christ for ever. Amen.

The chiastic reading:

  A. [16:25] Now to him that is of power to stablish you according to my gospel, and the preaching of Jesus Christ,

A'. [27] To God only wise, *be* glory through Jesus Christ for ever. Amen.

B. according to the revelation of the mystery, which was kept secret since the world began, [26] But now is made manifest, and by the scriptures of the prophets,

B'. according to the commandment of the everlasting God, made known to all nations for the obedience of faith:

I Tertius, who wrote this epistle, salute you in the Lord.

Paul's eyesight was bad, and he therefore often dictated his letters. Tertius, who wrote this letter for Paul, gives his name, probably because there are people in the church at Rome who know him.

Considering the complexity of this letter, I stand amazed that it could be dictated. The grace of God is given to the believer, not just to get us through our daily chores and activity, but to enable us to do what is beyond our natural abilities. God is not limited by our limitations, because limitations are not attributes of God. I believe that Paul's ability to compose this letter in his head is a testimony to the grace of God as much as it is to Paul's gift of mind.

VI

Concluding Remarks

A. PAUL'S TECHNIQUE IN BUILDING INVERTED SYSTEMS

There are several ways in which Paul builds inverted parallel systems.

a. He simply presents one side, inverts and presents the other side.
    This produces chiasma, which are similar in size and purpose to a paragraph. They are short enough to be held in working memory of most readers. There is only one chiasmus at a time, but when one ends another begins. Chiasmus is the basic literary unit. Without chiasmus the other forms could not exist. In this paper I have proposed some embedded chiasma. See pg. 70, and 161. This would appear to violate the principle of balance. We do not have Paul's criteria, but what he did was right. If Paul did this, and I believe that he did, then our criteria should allow for what he did.

b. He takes a chiasmus and extends its pattern of inversion.
    In this technique the original chiasmus becomes the center and the dominant system of a new and larger collective system. The extensions are not always as well-balanced as the center and therefore are not included as chiasma. They are similar in purpose to a chapter. There is normally only one at a time, and when one ends another begins. The extensions exist simultaneously with chiasma.

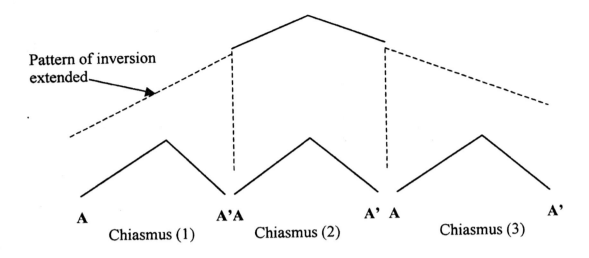

Pattern of inversion extended

A   Chiasmus (1)   A'A   Chiasmus (2)   A' A   Chiasmus (3)   A'

c. The third way is an expansion of the transition from one chiasmus to another. When placing a number of chiasma in series, it could be very choppy, with abrupt change between chiasma. In music and literature, that which makes a smooth transition between parts is called a segue. Paul makes this segue by introducing an idea at the end of one chiasmus, and repeating it in the beginning of the following chiasmus. Examples of this are:

> A'. [6:14] . . . for ye are not under the law, but under grace.
> B. [15] . . . shall we sin because we are not under the law, but under grace?

> A'. [7:12] Wherefore the law is holy, and the commandment holy, just, and good.
> B. [13] Was then that which is good made death unto me?

Sometimes a segue is expanded to make a transition to a larger segment in the letter, resulting in a TIP system that exists simultaneously with other chiastic structures. For example:

> [5:19] For as by one man's disobedience many were made sinners, so by the obedience of one shall many be made righteous. [20] Moreover the law entered, that the offence might abound.But where sin abounded, grace did much more abound:

> [5:21] That as sin hath reigned unto death, even so might grace reign through righteousness unto eternal life by Jesus Christ our Lord.

5:20 . . . But where sin abounded, grace did much more abound:

6:1 . . . Shall we continue in sin, that grace may abound?

5:20 Moreover the law entered, that the offence might abound.

6:15 shall we sin because we are not under the law, but under grace?

5:21   **a'.**   That as sin hath reigned unto death,

      b'. even so might grace reign through righteousness unto eternal life by Jesus Christ our Lord.

7:1–6

    a.   First husband [law and death]

    b.   Second husband Jesus [Christ our Lord]

In a transitional system, the primary side is short, the secondary side is an amplification of the first, and there is no attempt to balance the system. They provide an outline of where Paul is going next. When a TIP is completed, Paul introduces another one. For example:

A'. 7:5 For when we were in the flesh, the motions of sins, which were by the law, did work in our members to bring forth fruit unto death. 6 But now we are delivered from the law, that being dead wherein we were held; **that we should serve in newness of spirit, and not *in* the oldness of the letter.**

    A.   That we should serve in newness of spirit.

      B.   That we should serve . . . not *in* the oldness of the letter.

> **B'.** [7-25] Paul's attempt to serve Christ by the law

> **A'.** [8:1-8:30] Serving Christ by the Spirit of Christ

Most often there is only one of these at a time, but there are times when there are multiple systems operating simultaneously.

    d. Sometimes a segue between two extended chiasma is used to make a much larger TIP system. In this situation the primary side continues back and is not restricted to the chiasmus at hand, and the secondary side expands in an amplified way, resulting in a large, unbalanced system. Examples are E-TIP (1),[141] (2),[142] and (3).[143] With this type of system it is the norm for there to be multiple systems at a time.

Atypical Systems

    1. Paul lists a series of words, and then presents these concepts first in order and then in reverse order, producing an inversion.

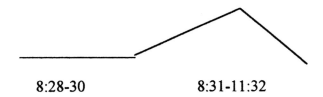

There is only one instance of this documented in Romans. See pg. 184.

    2. The primary side consists of a chiasmus, and the secondary side presents matched pairs starting from both extremes of the chiasmus and working towards the center. There is only one instance of this identified in Romans. See pg. 232.

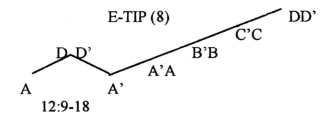

---

[141] Pg. 106–107
[142] Pg. 133–135
[143] Pg. 150–155

Because transitional systems center between two consecutive chiasma, they only exist in an otherwise chiastic document, and are a part of chiastic literature. They provide organization and threads of thought that unify the document.

3. There is one very large extended chiasmus that exists simultaneously with other extended chiasmus. It can be found on page 206–208.

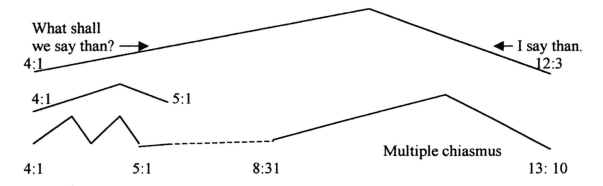

B. Inverted Parallelism as a Memory Technique

In Paul's day, parchment and ink were very expensive. Therefore, scholars could not make many drafts of their developing paper. Instead, they composed and edited their literary works in their heads. To help them do this, they were trained in memory techniques. For the Jew, chiasmus was the primary literary style and doubled as a memory technique. For example, 2:16–3:31 is an extended chiasmus. Paul presents the first side, which helped him recall what he wanted to say in the second half. He then produced another inversion, this time working his way back to 1:1. As he mentally worked backward, the first half prompted his memory, helping him recall the main ideas to be presented in the rest of Romans. At the end of chapter five he produced another inversion that helped him with the detail. As he proceeded he continued to add points of inversion, each helping him recall what was to come.

C. Paul's Expectations of His Readers

Did Paul expect the believers at Rome to detect all of this inverted parallelism?

As already stated, chiasmus was a part of everyday thought and speech in the Jewish community, but Paul's training under Gamaliel produced a scholar, whose abilities were far beyond his peers. The Corinthian believers said that his letters were mighty, and Peter said that they were hard to understand. These comments probably express the prevailing sentiment of the day. Paul taught some of the most difficult truths to understand. In addition to this he took the inverted order to a level beyond his audience.

There was probably no one else in the church of his day with a similar background. The Gentiles in the congregation would not even have the advantage of being familiar with chiasmus. As the letter to the Romans advances, the number of ideas being presented increases. At its peak that number reaches eight, and for several chapters, seven are maintained. I am convinced that Romans is one of the most complex chiastic documents ever written. It is little wonder that even church leaders like Peter had difficulty with these writings.

Paul could expect the Jewish believers to recognize many of the chiastic structures. I do not believe that he could have expected them to detect the many macro-systems. Only those students who were willing to spend years studying this document and were willing to wait on God could be expected to find such truths. They in turn would teach others just as Paul had been taught such things.

It has been about two thousand years since Paul dictated this letter. It is not because of a gift of mind, nor because of advanced degrees that this analysis is now presented. God has given the least of his servants grace, to do what that servant could not naturally do. At a time of God's choosing, and by an individual the world would consider foolish, Paul's literary style and technique are now made known.

D. The Value of Inverted Parallelism

In the introduction I said, "This paper is presented with the conviction that the awareness of form enhances our understanding of the text." Has this paper borne this out? Or have we just gone through an academic exercise that accomplishes nothing? Does knowing that Romans is written in inverted parallelism serve any purpose?

1. It answers some of the long-standing questions concerning Romans.

    a. Is Romans one continuous document, or is there a parenthetical portion? The answer: Romans is one continuous document.

    b. In chapter seven, did Paul struggle with sin as a Christian or unbeliever? Chapter 7:6 provides us with the general topic; "We do not serve Christ, our husband, in the oldness of the letter," the "we" being believers, Paul and the believers at Rome included. For his experience to illustrate this truth, Paul must have experienced this struggle as a believer.

    c. Is the "good" of 8:28 a general good, or is it one specific good? It is one specific good. It is the good of 2:10, the good that Paul did not have in chapter seven.

2. It makes it much easier to follow Paul's logic and therefore to understand his message. (The gospel leads to obedience).

    In extended chiasmus 2, the center is the unrighteous speech of the legalist, and both extremes have boasting. The accusations against the gospel are on the primary side, and God's declarations of His righteousness are on the secondary side. If we fail to recognize this system, it is doubtful that we would be aware of this aspect of Paul's argument. The importance of our speech is further developed in the system presented on page 141. This system centers in man's calling out to God for salvation. The primary side is "what shall we say then?" and the secondary side is "I say then." These emphases on speech would be totally missed if these systems were not first recognized.

    Throughout Romans, Paul consistently introduces the coming chiasmus with the closing statement of the previous chiasmus. Because of this, 6:23 introduces the two husbands: 7:1–6"The wages of sin is death," introduces the first husband "the Law," and the [charis] "grace of God is eternal life" introduces the second husband. This second husband is God's grace that comes through Jesus. Again, we would miss this if we failed to recognize the literary style, and failed therefore to identify the chiastic systems.

3. These systems clarify some otherwise confusing passages. For example:
    [2:14]For when the Gentiles, which have not the law, do by nature the things contained in the law, these, having not the law, are a law unto themselves: [15]Which shew the work of the law written in their hearts, their conscience also bearing witness, and *their* thoughts the mean while accusing or else excusing one another;

    and,

    [2:27] And shall not uncircumcision which is by nature, if it fulfil the law, judge thee, What Gentile did by nature the things in the law? What Gentile had the law written on his heart? Or what uncircumcised person fullfiled the Law?

    In TIP 2, these passages correlate with:
    [8:3] For what the law could not do, in that it was weak through the flesh, God sending his own Son in the likeness of sinful flesh, and for sin, condemned sin in the flesh: [4]That the righteousness of the law might be fulfilled in us who walk not after the flesh, but after the Spirit.

    And,

    [11:27]For this *is* my covenant unto them, when I shall take away their sins,We now know who these Gentiles are. They are believers under the new covenant and, indwelt by the Holy Spirit.

4. In some situations, form becomes essential to understanding the text. When the correlating parts are close or even adjacent we often see the relationship, even if we do not see the form. But when the correlating parts are far apart, we are unlikely to make the connection without the help of form. In these situations form becomes essential if we are to get the full intent of the text. For example: The many correlations between chapter five and chapter eight, especially the one correlating the two Adams with the flesh and the Spirit, provides additional insights.
    Noting the relationship between the first eight verses of chapter three and chapter nine will be helpful. I am looking forward to reading what others will have to say here.

I am confident that the correlation concerning the five words of 8:29–30 with chapters 9–11, will be the topic of discussion for some time, and will add to our understanding of these important truths.

In general, the ability to relate distant parts to each other will help many to understand and better interpret the book of Romans. Our knowing Paul's literary style will forever alter our understanding of this important document.

5. It demonstrates God's protective hand to preserve his Word.
The early church knew and understood chiasma and other forms of inverted parallelisms. Chiasma dripped from their speech and saturated their writings, yet even Peter had trouble with Paul's writings. The early church fathers used chiasma freely, but gave no indication that they realized the extent and complexity with which Paul used this literary style. Though the ages, professors of rhetoric, such as Augustine and Erasmus, labored to determine Paul's literary style. In the post-Reformation period, many pastors and authors applied their gifts, yet only bits and pieces have emerged. If this thesis stands it will be the first time since the ink flowed from Tertiuss' pen that Paul's literary style has been unveiled. In this context, it would have been impossible for someone to alter the text and not have raised havoc with the many correlations. The fact that these correlations are intact testifies to God's preservation of His Word.

6. It helps us understand salvation in the Old Testament.
Salvation in the Old Testament has been much misunderstood. The sacrifice of animals including the bull and goat of the Day of Atonement (Yom Kippur) could not take away sin. Since Christ had not yet died for sin, how were they saved, for without the shedding of blood there is no forgiveness of sin. Form helps us understand that Christ died for past sins; that is, for sins committed before the cross. The forgiveness of these past sins is illustrated for us with Abraham and David. We have more in common with Old Testament saints than we have differences. The Old Testament account is written for us who like them are given the righteousness of Christ, i.e. the Messiah, when we believe.

The olive tree in chapter eleven represents the work of the Holy Spirit, in both testaments, working through the promises. The olive tree, beginning with the original promise to Abraham in Genesis 12, includes all that are of promise, whether they lived before or after the cross. In chapter nine, not all descendents of Israel (Jacob) are of Israel. Only those of promise, like Isaac and Jacob, were saved. In chapter eleven, believing Gentiles are placed into the olive tree with believing Israel. Together, they benefit from the goodness of this spiritual tree. The eternal gospel that leads to obedience is what Paul is presenting in chapters nine through eleven.

E. Conclusion

The book of Romans is a complex arrangement of inverted parallelisms, both in its particular parts, and in the larger scheme of things. The particular parts are a series of chiasma, while the larger units are chiasma with extended patterns of inversion, transitional systems and extended transitional systems.

The complexity of Paul's form and the sheer volume of information presented in this paper will give some difficulty to those who wish to examine this material in depth. Completely new paradigms for understanding Romans and chiastic literature have been presented. Most of the systems presented here are very clear, but with so many, there are bound to be a few less clear examples.

Chiasmus is a term referring to balanced, symmetrical, inverted parallel systems. Excluded from this term are TIP and E-TIP, because they are not balanced. They should be recognized as significant elements of Romans, and given a recognized place in chiastic literature. The recognition of these systems would allow scholars to further develop criteria for the identification of macro-systems. The development of additional criteria would do much to reduce the subjectivity that now plagues this area of study. I recognize that, as additional data is accumulated from other documents, the distinction between TIP and E-TIP systems may have to be refined. I say that because the systems at the end of chapter eight and beginning of chapter nine do not clearly fit either, but share characteristics of both.

In addition to the presentation of inverted parallelisms, this paper has a limited amount of information I consider helpful for understanding Romans. This thesis neither stands nor falls based on this information. The two should be viewed as independent of one another.

The thesis statement of this paper has two parts. The first says:

The prevailing literary form of Romans is inverted parallelism, sometimes called chiasmus, and its many inverted systems are so placed together as to form multiple inverted parallelisms, two of which encompass the whole of Romans.

This does not rule out direct parallelism or other literary forms, but even they are most often components of inverted parallelisms. This portion of the thesis stands or falls on the existence of the proposed inverted parallelisms. A great number of observations have been presented to support these systems. Romans is saturated with many chiasma. Of the E-TIP systems, (1) and (2) encompass the whole of Romans, while others span less of the book, but are more detailed. If it were shown that some of these systems can be improved or that there are other inverted parallelisms that have not been identified in this paper, that would only strengthen this thesis. Only if it is shown that the proposed systems do not exist, would this portion of the thesis fail. Care has been taken not to call the macro-systems chiasma, and to document the pattern of inversion. Such patterns of inversion are not the product of my mind nor accidental, but they were authored by Paul and the Holy Spirit. They are intrinsic to Romans.

The second part of this thesis states:

Therefore every part is part of the whole, and the whole is not complete without every part.

Bible teachers, authors, and pastors have always had difficulty determining how Romans 9–11 relates to the rest of Romans. Many have concluded that these chapters do not, and have considered them to be parenthetical. As parenthetical these chapters are viewed as extra information, not related to the main theme of Romans. It is thought that Paul inserted this unrelated material into the text. This paper holds that these chapters are a part of the whole of Romans, and are not parenthetical.

The success or failure of this part of the thesis depends on whether or not the inverted parallelisms include all of Romans, especially Romans 9–11. Many of the extended transitional systems tie these chapters to the rest of the book, but extended transitional system (3) does so in great detail. It also becomes evident that the message of these chapters is essential to, and is an integral part of, the overall message of Romans. Indeed, chapters 9–11 are shown to be as much a part of Romans as any other part.

In the introduction it was said that much of what is in this paper is obvious, and can be verified by observation. I am convinced that this is true, and that this thesis will stand for that very reason.

"To God only wise, be glory through Jesus Christ for ever. Amen."[144]

Wayne Olson

---

[144] Romans 16:27

VII

Appendix

1. The Purpose of the Law
(From Page 129)

Now we know that what things soever the law saith, it saith to them who are under the law: that every mouth may be stopped, and all the world may become guilty before God. [20]Therefore by the deeds of the law there shall no flesh be justified in his sight: for by the law *is* the knowledge of sin.[145]

The Law may pronounce the blessing of eternal life upon the sinless, but it must also condemn the guilty, and all are guilty. Therefore the Law shall not justify (declare righteous) a sinner. That would be unrighteous!

To understand the purpose of the law we need to go back to the Old Testament. The children of Israel were heirs to the promises God made to Abraham,[146] and ratified in a formal contract (covenant).[147] With the promises there are no conditions: what God says, he will do. Four hundred and twenty years after the covenant was ratified, Moses delivered a message to the children of Israel.

---

[145] Romans 3:19–20
[146] Genesis 12:1–3
[147] Genesis 15:1–21

Then the LORD said unto Moses, Now shalt thou see what I will do to Pharaoh: for with a strong hand shall he let them go, and with a strong hand shall he drive them out of his land. [2]And God spake unto Moses, and said unto him, I *am* the LORD: [3] And I appeared unto Abraham, unto Isaac, and unto Jacob, by *the name of* God Almighty, but by my name JEHOVAH was I not known to them. [4]And **I have also established my covenant** with them, to give them the land of Canaan, the land of their pilgrimage, wherein they were strangers. [5]And I have also heard the groaning of the children of Israel, whom the Egyptians keep in bondage; and I have remembered my covenant. [6]Wherefore say unto the children of Israel, I *am* the LORD, and **I will** bring you out from under the burdens of the Egyptians, and **I will** rid you out of their bondage, and **I will** redeem you with a stretched out arm, and with great judgments: [7]And **I will** take you to me for a people, and **I will** be to you a God: and ye shall know that I *am* the LORD your God, which bringeth you out from under the burdens of the Egyptians. [8]And **I will** bring you in unto the land, concerning the which I did swear to give it to Abraham, to Isaac, and to Jacob; and **I will** give it you for an heritage: I *am* the LORD.[148]

In this passage there are seven "I wills of God, but there are no conditions, no ifs," just "I will." The next verse provides an interesting comment:

And Moses spake so unto the children of Israel: but **they hearkened not unto Moses** for anguish of spirit, and for cruel bondage.[149]

Many years later, God, speaking to Ezekiel the prophet, says:

A. And say unto them, Thus saith the Lord GOD; In the day when I chose Israel, and lifted up mine hand unto the seed of the house of Jacob, and **made myself known unto them** in the **land of Egypt**, when I lifted up mine hand unto them, saying,

B. I *am* the Lord your God; [6]In the day *that* **I lifted up mine hand unto them**, to bring them forth of the land of Egypt into a land that I had espied for them, flowing with milk and honey, which *is* the glory of all lands:

C. [7] Then said I unto them, **Cast ye away every man the abominations of his eyes**, and defile not yourselves with the **idols of Egypt**: I *am* the LORD your God.

---

[148] Exodus 6:1–8
[149] Exodus 6:9

C'. [8] But they rebelled against me, and would not hearken unto me: **they did not every man cast away the abominations of their eyes**, neither did they forsake the **idols of Egypt**:

B'. then I said, **I will pour out my fury upon them** to accomplish my anger against them in the midst of the land of Egypt. [9] But I wrought **for my name's sake**, that it should not be polluted before the heathen, among whom they *were,*

A'. in whose sight **I made myself known unto them**, in bringing them forth out of the **land of Egypt**.[150]

Israel's spiritual condition was that of being idol worshipers. With the worship of the idols of Egypt would come all of the abominable sexual practices. Israel's response is clear. They rebelled; they hearkened not. God was angry to the point that he would have destroyed them all right there and then, but for his name's sake, he did not. If he had destroyed them, he would have broken his promise to the fathers. Paraphrasing Romans 3:8: Are the children of Israel any better than the Egyptians? No, in no wise. They are therefore under the same condemnation. How does God deal with this?

For I will pass through the land of Egypt this night, and will smite all the firstborn in the land of Egypt, both man and beast; and against all the gods of Egypt I will execute judgment: I *am* the LORD. [13]And the blood shall be to you for a token upon the houses where ye *are:* and when I see the blood, I will pass over you, and the plague shall not be upon you to destroy *you,* when I smite the land of Egypt.[151]

The Old Testament sacrifices could never take away sin,[152] but they did prefigure the coming Christ who would.[153] God now delivers them by his grace and leads them to the Mount of God. The promises of God shall never fail, no matter how terrible human failure may be. He leads them on and blesses them because he is faithful to his promises, but He is angry because of their idols, which they have not gotten rid of. At the Mount of God, God gives them the covenant of the Law, which is Israel's marriage covenant with

---

[150] Ezekiel 20:5–9
[151] Exodus 12:12–13
[152] Hebrews 10:1–3
[153] Hebrews 8:5

the LORD. Within forty days, they broke that covenant and their idol (the golden calf of Egypt) was out in the open for everyone to see. By the Law is the knowledge of sin. They should have known how totally depraved they were, but the children of Israel continued to struggle with the acknowledgement of their own sinfulness. God told them:

> The LORD did not set his love upon you, nor choose you, because ye were more in number than any people; for ye *were* the fewest of all people: [8] But because the LORD loved you, and because he would keep the oath which he had sworn unto your fathers, hath the LORD brought you out with a mighty hand, and redeemed you out of the house of bondmen, from the hand of Pharaoh king of Egypt. [154]

> Understand therefore, that the LORD thy God giveth thee not this good land to possess it for thy righteousness; for thou *art* a stiffnecked people. [7] Remember, *and* forget not, how thou provokedst the LORD thy God to wrath in the wilderness: from the day that thou didst depart out of the land of Egypt, until ye came unto this place, ye have been rebellious against the LORD. [155]

It seems that one of the hardest truths for the redeemed to accept is the extent of their own sinfulness. There is nothing in the redeemed that God should desire them above anyone else. Until this is acknowledged it is not possible to fully understand the grace of God.

The purpose of the law has not changed: "by the law is the knowledge of sin."[156] In the Old Testament, God gave the law to those who had been saved by grace, through faith in the blood of the Lamb. In the New Testament, God writes the same law on the hearts of those who have been saved by grace through faith in the Lamb that takes away the sin of the world.[157] We should be careful to note that the Lamb of God does what the Old Testament sacrifices could not do: "Take away sin."

"By the deeds of the law there shall no flesh be justified in his sight."[158]

On the day of judgment, what will count is how God sees things. God is holy, just, and good. We are all sinners, the best of us are guilty before the Judge of all the earth. The book of Romans is telling us how God sees things.[159]

---

[154] Deuteronomy 7:7–8
[155] Deuteronomy 9:6–7
[156] Romans 3:20
[157] John 1:29
[158] Romans 3:20
[159] Romans 3:20; 4:2

2. PROPITIATION
(FROM PAGE 132)

In the Old Testament temple, the Law was kept in the Ark of the Covenant. The lid for this ark had two cherubim on it. The space between the cherubim and above the Law represented the dwelling place of God. From here God judged, sending fire to devour Nadab and Abihu[160] and the two hundred and fifty who in Korah's rebellion offered up incense.[161] Once a year, on the Day of Atonement, the high priest sprinkled this lid with the blood of a sacrifice. When the blood was applied on the "judgment seat," God was said to be propitiated; his just demands were met. At this point the "judgment seat" became the "mercy seat." The Greek word translated *propitiation* is also translated *mercy seat*.[162] In the center section of this chiasmus, God set forth His Son, Christ Jesus as propitiation, through faith in his blood. The blood of Christ satisfies the just demands of God, and faith appropriates its benefits. "To as many as received him, to them gave he the power to become the sons of God, even to them that believe on his name"[163] and "The soul that sinneth, it shall die."[164] The sinner who approaches God, trusting in his own merits dies, but those who come to him trusting in the blood of Christ have his death credited to their account and shall live with him.

In 3:1–8, God's righteousness was challenged. The response of the legalist: if your gospel is true, then God would be unrighteous. On this side of the extended chiasmus, that accusation is answered. God declares his righteousness through the sacrifice of propitiation. God is therefore righteous in His dealings with sinners. He judged the man who picked up sticks on the Sabbath and forgave David, who committed adultery and murder. This confuses the legalist, but is understood and appreciated by believers. The deciding factor is, "When I see the blood I will pass over you."[165]

The Law and the prophets witnessed concerning this righteousness. An example of this in the prophets is when Jeremiah refers to the Christ as, "The LORD our righteousness."[166]

---

[160] Leviticus 10:1–2
[161] Numbers 16:35
[162] Hebrews 9:5
[163] John 1:12
[164] Ezekiel 18:4
[165] Exodus 12:13
[166] Jeremiah 33:16

3. CHILDREN OF ABRAHAM

(FROM PAGE 143)

When the children of Israel (Jacob) brought their firstfruits to the priest they were to recite Deuteronomy 26:5–10, which begins this way: ". . . A Syrian ready to perish was my father . . ." Jacob, like Abram, was a Syrian. Abram's father made and sold idols, but Abram believed God and it was counted unto him for righteousness. Now, Gentiles like Abram can follow in his steps of faith and like Abram, their faith is counted unto them for righteousness. After this Abram walked by faith claiming the promises of God, and brought glory to God. Likewise, all who follow in his steps bring glory to God. With such a life God is well, pleased.

Abram did not live by the Law, because the Law was not yet given. The world and the flesh reason that without the Law, he would do whatever he wanted, and that he would want the pleasures of this world. Law seeks to produce obedience through fear of punishment, but trust in the LORD motivates the believer to do God's will. Obedience is one of the stated goals of the gospel. Abraham did what God wanted and brought glory to God. Because of this he meets the requirements for being blessed by God. To emphasize this, God renames Abram, whose name means *father*, to Abraham. Abraham means *father of many*. His faith in God led him to live a godly life and to be blessed.

1:1-4 Separated unto the gospel . . . for obedience to the faith among all nations.

Obedience was the result of the gospel in the lives of the Roman believers.

6:17 But God be thanked, that ye were the servants of sin, but ye have obeyed from the heart that form of doctrine which was delivered you. 18 Being then made free from sin, ye became the servants of righteousness.

Obedience was the result in general.

2:14 For when the Gentiles, which have not the law, do by nature the things contained in the law, these, having not the law, are a law unto themselves: 15 Which shew the work of the law written in their hearts . . .

27 And shall not uncircumcision which is by nature, if it fulfil the law, judge thee, who by the letter and circumcision dost transgress the law? 28 For he is not a Jew, which is one outwardly; neither *is that* circumcision, which is outward in the flesh: 29 But he *is* a Jew, which is one inwardly; and circumcision *is that* of the heart, in the spirit, *and* not in the letter whose praise *is* not of men, but of God.

Obedience is the result of the Holy Spirit.

8:3 For what the law could not do, in that it was weak through the flesh, God sending his own Son in the likeness of sinful flesh, and for sin, condemned sin in the flesh: 4 That the righteousness of the law might be fulfilled in us who walk not after the flesh, but after the Spirit.

15:18 For I will not dare to speak of any of those things which Christ hath not wrought by me, to make the Gentiles obedient, by word and deed.

Again, speaking of the gospel we read:

16:26 . . . made known to all nations for the obedience of faith.

If the gospel being preached does not produce obedience, then we can be sure that it is not the true gospel of Christ, and lacks the power of God unto salvation.

4. PROMISE AND WORKS
(FROM PAGE 143)

Many readers may not have a good understanding of promise and works. Promise is not merely a prediction. A prediction says something will happen, but does not indicate that the speaker is going to cause it to happen. In promise the one making the promise says, "I will do this," and is obligated to do whatever it takes to ensure that this does happen. When we talk about works and promise we are not talking about periods of time, but about two types of contracts formed between God and man. To illustrate works and promise, we will consider covenants made with the first two kings of Israel.

Saul (works)

1 Samuel 12:13–15

A. Now therefore behold the king

    B. whom ye have chosen,

    B'. *and* whom ye have desired!

A. and, behold, **the Lord hath set a king over you.**

A. [14] If ye will fear the Lord, and serve him, and **obey his voice,**

    B. and **not rebel against the commandment of the Lord,**

        C. **then shall** both ye and also the king that reigneth over you continue following the Lord your God:

A'. [15] But if ye will **not obey the voice of the Lord,**

    B'. but **rebel against the commandment of the Lord,**

        C'. **then shall** the hand of **the Lord be against you,** as *it was* against your fathers.

According to this covenant, Saul and the people are to fear, serve, and obey the LORD as conditions for Saul's kingship continuing from one generation to the next.

Two years later Saul offers up burnt offerings to the LORD. In so doing he violates the law. This breaking of the covenant cost Saul the kingship.

A. [13:13] And Samuel said to Saul, Thou hast done foolishly: **thou hast not kept the commandment of the Lord thy God, which he commanded thee:**

    B. for now would the Lord have **established thy kingdom** upon Israel forever.

    B'. But now **thy kingdom shall not continue:**

A'. the Lord hath sought him a man after his own heart, and the Lord hath commanded him *to be* captain over his people, because **thou hast not kept** *that* **which the Lord commanded thee.**

All covenants of works require that man do all that God says. A failure in just one point breaks the covenant.

For whosoever shall keep the whole law, and yet offend in one *point*, he is guilty of all.[167]

---

[167] James 2:10

David (promise)

Then Samuel took the horn of oil, and anointed him (David) in the midst of his brethren: and the Spirit of the Lord came upon David from that day forward. So Samuel rose up, and went to Ramah.[168]

There is no mention of any requirements made of David or the people as conditions for David's kingship to continue. The reason for this silence is that there were no conditions as there were with Saul. Elsewhere we read:

Psalms 89:27 Also I will make him (David) *my* firstborn, higher than the kings of the earth.

A. a. [28] **My mercy** will I keep for him for evermore,
    b. and **my covenant shall stand** fast with him.
    c. [29] **His seed** also will I make *to endure* forever,
    d. and **his throne as the days of heaven**.

  B. [30] If his children forsake my law, and walk not in my judgments; [31] If they break my statutes, and keep not my commandments;

  B'. [32] Then will I visit their transgression with the rod, and their iniquity with stripes.

A'. a'. [33] Nevertheless **my lovingkindness** will I not utterly take from him nor suffer my faithfulness to fail.
    b'. [34] **My covenant will I not break**, nor alter the thing that is gone out of my lips. [35] Once have I sworn by my holiness that I will not lie unto David.
    c'. [36] **His seed shall endure forever**,
    d'. and **his throne as the sun before me**. [37] It shall be **established forever as the moon**, and *as* a faithful witness in heaven. Selah.[169]

In this covenant, made with David, it is God who promises and must therefore keep the covenant. Since God will not break His promise, the kingdom stays with David and his descendants even when David or his descendents sin.

---

[168] 1 Samuel 16:13
[169] Psalm 89:30–34 is presented as chiasmus in *Chiasmus in the New Testament* pg. 149 by Nils W. Lund, Hendrickson, Peabody, Mass.

Saul sought to secure his kingship through works, but David secured his kingship through promise. The proper response to a covenant of works is to fall on our knees, acknowledging our sinfulness and our inability to do what is being asked. We should cry out for mercy, claiming the promises of God. The covenants, made with Abram and David, were covenants of promise. The new covenant is also a covenant of promise.

> [4:23] Now it was not written for his sake alone, that it was imputed [counted] to him; [24] But for us also, to whom it shall be imputed [counted], if we believe on him that raised up Jesus our Lord from the dead; [25] Who was delivered for our offences, and was raised again for our justification [Our being declared righteous].

All covenants of promise require faith in what is promised, and God gives grace in response to faith. Everything that was true in chapter four, concerning Abram's salvation before the cross, is true concerning the believer's salvation after the cross. The content of faith changes with increased revelation, but the principles remain the same. In chapter four, Paul is concerned with those aspects of the gospel that present-day believers hold in common with Old Testament saints, because of the covenants of promise. Present-day believers do have some benefits that the Old Testament saints did not have. These differences are not in view here.

5. SINS OF IGNORANCE VS. INTENTIONAL SIN
(FROM PAGE 156)

The law teaches us many things about sin and the sinner. For example, the words that describe it are telling. Sin: to miss the mark. Transgression: to cross the line. Iniquity: to disregard the law, etc. Each specific sin has its own name according to what was done: idolatry, Sabbath-breaking, or murder. There were certain sins, such as idolatry, sorcery, witchcraft, and adultery, for which the law provided no sacrifice, but required mandatory death.

It is also possible to look at sin by attitude. Sins of ignorance and willful sin are the two categories under attitude. Sins of ignorance (unintentional sin) are very difficult to define. Our English terms do not adequately express the limits of this category of sin.

Even the rabbis found it necessary to give this explanation:

By sins 'through ignorance,' however, we are to understand, according to the Rabbis, not only such as were committed strictly through want of knowledge, but also those which had been unintentional, or through weakness, or where the offender at the time realised not his guilt.[170]

For each sin committed through ignorance there was a sacrifice prescribed. There were other sacrifices offered up at special holidays, such as the Day of Atonement.

But only the high priest entered the inner room, and that only once a year, and never without blood, which he offered for himself and for the sins the people had **committed in ignorance**.[171] (NIV)

Every sin offering in Leviticus 4 and every trespass offering in Leviticus 5 was conditional. They were for sins committed through ignorance only.

Speak unto the children of Israel, saying, If a soul shall **sin through ignorance** against any of the commandments of the LORD *concerning things* which ought not to be done, and shall do against any of them.[172]

All Old Testament sin and trespass sacrifices, including the bull and goat of the Day of Atonement, were for sins of ignorance only.[173]

Willful sin, sometimes called presumptuous sin, is the other category. Numbers 15:24–29 lists the various sacrifices for sins of ignorance, then says:

But the soul that doeth *ought* **presumptuously**, *whether he be* born in the land, or a stranger, the same reproacheth the LORD; and that soul shall be cut off from among his people. Because he hath **despised** the word of the LORD, and hath broken his commandment, that soul shall utterly be cut off; his iniquity *shall be* upon him.[174]

For willful sins there was no sacrifice, only death to the sinner. It is to this that the author of Hebrews refers when he says:

---

[170] pg. 128 *The Temple*, Alfred Edersheim. Grand Rapids, MI. Reprint 1987
[171] Hebrews 9:7
[172] Leviticus 4:2
[173] Hebrews 9:7
[174] Numbers 15:30–31

For if we sin **wilfully** after that we have received the knowledge of the truth, there remaineth no more sacrifice for sins, [27] But a certain fearful looking for of judgment and fiery indignation, which shall devour the adversaries. [28] He that **despised** Moses' law died without mercy under two or three witnesses.[175]

In keeping with this, if a man killed another person accidentally, or in a moment of anger, God made provision in the law for him in a city of refuge, but if he laid in wait, that is if he committed first degree murder, there was no provision, only death.

He that smiteth a man, so that he die, shall be surely put to death. [13] And if a man lie not in wait, but God deliver *him* into his hand; then I will appoint thee a place whither he shall flee. [14] But if a man come presumptuously upon his neighbour, to slay him with guile; thou shalt take him from mine altar, that he may die.[176]

For such sins the law offers no atonement, no forgiveness, and no hope, but there are people in the Old Testament who were forgiven for such sins. David's killing of Uriah is a case in point. A case could be made that David's sin with Bathsheba was done in a moment of weakness, but his killing of Uriah was premeditated murder. In Psalm 51 David is seeking the mercy of God because of these sins. It is very interesting to note what he says about sacrifice.

For thou desirest not sacrifice; else would I give *it*: thou delightest not in burnt offering. [17] The sacrifices of God *are* a broken spirit: a broken and a contrite heart, O God, thou wilt not despise.[177]

David was not forgiven because of some priesthood ministry, nor because of an Old Testament sacrifice, but because he claimed the promises of God by faith. God promised,

If they shall **confess** their iniquity, and the iniquity of their fathers, with their trespass which they trespassed against me, and that also they have walked contrary unto me; [41] And *that* I also have walked contrary unto them, and have brought them into the land of their enemies; if then their uncircumcised hearts be humbled, and they then **accept** of the punishment of their iniquity: [42] **Then will I remember my covenant with Jacob, and also**

---

[175] Hebrews 10:26–28
[176] Exodus 21:12–14
[177] Psalm 51:16–17
[178] Leviticus 26:40–42

my covenant with Isaac, and also my covenant with Abraham will I remember; and I will remember the land.[178]

All Old Testament promises rest firmly on covenants of promise. These covenants point to the coming Christ, and as we have already seen, Christ died for past sins. It is only because of the promised atonement by the Christ that sins were forgiven in the Old Testament, and this was appropriated by faith.

Paul's enemies had accused him of teaching that believers should, "do evil that good may come."[179] This is a serious charge. This would be teaching people to sin willfully. If this were true, it would put Paul in the same category as Balaam who taught the people of Israel to sin.

6. THE COVENANT OF LAW AS A WEDDING VOW
(FROM PAGE 164)

At first glance 7:1–6 seems out of place. Paul has been talking about the accusation that he taught people to sin willfully. The remainder of chapter seven is concerned with Paul's experience with sins of ignorance. At Corinth and at Ephesus Paul debated in the synagogues. The unsaved Jew, who also knew the law, did not understand how Jews could become a part of the bride of Christ. To them this would be spiritual adultery. Spiritual adultery was a continuous theme of the Old Testament prophets as they called Israel to be faithful to the Lord. To the unsaved Jew it sounded like Paul was asking Jews to sin when he asked them to convert and become the bride of Christ. This would be a very troubling accusation for Jewish believers.

The Law was given to a redeemed people who had not gotten rid of their idols, and had many other behavioral traits that were offensive to God. From God's perspective the purpose of the Law was to bring about knowledge of sin, but from Israel's viewpoint it was to establish a more personal relationship between God and Israel. At the Mount of God, God set forth a proposal:

---

[179] Romans 3:8

Now therefore, *if* ye will obey my voice indeed, and keep my covenant, then ye shall be a peculiar treasure unto me above all people: for all the earth *is* mine: [6]And ye shall be unto me a kingdom of priests, and an holy nation. These *are* the words which thou shalt speak unto the children of Israel.[180]

The people accepted his proposal saying,

. . . All that the LORD hath spoken we will do.[181]

After God set forth his expectations, the children of Israel entered into a formal covenant with God, and God indicated his acceptance of their pledge by writing, with his finger, the Ten Commandments in stone.[182] According to Jewish tradition, God did this on the first Feast of Weeks (Pentecost) after the Passover in Egypt. The book of the covenant[183] is Israel's wedding vows, and she becomes the bride of Jehovah.

Behold, the days come, saith the LORD, that I will make a new covenant with the house of Israel, and with the house of Judah: Not according to the covenant that I made with their fathers in the day *that* I took them by the hand to bring them out of the land of Egypt; which my covenant they brake, **although I was an husband unto them, saith the Lord.**[184]

For thy Maker *is* thine husband; the LORD of hosts *is* his name; and thy Redeemer the Holy One of Israel; The God of the whole earth shall he be called.[185]

In a way, Israel is married to the Law. The reader will recognize that on the first Feast of Pentecost after the crucifixion, believers collectively became the bride of Christ. In the first covenant, Israel pledges to do all or die. In the second covenant Christ does all, yet he dies, the just for the unjust.

Those who knew the law, the Jews, had a problem. How could they become a part of the spiritual bride of Christ when they were already spiritually married to Jehovah through the law? Was their first marriage covenant invalid? No, the covenant was valid, but

---

[180] Exodus 19:5–6
[181] Exodus 19:8
[182] Exodus 34:1-8
[183] Exodus 19:1–23:33
[184] Jeremiah 31:31–32
[185] Isaiah 54:5

Christ fulfilled the law, with all of its requirements, even death for sin. When Christ died, he brought an end to the law as a covenant. Paul says in a later epistle:

> And you, being dead in your sins and the uncircumcision of your flesh, hath he quickened together with him, having forgiven you all trespasses; [14] **Blotting out the handwriting of ordinances that was against us**, which was contrary to us, and took it out of the way, nailing it to his cross.[186] With such authoritative forces hard at work to influence the decision-making process in the direction of evil, the flesh has no problem reigning, as long as God stays out of things. God does not accept banishment, but is actively involved in the lives of people.

In this sense the covenant of law died with Christ, and we are viewed as having died at the cross also. Death always ends the marriage contract.

7. THE WILL OF MAN
(FROM PAGE 171)

The flesh does not like God's intervention, because it loses its claim to sovereignty over the affairs of man. The flesh does not object to God, as long as God is a spectator, or gets involved only with man's permission. As far as the flesh is concerned, God can watch but he cannot interfere with the affairs of men without the permission of that person. There can be no outside authoritative interference in the decision-making process. The flesh (sin incarnate) reigns. Its cry is, *free agency* or in some cases, *freewill.* By these terms it means that God is banished to the bleachers as a spectator, not a player. Biblically, the situation is very different:

Emotional	The heart *is* deceitful above all *things,* and desperately wicked: who can know it?[187]
Intellectual	But if our gospel be hid, it is hid to them that are lost: [4] In whom the god of this world hath blinded the minds of them which be-

---

[186] Colossians 2:13–14

[187] Jeremiah 17:9

lieve not, lest the light of the glorious gospel of Christ, who is the image of God, should shine unto them.[188]

There is a way that seemeth right unto a man, but the end thereof are the ways of death.[189]

Spiritual

[1] And you *hath he quickened,* who were dead in trespasses and sins;

Experiential

[2] Wherein in time past ye walked according to the course of this world, according to the prince of the power of the air, the spirit that now worketh in the children of disobedience: [3] Among whom also we all had our conversation in times past in the lusts of our flesh, fulfilling the desires of the flesh and of the mind; and were by nature the children of wrath, even as others.[190]

No man can come to me, except the Father which hath sent me draw him: and I will raise him up at the last day.[191]

Nevertheless I tell you the truth; It is expedient for you that I go away: for if I go not away, the Comforter will not come unto you; but if I depart, I will send him unto you. [8] And when he is come, he will reprove the world of sin, and of righteousness, and of judgment: [9] Of sin, because they believe not on me; [10] Of righteousness, because I go to my Father, and ye see me no more; [11] Of judgment, because the prince of this world is judged.[192]

For it is God which worketh in you both to will and to do of *his* good pleasure.[193]

It should be clear from the above passages that man does not make his spiritual decisions in a vacuum, devoid of authoritative forces, but in a context of conflict between these authoritative spiritual forces of good and evil.

---

[188] 2 Corinthians 4:3–4
[189] Proverbs 14:12
[190] Ephesians 2:1–3
[191] John 6:44
[192] John 16:7–11
[193] Philippians 2:13

The will makes the right decision, when it agrees with God, and errs when it does what it thinks to be right.[194] Man is responsible for his decisions, which are made under the influence of both good and evil authoritative forces.

Law requires man to do all, and under law, man assumes that he can but law is weak through the flesh.[195] Law and man doing things in his own strength (freewill) go hand in hand. Promise, grace, and election also go hand in hand. Promise knows that man can not live righteously on his own and bring divine help. Law and promise do not mix because in law "faith is made void, and the promise made of none effect."[196]

Spiritually defeated, Paul cried out, "who shall deliver me from the body of this death?" Paul's answer was "Jesus Christ my Lord."[197] The Holy Spirit through direct involvement,[198] and through prayers of intercession,[199] now works to produce the righteousness of the law in Paul.[200] God, in answer to the Holy Spirit's prayer, works to glorify the believer. The flesh is not happy and objects to God's intervention, especially to chastisement and judgment.[201]

Under promise, the spiritual man understands that those condemned are condemned justly. He understands that those spared from judgment are saved by grace and are by nature no better than the condemned. Under works, the flesh sees that those condemned are no worse than the saved and thinks that God's judgment is unfair.

8. Firstfruits
(From Page 218)

Numbers 15:18 Speak unto the children of Israel, and say unto them, When ye come into the land whither I bring you, ¹⁹ Then it shall be, that, when ye eat of the bread of the land, ye

---

[194] Isaiah 55:8–9
[195] Romans 8:3
[196] Romans 4:14
[197] Romans 7:24–25
[198] Romans 8:1–4
[199] Romans 8:26–28
[200] Romans 8:4
[201] Romans 9:14,19

shall offer up an heave offering unto the LORD. ²⁰ Ye shall offer up a cake of the first of your dough *for* an heave offering: as *ye do* the heave offering of the threshingfloor, so shall ye heave it. ²¹ Of the first of your dough ye shall give unto the LORD an heave offering in your generations.

Individual firstfruits were always freewill offerings and heave offerings. They were not required, but when given they were waved before the LORD. Symbolically, they are given to God; God accepts them, and then gives them back. Christ as firstfruits from the dead is given to the LORD as a firstfruits offering. He then presents himself to the Father, who accepts this offering, and gives the Son back in resurrected life. Firstfruit offerings represent and sanctify (make holy) the whole. Christ as firstfruits sanctifies the rest of the spiritual harvest. The cake given from each batch of bread sanctified the rest of the batch.

9. THE OLIVE TREE
(FROM PAGE 220)

There was both a wild and domestic variety of the olive tree. The wild variety had a very hardy root, but poor fruit, while the domestic variety had good fruit, but a root that was not hardy. It was common to graft the domestic stock unto a wild root, but it was not normal to graft wild stock unto the domestic root. There was one exception to this. Sometimes when the domestic olive tree stopped bearing fruit, they would graft wild branches onto it, to rejuvenate the tree and increase the harvest of domestic fruit. This is what Paul is referring to. The olive tree is God's plan of redemption. The promises come through Abraham, the domestic root, and Israel the natural branches. The wild branches are the Gentiles. The wild branches have no natural goodness, but are sanctified because they are connected to the root. They are the adopted children of Abraham.[202] This is intended to increase the Jewish harvest. The olive tree spans both Old and New Testaments. It therefore represents the common salvation experience shared by saints of all time.[203]

---

[202] Romans 4:16–18
[203] Romans 4:23–25 Pg. 143–145.

10. THE NEW COVENANT
(FROM PAGE 221)

While this paper has mentioned the new covenant before, this is the first time that Paul has discussed it. The new covenant is a covenant of promise, and therefore an eternal covenant. Christ is the blessing of the Abrahamic covenant and the curse of the law.

> Christ hath redeemed us from the curse of the law, being made a curse for us: for it is written, Cursed *is* every one that hangeth on a tree: [204]

The blessings, offered to Israel under law, are conditioned on obedience. These blessings are ours in the New Covenant, because of Christ's obedience.[205]

> Now therefore, if ye will obey my voice indeed, and keep my covenant, then ye shall be a peculiar treasure unto me above all people: for all the earth *is* mine: 6And ye shall be unto me a kingdom of priests, and an holy nation. These *are* the words which thou shalt speak unto the children of Israel.[206]

Israel never obtained this because of their disobedience in worshiping the golden calf. Instead, God appointed Aaron and his sons as priest. Korah [207] did not accept God's judgement in disqualifying Israel from this blessing, and did not understand the grace of God in giving the priesthood to Aaron by promise. Remember that it was Aaron who made the golden calf in the first place. Korah wanted the priestly blessing for all Israel, but they could not have it, because they failed to meet the condition "**if.**" Aaron received this lesser priesthood, not because he was obedient, but because God is gracious. God bestowed it on him as an act of grace. This blessing is ours in Christ [208] because of His total obedience to the law. God bestows it on us as an act of grace. In addition to the blessings offered by the law, all of the promises of the new covenant are ours in Christ because God is faithful and cannot lie.

---

[204] Galatians 3:13
[205] Romans 5:19
[206] Exodus 19:5–6
[207] Numbers 16
[208] 1 Peter 2:9

11. Living Sacrifices
(From Page 225)

Paul's plea is for the believer to present his body, the home of the old nature, (the flesh), as a living sacrifice. Every living sacrifice had a companion sacrifice that died in its place.

The offering of Isaac by Abraham is a case in point.[209] The ram in the thicket was God's substitute that died for Isaac. The ram died for Isaac, and thereafter Isaac lived instead of the ram. It should also be noted that Isaac went willingly. Abraham, who was well over one hundred years old, could not have put his teenage son on the altar if the son resisted. It was one thing for Isaac to be the child of promise. It was quite another thing for Isaac to place himself on the altar of sacrifice.

The cleansing of the leper is another illustration of a living sacrifice.

And the LORD spake unto Moses, saying, ²This shall be the law of the leper in the day of his cleansing:

A. He shall be brought unto the priest: ³And the priest shall go forth out of the camp; and the priest shall look, and, behold, *if* the plague of leprosy be healed in the leper;

    B.   a. ⁴Then shall the priest command to take for him that is to be cleansed two birds alive *and* clean, and cedar wood, and scarlet, and hyssop:

        b. ⁵And the priest shall command that one of the birds be killed in an earthen vessel over running water:

    B'. a'. ⁶As for the living bird, he shall take it, and the cedar wood, and the scarlet, and the hyssop,

        b'. and shall dip them and the living bird in the blood of the bird *that was* killed over the running water:

---

[209] Genesis 22:1–14

A'. [7] And he shall sprinkle upon him that is to be cleansed from the leprosy seven times, and shall pronounce him clean, and shall let the living bird loose into the open field.[210]

The earthen vessel is the symbol for the body,[211] and water is the symbol for the Holy Spirit.[212] The vessel must experience a twofold cleansing, by water and the blood. The clean bird that dies represents "propitiation through faith in his blood."[213] The earthen vessel represents the leper before cleansing. The cedar wood represents that which is incorruptible and the scarlet speaks of blood atonement. The living sacrifice represents the leper during and after cleansing. Imagine how the living sacrifice must have felt when being dipped in the blood of the atoning sacrifice. One heavenly creature dies, while the other, dipped in the blood of the first is set free to live a heavenly life. Paul was saved on the Damascus road. Later frustrated with trying to live the Christian life by the law, Paul wrote:

O wretched man that I am! Who shall deliver me from the body of this death?[214]

This is the cry of the spiritual leper, unclean, unclean, and knowing all too well that according to the Law his uncleanness means a very certain and miserable death. Defiled like the leper, he needed cleansing. He placed himself on the altar and therefore can say:

I am crucified with Christ: nevertheless I live; yet not I, but Christ liveth in me: and the life which I now live in the flesh I live by the faith of the Son of God, who loved me, and gave himself for me.[215]

This is the song of the spiritual leper after cleansing. It is the body that gets put on the altar, and is condemned to death because of sin. It is the mercy of God that withholds the much-deserved judgment, and places it on another.

All we like sheep have gone astray; we have turned every one to his own way; and the Lord hath laid on him the iniquity of us all.[216]

---

[210] Leviticus 14:1–7, Lund shows that Lev. 14:10–49 is chiastic. *Chiasmus in the New Testament,* pg. 52–56, Hendrickson, Peabody, Mass. 1992

[211] Isaiah 12:3, 44:3 John 7:37–39

[212] 2 Corinthians 4:7

[213] Romans 3:25

[214] Romans 7:24

[215] Galatians 2:20

[216] Isaiah 53:6

When we come to recognize that it is only by God's sovereign mercy that we have life, and that we were condemned to die, but dipped in Christ's blood we have a new life and a new song, it is only then that we can view each moment as his.

The world through outside pressure should no longer mold us into its image, but the Holy Spirit transforms the inner man producing Christlike ones. Paul's desire in chapter seven was to do the will of God and thereby please God. Once transformed, the believer "may prove what is that good, and acceptable, and perfect, will of God."

Apart from this transformation the believer is like Paul in chapter seven, "carnal, sold under sin." And when he would do good, evil is present with him. The truth of the matter is:

> For they that are after the flesh do mind the things of the flesh; but they that are after the Spirit the things of the Spirit. [6] For to be carnally minded *is* death; but to be spiritually minded *is* life and peace. [7] Because the carnal mind *is* enmity against God: for it is not subject to the law of God, neither indeed can be. [8] So then they that are in the flesh cannot please God.[217]

The believer who desires to rise above the defeat of chapter seven must heed Paul's plea in chapter twelve.

---

[217] Romans 8:5–8

To order additional copies of

the
Unfolding
of
Romans

Have your credit card ready and call:

1-877-421-READ (7323)

or please visit our web site at
www.pleasantword.com

Also available at:
www.amazon.com
and
www.barnesandnoble.com